EXPRESSIONS OF
AUSTRONESIAN
THOUGHT AND EMOTIONS

EXPRESSIONS OF
AUSTRONESIAN
THOUGHT AND EMOTIONS

EDITED BY JAMES J. FOX

Australian
National
University

PRESS

ANU PRESS

Published by ANU Press
The Australian National University
Acton ACT 2601, Australia
Email: anupress@anu.edu.au
This title is also available online at press.anu.edu.au

A catalogue record for this book is available from the National Library of Australia

ISBN(s): 9781760461911 (print)
9781760461928 (eBook)

Cover design and layout by ANU Press. Cover photograph: Woman from the Island of Flores by James J. Fox.

To the memory of Michelle Z. Rosaldo

Contents

Figures and tables

1

Towards a comparative study of the structure of sentiment among the Austronesians[1]

James J. Fox

Introduction

The chapters in this volume offer a contribution to the comparative study of Austronesian conceptions of thought and emotions. These papers vary in their approach, their focus and in the particular societies they examine, but they also point to a variety of similar cultural patterns. While their diversity suggests different avenues for exploration of a complex subject, their common features combine to highlight critical areas of research.

As a collection, these papers are also intended to focus—or, more exactly, refocus—attention on the study of Austronesian ideas of thought and emotions for which there is already an impressive literature and an array of valuable research. In introducing these papers, the first task is to recognise this previous research and to relate elements within this literature to the

---

1   Rodney Needham, my D.Phil. supervisor at Oxford, came to prominence with the publication of his book *Structure and Sentiment* (1962). Years later, after the publication of his book *Belief, Language and Experience* (1972), he set to work on a book he said would be entitled *The Structure of Sentiment*. His intent was, I believe, to examine the structural patterning of categories of thought and the emotions, but he never completed this book and never revealed its contents. Without any certain idea of the substance of this work, I have chosen to insinuate his title into this introduction as a personal link to the comparative effort I imagine he had hoped to provoke.

chapters in this volume. The foundation for the study of Austronesian thought and emotions has been well laid and, therefore, to move forward, in a comparative framework, it is essential to recognise and acknowledge contributions of potential significance.

Selecting a starting point

Contrary to the assertion that there has been relatively little research done on the ethnography of Austronesian thought and emotions, it is possible to point to a considerable and remarkably varied literature on thinking and feeling among Austronesian-speaking populations. This literature combines substantial studies in anthropology and linguistics that offer a valuable starting point from which to consider the contributions offered in this volume.

A useful starting point to consider the trajectories of these previous studies and the particular legacies they bequeathed to the field is the remarkable confluence of publications—an exceptional burst of original papers on Austronesian thought and emotions—that appeared at virtually the same time in the early 1980s. Seen in retrospect, these varied papers offer a wealth of observations and insights for comparative consideration.

The first of these publications is the pioneering volume *Culture Theory: Essays on mind, self and emotion*, edited by Richard A. Shweder and Robert A. LeVine, which was published in 1984, comprising the papers of a Social Science Research Council conference held in 1981. Richard Shweder, in his 'Preview', defined the most general goal of the volume as presenting 'a broad-gauged and accessible discussion of theories of culture' in relation to 'research issues in the development of mind, self and emotion' (1984: 1).

The volume certainly achieved this goal. It was a genuinely seminal work that offered a substantial critique of previous behavioural-oriented research and provided a rich diversity of views setting out various directions—not all compatible—for future research. Significantly, among the contributions in this volume were three important papers by key researchers who focused on their Austronesian ethnographies. Remarkably, each of these contributors traverses similar grounds in separate ways.

Robert Levy was the first of these Austronesianist contributors. Threading his way between supporters and denigrators of the study of the emotions, Levy argues for 'a general person-oriented ethnography' attuned to the features of each community (Levy 1984: 216). Although wideranging in its general discussion, the essay repeatedly and specifically draws on Levy's crucial fieldwork in Tahiti to illustrate its general argument. In distinguishing between 'hypocognised' feelings—nonspecific, general 'underschematised emotional domains'—and 'hypercognised' classifications of feelings, he singles out, for Tahiti, the categories of anger, shame and fear as 'hypercognised'. He relates this distinction to modes of control—feelings controlled 'by not being known', in contrast to feeling known in obsessive detail. Thus, hypercognition 'involves a kind of shaping, selecting, and standardizing, a familiar function of cultural symbols and forms' (Levy 1984: 227).

Another of the contributors was Clifford Geertz. In his essay, 'From the native's point of view', Geertz argues that the 'concept of person' is 'an excellent vehicle … to go about poking into another people's turn of mind'. He describes the 'intellectual vitality' of Javanese labourers to theorise over 'relations between reason and passion' couched in a contrast between 'inside' and 'outside':

> [T]wo sets of phenomena—inward feelings and outward actions …
> regarded not as functions of one another but as independent realms of being
> in no part to be put in proper order independently. (Geertz 1984: 126–7)

He compares these Javanese conceptions with what he encountered in Bali: 'a bifurcate conception of the self … an inner world of stilled emotion and an outer world of shaped behaviour … a persistent and systematic attempt to stylize all aspects of personal expression' (Geertz 1984: 128). In this context, Geertz retranslates the Balinese term *lek*, normally translated as 'shame', as 'stage fright': 'the fear that, for want of skill or self-control, or perhaps by mere accident, an aesthetic will not be maintained, that the actor will show through his part' (1984: 128–30).

The third of these three distinguished Austronesian contributors to the volume was Michelle Rosaldo, whose ethnographic focus was concentrated on the Ilongot of Luzon in the Philippines. She notes that her comments are further reflections on her monograph *Knowledge and Passion* (1980). Her essay is no less wideranging or challenging in its analysis than the others in the volume. She argues for an intimate interpenetration of thought and affect: 'feeling is forever given shape through thought and that thought is laden with emotional meaning' (Rosaldo 1984: 143). At the core of the Ilongot person is a self, identified with the heart, who is both inwardly hidden and outwardly active:

> Thus Ilongots see the *rinawa* or (heart) [*nyawa*] as something that responds and acts within the world but also claim that actions of the 'heart' are often hidden, inexplicable, opaque, autonomous. (Rosaldo 1984: 145)

Intriguingly, she touches on a similar array of emotions as Levy and Geertz—shame, fear and anger:

> Ilongots are concerned primarily not to protect but rather to assert the potency of equal, 'angry' hearts in everyday affairs. Thus, Ilongot 'shame' is not a constant socializer of inherently asocial souls but an emotion felt when 'sameness' and sociality are undermined by confrontations that involve such things as inequality and strangeness. (Rosaldo 1984: 149)

She goes on to call for a cross-cultural study not of 'shame', but of the diversity of 'shames'.

Each of these contributors was able to give ethnographic elaboration to their papers: Levy, in his monograph *Tahitians: Mind and experience in the Society Islands* (1973); Geertz, particularly in his study *Person, Time and Conduct in Bali* (1966); and Rosaldo, in her masterful monograph, *Knowledge and Passion: Ilongot notions of self and social life* (1980). This monograph is perhaps the most extensive, subtle and insightful exploration of the thought and emotions of any Austronesian-speaking population—a model of its kind that rewards careful consideration.[2]

The second volume for consideration is the special issue of *Ethos* that appeared in 1983 organised by Robert Levy on 'Self and Emotion', a collection that refers to the *Culture Theory* volume, which was, at the time, in press. Apart from Levy's introduction, this *Ethos* collection contains a further key Ilongot essay by Michelle Rosaldo, on 'The shame of headhunters and the autonomy of self', and another important essay, by Ward Keeler, on 'Shame and stage fright in Java', which draws on both Clifford and Hildred Geertz's work on Bali and Java.

In his introduction, Levy puts forward an argument for Rosaldo's ideas about the cultural patterning of the emotions in different societies while rejecting the stereotyping of an entire society by particular emotional valency. In her essay, Rosaldo pursues her ethnographic reflections specifically on the Ilongot conceptions of shame (*bétang*), providing

---

2   Here I should declare a personal involvement that undoubtedly colours my judgement: Shelly Rosaldo was my first PhD student at Harvard. Her energy, talent and intelligence were extraordinary and her tragic death, while doing fieldwork among the Ifugao, was an incalculable loss.

a detailed, complex and marvellously nuanced examination of shame in relation to 'fear' (*kayub*), as well as 'humility, respect and honour' (*tu'ngan*): shame as a stimulus for action and as a prod for emulation as well as a constraint on behaviour. Shame creates a 'heaviness' that controls anger, but gives rise to a 'lightness' when that anger is released.

Following the general theme of the volume, Keeler discusses the polarities of shame (*isin*) and fear (*wedi*) for the Javanese. For a child, the acquisition of the proper awareness of the sentiment of shame is crucial to learning to negotiate social interaction. Showing that one knows shame (*ngerti isin*) demonstrates, especially to outsiders, that one is conscious of one's position in society. Without this awareness, social situations can cause fear, but fear is more than an emotional relationship to the strangers; fear is also a form of respect towards one's elders. As different as these polarities of fear and shame are among the Ilongot and the Javanese, they gravitate in a similar dimension.

The third publication in this consideration is *Person, Self, and Experience: Exploring Pacific ethnopsychologies*, edited by Geoffrey M. White and John Kirkpatrick (1985), published only a year after the Shweder and LeVine volume. This book grew out of a symposium held in 1982 at the annual meetings of the Association of Social Anthropology in Oceania. In it, many of the same issues raised in the *Culture Theory* and *Ethos* volumes were further explored by various researchers in relation to the specific Austronesian societies they had studied. It is instructive, therefore, to point to these same notions—the bodily locus of thought and emotion and the highlighting of specific feelings—in the succession of papers in the volume.

In the first paper of the volume, Catherine Lutz summarises key aspects of her research on Ifaluk, which she later elaborated on in her monograph *Unnatural Emotions* (1988). One aspect of the analysis of emotions, which she emphasises, is the crucial relationship of the person to the body:

> On Ifaluk, as elsewhere, the body's structure and well-being are seen to be involved in an inseparable and systematic way with psychosocial well-being … 'the emotional mind' of Ifaluk ethnopsychology is solidly embedded in moral and social life … and in the physical body … Traditionally, all thought/emotions (*nunuwan*) and 'will/emotion/desire' (*tip-*) were believed to be experienced in the 'gut' … The 'gut', as the traditional seat of thought, feeling, and will, is seen in a very real sense as the link between mind and body or, more accurately, as the core of the self in both its physical and mental functioning. (Lutz 1985: 52–3)

Geoffrey White, in his essay on the ethnopsychology of A'ara on Santa Isabel in the Solomon Islands, reinforces Lutz's insistence on the importance of the image of the body in the expression of sentiment: 'The human body is a potent symbol of personal well-being. A'ara speakers extend certain core concepts of bodily experience to the domain of social experience' (1985: 333).

White also raises the issue of the complexities of analysis required in the consideration of the relations between persons and spirits—a common feature of the social life in many Austronesian societies. Peter Black, writing on the population of the island of Tobi in Micronesia, takes up this issue in regard to fear prompted by ghosts, anger and shame. Among the Tobi population, intense shame leads to the expression of anger, which is regarded as 'acting like ghosts' (Black 1985: 282).

Like other contributors, John Kirkpatrick argues that shame (*hakā'ika*) 'deserves a prominent place in an account of Marquesans' interactions and experience', but such *hakā'ika* can only be understood in 'the matrix of cultural knowledge in which it is embedded' (1985: 83). He goes on to examine *hakā'ika* in relation to two other prominent Marquesan terms, *kā'oha* ('concern' towards others) and *keitani* ('envy' by another towards oneself). He quotes an informant's description of *hakā'ika* that gives this emotion a locus and intensity: 'The guts tremble; one fears; one doesn't want to go [i.e. continue] ... the belly thinks' (Kirkpatrick 1985: 89).

Similarly, Karen Ito, in her essay on Hawaiian affective bonds, argues that the 'Hawaiian concept of self is grounded in affective social relations' and 'these social relations are not confined to humans but include the spiritual and natural worlds as well' (1985: 301). She goes on, however, to give a central locus to these affective sentiments:

> The importance of affect for Hawaiian social relations and self concept is most clearly demonstrated in the concept of *na'au* which literally means one's innards and more generally refers to one's heart, mind or affections. One's *na'u* is the seat of one's intelligence, feeling and sincerity. It is important that a person act 'with heart' sincerely, affectionately, thoughtfully, and without reservation in the extension of self. (Ito 1985: 301)

In contrast to the various analyses of specific emotions, Eleanor Gerber's paper on the examination of 44 named Samoan emotions—grouped in four clusters by informants' judgements on relative similarity—offered, at the time, another methodological approach for an ethnographic assessment of affect that stimulated further research by Karl Heider, particularly for the Minangkabau (1981, 2011). The study of 'domains of emotion', their activation as strong affect and their culturally contextual similarities provided another ethnographic dimension for comparison among Austronesian-speaking populations.

In retrospect, one can recognise in these dozen or so papers—all written at roughly the same time—a remarkable configuration of observations and insights that provide an exceptional perspective for the comparative consideration of Austronesian thought and emotions. Following Levy, it may well be that, among Austronesian populations, certain emotions tend to be 'hypercognitised'—'shame', 'fear' and 'anger' among them. It is also seemingly significant that there appears to be a locus for emotions among Austronesians in what is variously called the 'heart', 'gut' or 'belly'. Also significant is the repeated observation that thinking and feeling are intertwined within the body and that key emotions are frequently elaborated in metaphoric bodily expressions. Equally important is the critical observation that each of a culture's key emotions has multiple, subtle dimensions and understanding derives from the careful consideration of the emotions in relation to each other.

In this context, it is valuable to consider Karl Heider's two studies, *Landscapes of Emotion: Mapping three cultures of emotion in Indonesia* (1981) and *The Cultural Context of Emotion: Folk psychology in West Sumatra* (2011), both of which are interesting experiments in analysis. His study—particularly his first study—is focused on the Minangkabau of West Sumatra, although he also considers Indonesian as spoken by Minangkabau and Javanese. Based on a combination of questionnaires and work with different groups of informants, this study examines a lexicon of 200 words for emotion and attempts to map connections among them. The result is what Heider describes as a 'cognitive map of emotion words' (1981: 40)—a global landscape of emotional relations primarily in Minangkabau. As a Malayic language, Minangkabau is closely related to Indonesian (and Malay). Consequently, although minor differences emerge, it is difficult to disentangle these differences from within the methodology and to discern their significance.

Heider divides this lexical landscape into 44 tighter clusters of emotional relations and devotes the second half of his *Landscapes* volume to examining these separate clusters, each primed to particular terms— 'surprise' (M: *takajuik*; I: *terkejut*), 'happy' (M: *sanang*; I: *gembira*), 'desire'

(M: *suko*; I: *ingin*)—of high saliency ('prototypicality') as defined by his informants, which extend from a core of related terms to a range of other terms. The value of this analysis is its emphasis on the dynamics of the formation of emotions, considering the way in which particular emotions form 'way stations' leading to other emotions.

Heider's second book builds on his earlier work but delves much more deeply into the ethnographic sense of the particular emotion clusters outlined in the first volume.

The possibilities of comparison: A relational analysis of shame and fear

The accumulation of ethnographic accounts of Austronesian thought and emotion provides marvellous insights but does not, of itself, provide a comparative perspective. The question is whether such a comparative perspective is possible and, if it is possible, how it can possibly be achieved. Is it possible, for example, to compare Gerber's general findings on Samoa with Heider's findings on the Minangkabau and consider how particular emotions relate to one another within their wider cultural domains? In this regard, I would like to consider the emotions of shame and fear (and anger), already identified variously by many ethnographers of different Austronesian societies, as hypercognitised emotions or as emotions of a high saliency.

Shame, in particular, has significant valency among Austronesians. There is hardly an extended ethnography of an Austronesian people that does not touch on, and often elaborate on, the social importance of shame. More than anger or fear, shame is a learned emotion. Its circumstances, causes and conditions vary from society to society (and indeed within a society), and all of this needs to be taught from an early age. Often it would seem that the learning of shame sets the basis or prerequisite for further emotional learning. Hollan and Wellenkamp, for example, in their ethnography of the Torajan life cycle, *The Thread of Life* (1996), devote considerable attention to the development of shame, which, in the case of the Torajans, relates particularly and initially to sexual conduct. Hollan and Wellenkamp set out this development clearly: 'Soon after children develop a sense of shame (*siri'*) … they begin to feel modest in front of members of the opposite sex, especially opposite-sex siblings' (1996: 56). As they go on to explain:

> Although it is considered pointless to teach or discipline children before they are capable of experiencing shame and of 'hearing' their parents' words of advice ... once children have attained such capacities, parents are thought to be responsible for providing them with proper instruction. (Hollan and Wellenkamp 1996: 137–8)

In the words of one Torajan informant: 'Once we know shame, we must be taught by our father and our mother ... As long as one is human, one must have shame. But parents add to it' (Hollan and Wellenkamp 1996: 135). Eventually, a range of other complex emotional conduct is inculcated on this initial foundation. Initially, as Hollan and Wellenkamp point out, parents can only rely on 'frightening' or 'shaming' children to control them. Thus, shame and fear are linked and learned at an early age.

Of other ethnographers, Keeler is perhaps the most explicit in linking shame/embarrassment (*isin*) with fear (*wedi*) among the Javanese, although, in fact, this only restates Hildred Geertz's exposition on the socialisation of Javanese emotions. As she writes:

> Javanese children are *taught* how to be *wedi* and *isin*; they are praised for being *wedi* to their elders and *isin* to their betters ... They learn *wedi* first ... [and] As they grow older *isin* is taught to them. (Geertz 1959: 233)

Rosaldo is equally explicit in her description of the core emotions taught to Ilongot children. In her discussion of early development of knowledge, she writes:

> [O]bedience to the demands of another grows from 'fear' or *kayub*, and from *bētang*, a word whose sense includes aspects of the English 'respect', 'embarrassment' and 'shame' ... 'Fear' and 'shame' are understood by adults as the condition of obedience. (Rosaldo 1980: 70)

Lutz provides an extended and nuanced discussion of the relationship between the key emotions of shame/embarrassment (*ma*), fear/anxiety (*metagu*) and compassion/love/sadness (*fago*) among the Ifaluk. The Ifaluk ideal is to be a 'gentle', 'calm and quiet' person and not to be 'hot-tempered'. Feelings of *fago*, *ma* and *metagu* are the means by which a person is able to be such a calm person (Lutz 1988: 176–90).

Among the Marquesan informants, according to Kirkpatrick, this relationship is direct: 'in shame, the belly trembles in fear' (1985: 89). Among the Rotenese in eastern Indonesia (Fox, Chapter 5, this volume), rituals require the pairing of terms, including all key emotions. As such, the term for 'shame' (*mae*) pairs with the term for 'fear' (*bi*) so that, at critical junctions of ritual uncertainty, the formal injunction to participants is *boso bi ma boso mae*: 'do not be fearful, do not be ashamed'. Valerio Valeri describes this connection between fear and shame among the Huaulu of Ceram in terms of its converse: 'Being unashamed in the eyes of the others may occur just like being unafraid' (2000: 404).

Casting the examination of emotions in a wider context for Samoa, Gerber locates the emotions of shame (*māsiasi*) and fear (*fefe*) in close relationship to one another and in the same cluster (Cluster 4) with emotions of shyness (*matamuli*), worry (*popole*) and hurt (*mafatia*). Anger and jealousy are in a separate cluster (Gerber 1985: 140). Interestingly, Lutz, who has carried out a cluster analysis of Ifaluk emotions, also locates shame/embarrassment (*ma*) in the same cluster (Cluster 2) with fear/anxiety (*metagu*)—a cluster that also includes terms for discomfort (*lugumet*), fright (*rus*) and disappointment (*bobo*), which are all emotions of negative valence (1982: 116). Similarly, Heider, in his examination of the relationship among named Minangkabau emotions, draws the connection between shame (*malu, segan*) and fear (*takut*) more emphatically, arguing for a 'close association of "fear" and "shame"' (2011: 142), and going so far as to assign the gloss 'shame' as another translation for the word *takut*. In his second volume, *The Cultural Context of Emotion*, Heider provides an extended and nuanced discussion, in succession, of these two terms (2011: 127–46).

Certainly, an impressive array of ethnographers has separately but cogently pointed to a significant relationship between shame and fear among Austronesian populations—from Sumatra and Java through eastern Indonesia to the Pacific. This in itself is of interest but perhaps, more importantly, such observations suggest that, to reach an understanding of Austronesian emotions, they have to be approached not individually as separate sentiments but relationally one to another within a wider context.

Linguistic research on Austronesian thought and emotions: Various starting points

Linguistic approaches to the study of Austronesian thought and emotion are certainly as various as those in anthropology. Often of a comparative focus, these studies frequently differ in their scope and direction. One particularly productive starting point for linguistic comparisons is the paper by James Matisoff 'Hearts and minds in South-East Asian languages and English' (1986). Directed to the comparative examination of various languages in South-East Asia—mainly belonging to the Sino-Tibetan language family (Burmese, Lahu, Jingpho), but also Thai—Matisoff calls attention to what he describes as 'psycho-collocations': the lexico-semantic designation of mental activities and personal qualities by metaphoric associations with bodily parts. In his scheme, a 'psycho-term' (psycho) is combined with a 'psycho-mate' (mate) to produce a 'psycho-collocation' (psi-collocation). He illustrates this with two simple examples:

Language	Phrase	Psycho	Mate	Psycho-collocation
Lahu	*ni-ma-lù*	'heart'	'ruin'	'be depressed'
		Mate	**Psycho**	
Thai	*wáj caj*	'keep'	'heart'	'trust in'

While such psycho-collocations may be universal in languages, they differ significantly among languages, although similar general patterning may occur within related groups of languages. Certainly, Matisoff's observations are relevant to Austronesian languages. He has given a focus to what has been reported on and described by linguists, anthropologists and especially dictionary compilers.

For comparative purposes, it is useful to begin with a discussion of similar psycho-collocations among Austronesian-language speakers in Taiwan. In a valuable short paper (2002), Shuanfan Huang has provided excellent examples of such psycho-collocations among the Tsou. A key element of his argument is that the Tsou language possesses no means of nominalising emotional concepts: 'emotion concepts must be realized syntactically as verbs and can never be nominalized' (Huang 2002: 171–2). Hence, Tsou does not and cannot exploit what Lakoff and Johnson (1980) call 'ontological metaphors'. Although perhaps not as pronounced as in Tsou, this is a tendency evident in other Austronesian languages as well.

Instead, in Tsou, emotions and processes of thought are expressed in relation to the body. 'The body part most intimately associated with cognition (thinking or intending) or feeling in Tsou is *koyu* "ear", the seat of Tsou emotion and mentation' (Huang 2002: 172). Various examples of this are the following:

- *micu nae'o co koyu-taini*: 'she has been sad' (lit.: his/her ear has been sad)
- *os'o cong'eneni koyo 'e*: 'I feel distressed about my children' (lit.: my ear aches for my children)

- *ci os'ko cohivi co koyu-'u?* 'How do you know what I think?' (lit.: how do you know my ear?)

- *ci na'on kuici koyu?* 'Why are you in such a bad mood?' (lit.: why are your ears so bad?)

From his linguistic analysis, Huang goes on to suggest that 'grammatical models involving prefixation in Tsou make it far more sensitive to the co-presence of emotions and behaviour responses at the expense of physiological effects in emotional experience' (2002: 182).

Indonesian (Malay) provides an extensive array of recognisable psycho-collocations. As is common among western Austronesian populations, here, the liver (in Indonesian: *hati*; Proto-Malayo-Polynesian: **qatay*) provides the basis for a significant number of psycho-collocations. Just a few of these psycho-collocations (from Echols and Shadily 1992: 206–7), of which there are many, are sufficiently illustrative:

hati bejar	'courageous, encouraged'
hati bercagak	'insincere'
hati berkarat	'corrupted'
hati buntu	'afraid, uneasy'
hati beku	'cold-hearted, unhappy'
hati kecut	'timid'
berhati berjantung	'to be sensitive, compassionate'
berhati dendam	'to be revengeful'
berhati-hati	'to be careful'
berhati rawan	'to be depressed, melancholy'
berhati tungau	'to be cowardly'
berhati walang	'to be concerned, anxious'

This list offers an illustration of the use of *hati* as a marker of emotions in Malay and Indonesian. Linguist Cliff Goddard has written far more extensively on the use of *hati* as a 'key word in the Malay vocabulary of emotion' (2001: 167–95). His study highlights the extraordinary range and nuanced usage of this body term (see also Goddard 1996).

As a Malayic language, Iban shows many similarities to Indonesian (Malay). Clifford Sather, in his contribution to this volume (Chapter 3), lists a variety of Iban psycho-collocations that are based on the liver/heart (*ati*) as 'the principal seat of sentient awareness'. Among the Iban psycho-collocations he cites are the following:

gaga ati	'happy'
pengerindu' ati	'glad'
tusah ati	'sad'
sinu' ati	'pity'
penakut ati	'frightened'
pengerawan ati	'nervous, fearful'
pengirau ati	'worried, anxious'
pemerani ati	'courageous'
tembu' ati	'contented'
penaluk ati	'obedient'
pengangkun ati	'steadfast, loyal'
chemuru ati	'jealous'
pengaru' ati	'suspicious'
bebulu ati	'ill-natured'
begedi' ati	'hate'

Recognising the relationship with Malay, Sather goes on to cite various Iban expressions that share a close resemblance to their Malay equivalent. Thus, for example, he notes:

> *ambil hati* (fetch + heart) in Malay and *ngambi' ati* (fetch + heart) in Iban have roughly the same meaning: 'to attract' or 'win the affections of'. Similarly, *bakar hati* (burn + heart) in Malay and *panas ati* (hot + heart) in Iban both mean 'hot-tempered'; *busok hati* (rotten + heart) in Malay and *jai ati* (bad + heart) in Iban both mean 'quick to take offence', 'ill-natured'; and *sakit hati* (sick + heart) in Malay and *pedis ati* (hurt + heart) in Iban both mean 'annoyed', 'angry'.

He also notes where similarly constructed idiomatic expressions differ: '*besar hati* (big + heart) in Malay has a slightly different meaning to *besai hati* (big + heart) in Iban'. Finally, but equally importantly, he notes where there appear to be no equivalences:

> In Iban, there are no precise counterparts of the Malay *kecil hati* (small + heart) or of *puteh hati* (white + heart), while there are no apparent counterparts in Malay of the Iban expressions *pengaru' ati* (scratchy + heart), *bebulu ati* (to have hair + heart) or *ensiban ati* (splinter/thorn in the flesh + heart).

In identifying both the metaphoric similarities and the differences in these expressions of emotions between Malay and Iban, Sather also points to other bodily loci for the expression of emotions—particularly the 'gall bladder' (*empedu*; Proto-Malayo-Polynesian: *qapeju*) for 'shame' and the 'bones' (*tulang*) for feelings of strength or weakness. All of these emotions arise and emanate from within (*di dalam*).

Michelle Rosaldo concludes her Ilongot study, *Knowledge and Passion*, with an extended glossary (1980: 236–57) of the key terms she discusses in her ethnography. Under each of some 80 key terms, she provides a number of Ilongot sample sentences 'culled from texts, lexical interviews and notes on conversations' (Rosaldo 1980: 236). Her translations of these sentences are intended to give 'a sense of the lively and often "literal" ways that apparent "metaphors" tend to be seen' (Rosaldo 1980: 236). Among these key terms are a host of expressions for specific emotions that show clearly their basis as psycho-collocations.

For the Ilongot, *rinawa*, which Rosaldo glosses as 'heart', is the primary bodily focus of the emotions. (It is a reflex of the term *nyawa*, which more generally, in other Austronesian languages, is associated with 'breath' or 'spirit' and serves as another common psychosomatic linguistic operator for the expression of cognitive and emotional states. See Sather, Chapter 3, this volume.) In her glossary, Rosaldo gives a plethora of usages of this *rinawa* for the different expression of sentiments. As she explains, *rinawa* can be used verbally to mean 'like, want'. Here are a variety of the uses of *rinawa* in a selection of different sample sentences forming psycho-collocations based on various verbal 'mates':

> *rinawa* ('to will, want, to take heart')
>
> *Nu 'away rinawa mesigalan ma tu'u*: 'A person without a heart gets thin.'
>
> *Nan'irinaway de*: 'Their hearts are joined, they are in love.'
>
> *'aleng* ('to be bored, weakened, sullen, dull')
>
> *Nu si ligetka 'un'a' aleng ta rinawan*: 'If you are angry, your heart grows weak and dull.'
>
> *dikrat* ('to be startled, made to jump, be distressed')
>
> *Dimikrat ma rinawak 'eta'gi kimeyeb*: 'My heart was startled and rose with sudden distress.'
>
> *kemnu* ('to be disappointed')
>
> *Kimemnuy ma rinawak*: 'My heart was disappointed, saddened.'
>
> *ngalemken* ('to tense, clutch, be angry')
>
> *'Engngalemkem ma rinawak nu meligetanak*: 'My heart clutches with anger.'

ruyuk ('to lengthen, be long, be happy')

'Awana 'unsipēka nu 'ed mangruyuk ma rinawan: 'You won't be happy, if our heart does not lengthen.'

As one moves eastward, the bodily focus for thought and emotion shifts towards a more general inner organ of the body, which is variously identified as 'inside', 'inner core', 'heart' or even sometimes 'belly' or 'gut'.

For Rotenese, this organ is referred to as the *dale(k)* (lit.: 'the inside') and, as such, it serves as the linguistic basis for a range of sentiments, a few of which are illustrative of this psycho-collocation (for an extended discussion, see Fox, Chapter 5, this volume):

dale malole: 'good-hearted, kind'
dale maloak: 'open, generous'
dale hedi: 'sad, sick at heart'

For Tetun speakers on Timor, this organ of thought and feeling is referred to by a cognate term, *laran*, which means 'inside' and is implicated in similar psycho-collocations. The following examples (cited by Grimes, Chapter 6, this volume) closely parallel those of the Rotenese:

nia laran di'ak: 'he is good-hearted, kind'
nia laran maluka: 'he is open, generous, helpful'
nia laran moras: 'he is offended, sickened'

Although there are notable similarities in the bodily expression of some emotional idioms in Rotenese and Tetun, the differences between these closely related languages are equally pertinent. Tetun directs the expression of emotions to a wider array of body parts than Rotenese, which relies more heavily on expressions based on 'inside' (*dale*) and 'stomach/belly' (*tei*). Thus, for example, as Grimes notes, in Tetun, 'anger' is associated with 'breath' or 'life force' (*nawan*), as in the expression *nia nawan badak*: 'he is quick to get angry'. Among the Rotenese, anger is conceived as a 'storm' that sweeps over a person, but a person inclined to ill temper and anger is described as *dale nasa-meluk*: 'bitter-hearted'. For the Tetun, 'selfishness' is located in the 'liver' (*ate*), as indicated by Grimes:

ema ne'e, ate kabahat: 'this person is very selfish/unsharing/stingy'
eme ne'e, ate fa'ek: 'this person is self-centred'

For the Rotenese, a similar attribution is associated with the paired terms 'inside/heart'//'stomach/belly' (*dale*//*tei*); a selfish person is someone who only follows 'the *dale*'s wish and the *te'i*'s desire' (*dale hi ma tei nauk*).

For the Buli of Halmahera, whose language is classified as belonging to the South Halmahera–West New Guinea subgroup of Austronesian, a similar body organ is identified as the *uló*, which is glossed as 'the inner core, feeling, heart, consciousness'. Bubandt, writing of the Buli (2015: 125), provides a range of usages of this term 'to express a wide range of emotional and cognitive states':

> *uló loló*: 'to wish for, to like, to have in the inner core'
> *uló ya senga*: 'to be happy'
> *uló ya kangelá*: 'to be troubled, sad'
> *uló ya amici*: 'to be jealous, envious'
> *uló ya mafia*: 'to be a good person'
> *uló ya mafia*: 'to be a bad person, to have a bad inner core'
> *uló ya neto*: 'to remember'
> *uló ya lal*: 'to be undecided, to have many inner cores'

For the Dobu, this bodily inner core is referred to as *nua*, a term glossed as 'mind'. Dozens of compound expressions for thought and emotion rely on *nua* to create the appropriate psycho-collocation. Susanne Kuehling (Chapter 7, this volume) cites a variety of these expressions:

> *nua-mwauta*: 'descending, to be humble'
> *nua-tue*: 'climbing up, to be boastful'
> *nua-mwau*: 'heavy, to be worried'
> *nua-siwalowa*: 'calm and quiet, to be at peace'
> *nua-'iyowana*: 'wandering aimlessly, to be confused'

Malinowski, in his classic study, *The Argonauts of the Western Pacific* (1922), translated the term *nanola* as 'mind' among the Trobrianders and, following his informants' comments, identified this organ with the larynx, but he went on to explain that all knowledge, especially magical formulae, resides in the belly and from there rises to the mind. Whereas this understanding represents Trobriand conceptions, the term *nanola* (root: *nano*) is in fact a reflex of the Proto-Oceanic (POc) **lalo* and Proto-Malayo-Polynesian (PMP) **dalem*, meaning 'inside' (see Osmond 2016: 523–33). Following Malinowski's work, Gunter Senft carried out a systematic examination of terms for the body and their use in the expression of thought and emotions (1998). (His Appendix A, 'Kilivila body-part terms', is particularly useful: Senft 1998: 94–103.) Of more than 50 such idiomatic expressions, a majority rely on the root *nano-* (translated as 'larynx'), although key expressions also refer to the body (*vovo-*) as a whole, the head (*daha-*) and the belly (*lopo-*) (Senft 1988: 77).

Senft quotes one of his informants whose comments replicate what Malinowski's informants told him: 'If I whisper magic, the magical formulae will go from my lopo to my nano' (1998: 89). A few of the many psycho-collocations based on *nano-* that encompass a range of emotions and cognitive states are expressions such as:

i-polu nanom: 'it makes you jealous' (boils the mind)
i-kaikai nanosi: 'it irritates them' (it 'lightens' the mind)
i-mwau nano-gu: 'I am sad' (my mind is heavy)
bi-manum nanomi: 'you won't be angry' (your minds will be soft)
i-taki nanola: 's/he is obsessed'
i-yogagi-si: 'it upsets him/her' (it spoils him/her)

Although not all Austronesian emotions or cognition are expressed through psycho-collocations, it is impossible to consider the expression of such personalised processes without reference to these linguistic forms. Psycho-collocations and body metaphors may well constitute linguistic universals; the expression of these in relation to different body parts—ear, liver, heart, head, inside, belly, larynx—among Austronesian speakers is of comparative interest.

In the fifth volume of *The Lexicon of Proto Oceanic*, focused on mind and body, Meredith Osmond surveys the variety of body-part metaphors used in the lexical expression of the emotions, as well as cognitive states and their distribution among Oceanic languages (2016: 519–34). The two most prominent of these lexical resources are based on the roots **qate* (most closely associated with the 'liver') and **lalom* (associated with 'inside' or 'mind').

The modifying terms used in relation to these body parts comprise a relatively small repertoire—'good', 'bad', 'heavy', 'big', 'small', 'hot' or 'hard'—to invoke feelings of happiness, sadness or anger. To which may be added, more generally, terms that describe further qualities such as 'soft', 'cool', 'firm' or 'watery', as well as aspects of motion such as 'descending', 'dropping', 'trembling' or 'quivering', together with bodily actions based on 'eating', 'swallowing' or 'holding'.

In addition to the key body-part terms, *qate and *lalom, other body-part terms occur: 'mouth' (POc: *qawa), 'face' (POc: *nako), 'eye' (POc: *mata), 'skin' (POc: *popo), 'head' (POc: *daba) and 'throat/voice' (POc: liqoR).[3] Interestingly, the expression for 'doubt' or 'hesitation'—'to be of two minds/heads' (*lalo *rua-rua)—is as common in Oceania as it is elsewhere among Austronesian speakers (Ross and Osmond 2016: 559–61). The survey also identifies where lexical substitutions have occurred. Thus, for example, *nua ('mind, inside'; POc: *nuka) has replaced *lalom in the Papuan tip languages including Dobu (see Kuehling, Chapter 7, this volume).

It is important to recognise the relational aspects of these various local conceptions of the emotions in relation to different body parts and how they are patterned differently across the Austronesian-speaking world. Among the Rotenese, the 'eyes' (mata) serve as the locus for the expression of key emotions, both positive and negative. Hence, a person's integrity as well as their 'shame' are said to be seen in their eyes. By contrast, among the Huaulu of Ceram, 'shame' as a form of ugliness is considered to be visible on the 'skin' (Valeri 2000: 405). This idea of 'skin' as the manifest expression for states of being, particularly shame, can be found among Austronesian speakers on islands on both sides of New Guinea (see Strathern 1977 for similar notions among non-Austronesians, from whom the idea may have originated). Richard Eves, in his ethnography *The Magical Body*, which looks at the Lelet of New Ireland, discusses the idea of 'skin' as a 'metonym for the body' that discloses 'inner states of the person to the world' where what is 'inside is made visible on the outside' (1998: 28). It follows, therefore, that 'shame is said to cover up or inhere in the skin and to be made manifest in bodily dispositions and comportments' (Eves 1998: 126). Suzanne Kuehling (Chapter 7) aptly describes the skin as the 'almost public messaging board' among the Dobu.

Given the prominence associated with the 'ear' among the Tsou, it is perhaps worth noting the pertinent general observation made by Osmond and Pawley in regard to the linguistic expression of the senses in the chapter of *The Lexicon of Proto Oceanic, Volume 5*, devoted to perceptions:

---

3   Robert Blust, in his discussion of body-part terms and their extensions (2013: 321–7), gives particular attention to metaphors based on the 'eye' (Proto-Austronesian: *maCa), but also to metaphors of the 'gall' and 'liver'.

Comparison of a large sample of Oceanic languages shows that most verbs of sensing have remained dedicated to a single sense. For most people, sight is the primary source of objective data about the world, and evidently was treated as such by Proto Oceanic speakers. We have no examples from a sample of many dozens of languages where a verb meaning 'see' has extended its meaning to other senses, although it can carry a cognitive meaning like 'know' or 'recognise'. In contrast, *roŋoR 'hear' is the most semantically elastic of the sense terms. In some languages of the Solomons, Vanuatu and Polynesia, reflexes, still with the primary meaning 'hear', can be extended to 'smell', 'taste' and 'feel', although never to 'see'. (Osmond and Pawley 2016: 516)

Contributions to a comparative endeavour

This volume is an attempt to rekindle interest in the comparative study of thought and the emotions specifically in reference to Austronesian-speaking populations. Although this is rarely defined as a specific research area, the weight of ethnographic research that has already been done points to a tantalising array of patterned similarities. The agenda is open and invites further research.

As part of this agenda, the chapters in this volume offer different approaches to this research. They are ethnographic explorations based on long personal engagement with different societies over a wide stretch of the Austronesian world, from Sumatra, Borneo and Sulawesi to Rote and Timor and to Dobu in Melanesia. As a collection, these chapters cover both the western and eastern regions of the Austronesian-speaking world.

The first three chapters in this volume focus on societies in western Austronesia. Minako Sakai's paper (Chapter 2) on the Gumay of South Sumatra touches on the Malayic world of *perasaan* from the term *rasa*, which most Malay dictionaries take at least a column to attempt to explicate—a term that shades from feeling and sensation to personal experience. It also deals with the significance of dreaming (*mimpi*) and visions (*ginaan*) set within a social context that communicates across an urban–village continuum.[4] Clifford Sather's paper (Chapter 3) is

---

4   Minako Sakai's excellent ethnography of the Gumay based on her ANU dissertation, 'The nut cannot forget its shell: Gumay identity, Islamisation and outmigration in South Sumatra', has been published in Indonesian (*Kacang Tidak Lupa Kulitnya: Identitas Gumay, Islam dan Merantau di Sumatera Selatan*, 2017) but not yet in English.

a beautiful, extended disquisition on the equally elusive idea of love (*rindu, kasih*) among the Iban of Borneo. It is also an extension of his stunningly comprehensive monograph *Seeds of Play, Words of Power* (Sather 2001), which examines a large corpus of shamanistic texts that illustrate the cosmic conceptions of a lived-in spirit world. Roxana Waterson's paper (Chapter 4) offers a concerted argument for the study of empathy, whose learning she examines in children's accounts of their personal participation in the crucial rituals of the Toraja of Sulawesi. Waterson draws on decades of research among the Toraja, ethnographically encapsulated in *Paths and Rivers: Sa'dan Toraja society in transformation* (2009), to situate her research, while pointing to new comparative directions for the study of empathy illustrated in the recent collection of papers edited by Douglas W. Hollan and C. Jason Throop, *The Anthropology of Empathy* (2011). For all three of these chapters, there is a further linking theme that focuses on the shared emotions that derive from participation in key rituals.

The three chapters in this volume that deal with societies in eastern Austronesia are concerned to define a range of cognitive and emotional categories, a majority of which relate to the body and, as such, provide the underpinnings of a conception of the human person. Fox's paper (Chapter 5) examines the linguistic bases for the notion of an 'inner person' and the 'outward' representation of that person within Rotenese society. He draws, in particular, on the evidence of Rotenese ritual language that gives formal expression to the categorisation of thought and emotion (Fox 2014, 2016). Barbara Dix Grimes (Chapter 6) offers a similar examination of the expression of thought and emotion, among the Tetun of Timor, not as abstract 'feelings', but as 'body talk'. Her conclusion is that, among the Tetun, this body talk asserts social-emotional agency: 'as agents act, their social-emotional states are read from their bodies'. Susanne Kuehling (Chapter 7) extends these same ideas to Dobu. Her analysis, set within a comparative perspective based on fieldwork on Yap as well as on Dobu, links attitudes about posture to the expression of the 'inner' person, arguing the case for the 'Austronesian body as a site for sociality'.

All of these chapters contribute to an ethnographic understanding of a particular Austronesian-speaking population. Through such contributions, the comparative effort builds slowly, piece by piece, ethnography by ethnography. Fortunately, for the field as a whole, superb ethnographies continue to be written that cover the whole of the Austronesian-speaking world. Each of these ethnographies sets out to 'capture the grain of the wood' of a particular way of life and, in so doing, offers a distinctive presentation. The critical issue, for the comparative effort, is to recognise similar patterning in different contexts. An essential stricture is to continue to read and re-read this proliferation of ethnographies.

This rich ethnographic proliferation has prompted a high degree of specialisation. Developing expertise in the field of Borneo research is as daunting a task as developing expertise in the field of Oceanic research, or of Malagasy or of Moluccan research. Comparative Austronesian has, as a result, become divided by its regional competencies. For comparative purposes, a regional focus has, however, to be considered in relational perspective. Although regions may possess distinctive aspects, no region can be easily circumscribed. All regions share features of a common heritage that extends, in degrees, to other regions. Eastern Indonesia offers a particularly apt illustration of comparative complexity. As a geographic region, it comprises various distinct island subregions; it forms a linguistic transition zone within the Austronesian world (Donohue and Grimes 2008). In its more recent historical and colonial features, it has much in common with the islands of Indonesia and South-East Asia, but, in basic social structure, it shares more features with Oceania than it does with closer islands to the west (Fox 2015). Another essential stricture required for the comparative endeavour is the need to read across ethnographic regions—not simply in the attempt to recognise similarities, but rather to recognise the transformations that have given rise to differences in the Austronesian world.

References

Black, Peter W. 1985. 'Ghosts, gossip, and suicide: Meaning and action in Tobian folk psychology'. In Geoffrey M. White and John T. Kirkpatrick (eds) *Person, Self, and Experience: Exploring Pacific ethnopsychologies*, pp. 245–300. Berkeley, CA: University of California Press.

Blust, Robert. 2013. *The Austronesian Languages*. Canberra: Asia-Pacific Linguistics. Available from: hdl.handle.net/1885/10191 (accessed 28 July 2017).

Bubandt, Nils. 2015. *The Empty Seashell: Witchcraft and doubt on an Indonesian island*. Singapore: NUS Press.

Donohue, Mark and Charles E. Grimes. 2008. 'Yet more on the position of the languages of eastern Indonesia and East Timor'. *Oceanic Linguistics* 47(1): 114–58. doi.org/10.1353/ol.0.0008.

Echols, John M. and Hassan Shadily. 1992. *Kamus Indonesia Inggris* [*Indonesian–English Dictionary*]. Jakarta: Penerbit PT Gramedia Indonesia.

Eves, Richard. 1998. *The Magical Body: Power, fame and meaning in a Melanesian society*. Amsterdam: Harwood Academic Publishers.

Fox, James J. 2014. *Explorations in Semantic Parallelism*. Canberra: ANU Press. doi.org/10.22459/ESP.07.2014.

Fox, James J. 2015. 'Eastern Indonesia in Austronesian perspective: The evidence of relational terminologies'. *Archipel* 90: 189–216. doi.org/10.4000/archipel.381.

Fox, James J. 2016. *Master Poets, Ritual Masters: The art of oral composition among the Rotenese of eastern Indonesia*. Canberra: ANU Press. doi.org/10.22459/MPRM.04.2016.

Geertz, Clifford. 1966. *Person, time and conduct in Bali: An essay in cultural analysis*. Cultural Report Series No. 14. Southeast Asian Series. New Haven, CT: Yale University. [Reprinted in Geertz, Clifford. 1973. *The Interpretation of Cultures*, pp. 360–411. New York: Basic Books.]

Geertz, Clifford. 1984. 'From the native's point of view: On the nature of anthropological understanding'. In Richard A. Shweder and Robert A. LeVine (eds) *Culture Theory: Essays on mind, self and emotion*, pp. 123–36. Cambridge: Cambridge University Press.

Geertz, Hildred. 1959. 'The vocabulary of emotion: A study of Javanese socialization'. *Psychiatry* 22: 225–37. doi.org/10.1080/00332747.195 9.11023175.

Gerber, Eleanor Ruth. 1985. 'Rage and obligation: Samoan emotion in conflict'. In Geoffrey M. White and John T. Kirkpatrick (eds) *Person, Self, and Experience: Exploring Pacific ethnopsychologies*, pp. 121–67. Berkeley, CA: University of California Press.

Goddard, Cliff. 1996. 'The "social emotions" of Malay (Bahasa Melayu)'. *Ethos* 24(3): 426–64. doi.org/10.1525/eth.1996.24.3.02a00020.

Goddard, Cliff. 2001. 'Hati: A key word in the Malay vocabulary of emotion'. In Jean Harkins and Anna Wierzbicka (eds) *Emotions in Crosslinguistic Perspective*, pp. 167–95. Berlin: Mouton de Gruyter. doi.org/10.1515/9783110880168.167.

Heider, Karl. 1981. *Landscapes of Emotion: Mapping three cultures of emotion in Indonesia*. New York: Cambridge University Press.

Heider, Karl. 2011. *The Cultural Context of Emotion: Folk psychology in West Sumatra*. New York: Palgrave Macmillan. doi.org/10.1057/9780230337596.

Hollan, Douglas W. and C. Jason Throop. 2011. *The Anthropology of Empathy: Experiencing the lives of others in Pacific societies*. New York: Berghahn Books.

Hollan, Douglas W. and Jane Wellenkamp. 1996. *The Thread of Life: Torajan reflections on the life cycle*. Honolulu: University of Hawai'i Press.

Huang, Shuanfan. 2002. 'Tsou is different: A cognitive perspective on language, emotion, and body'. *Cognitive Linguistics* 13(2): 167–86. doi.org/10.1515/cogl.2002.013.

Ito, Karen L. 1985. 'Affective bonds: Hawaiian interrelationships of self'. In Geoffrey M. White and John T. Kirkpatrick (eds) *Person, Self, and Experience: Exploring Pacific ethnopsychologies*, pp. 301–27. Berkeley, CA: University of California Press.

Keeler, Ward. 1983. 'Shame and stage fright in Java'. *Ethos* 11(3): 152–64. doi.org/10.1525/eth.1983.11.3.02a00040.

Kirkpatrick, John T. 1985. 'Some Marquesan understandings of action and identity'. In Geoffrey M. White and John T. Kirkpatrick (eds) *Person, Self, and Experience: Exploring Pacific ethnopsychologies*, pp. 80–120. Berkeley, CA: University of California Press.

Lakoff, George and Mark Johnson. 1980. *Metaphors We Live By*. Chicago: University of Chicago Press.

Levy, Robert I. 1973. *Tahitians: Mind and experience in the Society Islands*. Chicago: University of Chicago Press.

Levy, Robert I. 1983. 'Introduction: Self and emotion'. *Ethos* 11(3): 128–34. doi.org/10.1525/eth.1983.11.3.02a00020.

Levy, Robert I. 1984. 'Emotion, knowing and culture'. In Richard A. Shweder and Robert A. LeVine (eds) *Culture Theory: Essays on Mind, Self and Emotion*, pp. 214–37. Cambridge: Cambridge University Press.

Lutz, Catherine. 1982. 'The domain of emotion words on Ifaluk'. *American Ethnologist* 9: 113–28. doi.org/10.1525/ae.1982.9.1.02a00070.

Lutz, Catherine. 1985. 'Ethnopsychology compared to what? Explaining behaviour and consciousness among the Ifaluk'. In Geoffrey M. White and John T. Kirkpatrick (eds) *Person, Self, and Experience: Exploring Pacific ethnopsychologies*, pp. 35–79. Berkeley, CA: University of California Press.

Lutz, Catherine. 1988. *Unnatural Emotions: Everyday sentiments on a Micronesian atoll & their challenge to Western theory*. Chicago: University of Chicago Press.

Malinowski, Bronislaw. 1922. *The Argonauts of the Western Pacific*. London: Routledge & Kegan Paul.

Matisoff, James. 1986. 'Hearts and minds in South-East Asian languages and English: An essay in the comparative semantics of psycho-collocations'. *Cahiers de Linguistiques—Asie Orientale* 15: 5–57.

Needham, Rodney. 1962. *Structure and Sentiment: A test case in social anthropology*. Chicago: University of Chicago Press.

Needham, Rodney. 1972. *Belief, Language and Experience*. Chicago: University of Chicago Press.

Osmond, Meredith. 2016. 'Body part metaphors'. In Malcolm Ross, Andrew Pawley and Meredith Osmond (eds) *The Lexicon of Proto Oceanic. Volume 5: The culture and environment of ancestral Oceanic society. People—Body and mind*, pp. 519–34. Canberra: Asia-Pacific Linguistics.

Osmond, Meredith and Andrew Pawley. 2016. 'Perception'. In Malcolm Ross, Andrew Pawley and Meredith Osmond (eds) *The Lexicon of Proto Oceanic. Volume 5: The culture and environment of ancestral Oceanic society. People—Body and mind*, pp. 489–518. Canberra: Asia-Pacific Linguistics.

Peletz, Michael G. 1996. *Reason and Passion: Representations of gender in Malay society.* Berkeley, CA: University of California Press.

Rosaldo, Michelle Z. 1980. *Knowledge and Passion: Ilongot notions of self and social life.* Cambridge: Cambridge University Press. doi.org/10.1017/CBO9780511621833.

Rosaldo, Michelle Z. 1983. 'The shame of headhunters and the autonomy of self'. *Ethos* 11(3): 135–51. doi.org/10.1525/eth.1983.11.3.02a00030.

Rosaldo, Michelle Z. 1984. 'Toward an anthropology of self and feeling'. In Richard A. Shweder and Robert A. LeVine (eds) *Culture Theory: Essays on mind, self and emotion*, pp. 137–57. Cambridge: Cambridge University Press.

Ross, Malcolm and Meredith Osmond. 2016. 'Cognition'. In Malcolm Ross, Andrew Pawley and Meredith Osmond (eds) *The Lexicon of Proto Oceanic. Volume 5: The culture and environment of ancestral Oceanic society. People—Body and mind*, pp. 535–66. Canberra: Asia-Pacific Linguistics.

Ross, Malcolm, Andrew Pawley and Meredith Osmond (eds). 2016. *The Lexicon of Proto Oceanic. Volume 5: The culture and environment of ancestral Oceanic society. People—Body and mind.* Canberra: Asia-Pacific Linguistics.

Sakai, Minako. 2017. *Kacang Tidak Lupa Kulitnya: Identitas Gumay, Islam dan Merantau di Sumatera Selatan [The Nut Cannot Forget its Shell: Gumay identity, Islamisation and outmigration in South Sumatra].* Jakarta: Yayasan Pustaka Obor Indonesia.

Sather, Clifford. 2001. *Seeds of Play, Words of Power: An ethnographic study of Iban shamanic chants.* Kuala Lumpur: Tun Jugah Foundation and Borneo Research Council.

Senft, Gunter. 1998. 'Body and mind in the Trobriand Islands'. *Ethos* 26(1): 73–104. doi.org/10.1525/eth.1998.26.1.73.

Shweder, Richard A. and Robert A. LeVine (eds). 1984. *Culture Theory: Essays on mind, self and emotion*. Cambridge: Cambridge University Press.

Strathern, Andrew. 1977. 'Why is shame on the skin?' In John Blacking (ed.) *The Anthropology of the Body*, pp. 99–110. London: Academic Press.

Valeri, Valerio. 2000. *The Forest of Taboos: Morality, hunting and identity among the Huaulu of the Moluccas*. Madison: University of Wisconsin Press.

Waterson, Roxana. 2009. *Paths and Rivers: Sa'dan Toraja society in transformation*. Singapore: NUS Press. doi.org/10.1163/9789004253858.

White, Geoffrey M. 1985. 'Premises and purposes in a Solomon Islands ethnopsychology'. In Geoffrey M. White and John Kirkpatrick (eds) *Person, Self, and Experience: Exploring Pacific ethnopsychologies*, pp. 328–66. Berkeley, CA: University of California Press.

White, Geoffrey M. and John Kirkpatrick (eds). 1985. *Person, Self, and Experience: Exploring Pacific ethnopsychologies*. Berkeley, CA: University of California Press.

2

Fostering affinity through dreams and origin ritual practices among the Gumay of South Sumatra, Indonesia

Minako Sakai

Introduction

The Gumay people are a highland Malay-speaking ethnic group in the province of South Sumatra in Indonesia.[1] The most fundamental emotion for the Gumay is their respect for their ancestors and the origin villages associated with their ancestors, which are known as *dusun laman*. Remembering one's origin (Sakai 1997, 2002, 2006, 2009) is the most important obligation as a Gumay. Remembering one's origin means maintaining their relationship with the *dusun laman* through regular visits. *Dusun laman* generally refers to a hamlet to which Gumay people, living and deceased, belong, and is a place strongly affiliated with Gumay origins. Affinity and strong emotion are evoked when Gumay people return to their *dusun laman*. They celebrate their link to a *dusun laman* by holding

---

1   Before 2000, Gumai was the common spelling used in official documents. However, after the democratisation of Indonesia and the revival of regional culture, Gumay has become the preferred spelling. I have used Gumai in my earlier research publications, but, reflecting the change in the field, I use Gumay in this chapter.

a *sedekah* or ritual feast gathering. People express their happiness, safety and peacefulness when they return to their *dusun laman*. Thus, closeness and affection are not limited to expressions of romantic love.

The aim of this chapter is to explain how people's affinity with their *dusun laman* is expressed through kinship relations and emotional categories such as dreams (*mimpi*), visions (*ginaan*) or feelings (*perasan*). Dreams and visions often convey conscious and unconscious affinity with the origin village and messages in dreams and visions frequently lead to the formation of figurative kinship terms to revive and strengthen their links to *dusun laman*. Such figurative relations are not limited to Gumay people, but also may be applied to non-Gumay people such as myself who have developed strong emotional ties with Gumay people.

I conducted 20 months of fieldwork in Gumay Talang, located near the city of Lahat, in Indonesia's South Sumatra Province. I lived with two important Gumay families throughout this period, and was adopted as their daughter. My figurative adoption took place because I developed strong relations, as I will outline in two of the case studies in this chapter. Even after my initial fieldwork, I have maintained close contact with these two families over the past two decades through short visits and, increasingly, through the use of mobile phones. I made a short visit to Gumay Talang in August and in November 2015 to update and check my ethnographic data.

The structure of this chapter is as follows: the first section will provide an overview of the South Sumatran highlands and the origin stories of the Gumay. The second section will discuss the ways Gumay formalise affinity and affection including kinship relations and the ritual practice of *sedekah*. The third section consists of case studies that illustrate how affinity and affection are embodied in kinship relations, ritual practices and spatial connections with, and expressed desire to return to, one's origins (*dusun laman*). I will argue that dreams and feeling provide an opportunity for the Gumay to remember their affinity with *dusun laman*, despite the increasing influence of Islamisation in the everyday life of the Gumay (Sakai 1997, 2002, 2009, 2017a, 2017b).

Overview

There are three main clusters of Gumay villages in South Sumatra Province: Gumay Ulu, Gumay Lembak and Gumay Talang. These names were originally used as an administrative unit (*marga*), prior to the 1980s. All three clusters are located in the district of Lahat. Gumay Talang, the newest cluster of 14 villages, is about 15 km from the city of Lahat. These 14 villages became an administrative unit known as *kecamatan* (subdistrict) around 2008. While there is no specific statistical record available regarding the total Gumay population in Indonesia, the 2010 census shows the population of Gumay Talang was 9,804.[2] This population size is small for Indonesia, but an ethnographic study of Gumay is important in understanding the South Sumatran population. This is because Gumay people share general cultural traits of highland Malay speakers in a region in which numerous ethnic groups have long co-resided. For example, Gumay people have ancestral relations with neighbouring Besemah and Semendo people living in South Sumatra Province (Collins 1979: 20–35). Gumay also share general cultural traits with other nearby ethnic groups such as Empat Lawang, Belido, Lintang and Kikim in South Sumatra and Bengkulu and Lampung.

The name Gumay is widely known in the South Sumatra, as they are believed to be the oldest ethnic group in the region. The Gumay people claim to have migrated from Palembang and spread widely along nine major rivers (*Batang Hari Sembilan*) in southern Sumatra. According to their oral narratives, their founding ancestor, Diwe Gumay, was the first to descend from the Bukit Segungtang (Segungtan Hill) in Palembang on the night known as Malam Empat Belas. The descendants of the founding Gumay have moved upstream along major rivers, looking for fertile land and have settled in the highland areas near Lahat. Gumay people have spread through southern Sumatra, as Gumay ancestors have formed alliances with guardians of the important spheres of sea, sky and forest.[3]

The importance of these oral narratives is represented by the continuing practice of the monthly ritual Sedekah Malam Empat Belas (Sakai 2003). The ritual, to commemorate Diwe Gumay's descent, is conducted by the

---

2   'Lahat (Regency, Indonesia): Population statistics and location in maps and charts', available from: www.citypopulation.de/php/indonesia-admin.php?adm2id=1604 (accessed 7 August 2015). The estimated population in 1994 was 8,281 (Sakai 1997: 44).

3   See Sakai (1997: 45) on Gumay's relationship with the four important spheres.

Jurai Kebali'an, the most important Gumay ritual specialist, who traces his genealogy to Diwe Gumay. This monthly ritual is considered to be the most important occasion for the Gumay to return to *dusun laman* and seek blessings from their ancestors.

The term Jurai Kebali'an consists of *jurai*, which means 'descendants', and *kebali'an*, meaning 'to return'. His house, located in Endikat Ilir village in Gumay Talang, is believed to be the house to which all Gumay descendants should return, and the monthly ritual attracts 200–500 participants—predominantly visitors from outside the immediate cluster of Gumay Talang. The ritual is to ask for blessings from guardians and ancestral spirits so that Gumay descendants will be protected and given an ample livelihood (*rezeki*). The Jurai Kebali'an conducts a series of rituals as the guardian of this earth (*junjungan di bumi*) on behalf of his descendants. He is responsible for the wellbeing and livelihood of the Gumay and other ethnic groups in the region. The presentation of offerings and sacrificial animals and the burning of the tree resin benzoin (*menyan*) constitute the core of this ritual. The majority of the Gumay and other highlanders are cash-crop farmers producing coffee, rubber and agricultural products, and their livelihood sources are closely linked to forests and the land.

Although the upkeep of *adat* (customs) matters is important for the Gumay, the South Sumatran highlanders are Muslims and Islamisation processes have penetrated into the highlands. On the surface, Islamic values and teaching dominate the ways of life among the Gumay.[4] Harvest rituals, marriage ceremonies and funerals are all conducted according to Islam. But the importance of ancestors and origin villages continues to influence the majority of the population. Unexpected illnesses, deaths of family members, misfortune and accidents are often linked to a breach of their tradition and customs. Various Gumay ritual specialists, known as Jurai Tue and Mimbar, look after matters related to ancestors—now usually called *adat*. The succession of these ritual specialists is through genealogical connections and, despite increasing Islamisation in contemporary Indonesia, I have found that younger generations of Gumay have continued to respect and maintain their roles as ritual specialists over the past 20 years of my research (Sakai 2017b).

---

4   For example, the practice of oral epics known as *guritan* at the time of mourning among the Besemah people has almost ceased and has been replaced with Islamic Qur'anic recitation of *yasinan*. See Collins (1998).

One of the main obstacles to ethnographic research in this region has been secrecy around the knowledge related to ancestors. Only ritual specialists are allowed to have the knowledge of *adat* matters. Furthermore, calling the names of ancestors is closely linked to invoking the ancestral spirits, and people are generally reluctant to talk about ancestors or genealogies without seeking permission from the ancestors. Talking about Gumay genealogies and ritual practice to a total stranger, such as a foreign anthropologist, was unthinkable until the last Jurai Kebali'an, the late R. A. Rumsyah Amasin, wholeheartedly supported my research in 1994. He was concerned that secrecy would eventually lead to the disappearance of *adat* knowledge among the Gumay. There was a general view in the South Sumatran highlands that widespread Islamisation had led to the discontinuity of the Besemah descendants (*putus jurai*), as ritual specialists of the major clans (*sumbai*) ceased to function in daily matters. Because Pak Rumsyah endorsed my research, I was given permission to observe rituals and talk to the most knowledgeable ritual specialists (Jurai Tue and Mimber). He also asked one of his daughters, Yulia, to accompany me, to show his full support of my research. I still experienced some initial doubts from ritual specialists, but my 20-month stay in the field certainly contributed to the formation of close relations with the Gumay community, particularly the two Gumay families with whom I was staying. For reasons I discuss in the next section, I was adopted as a daughter by two key Gumay families and my putative family relations opened up my entry to the Gumay community. These were the family of the Jurai Kebali'an in Endikat Ilir village, Pak Rumsyah, and the family of the late Haji Hasan Basri in Lahat city. Haji Hasan Basri, whose mother was from the Lubuk Sepang village of Gumay Lembak, had served as a member of the local parliament for the Golkar Party. His wife had also served as a member of the local parliament for two periods and was actively involved in civil organisations in Lahat. Two of their daughters were working as senior schoolteachers in Lahat and, consequently, the Hasan Basri family was known and well respected in Lahat city. Although Haji Hasan Basri was a Muslim pilgrim and was strongly against un-Islamic practices, he was very interested in knowing the history of the Gumay and their associated rituals. Consequently, he was very supportive of my stay in his house and was a discussant in my research.

Affinity and affection among the Gumay

Now let me explain the importance of origins among the Gumay and how genealogical relations are shown and expressed by putative kinship relations through adoption. Dreams are often interpreted as evidence of the existence of mutual strong emotional ties, which justify the formation of putative kinship relations.

Generally speaking, the Gumay can trace their genealogical connections to any of the ancestors. Genealogical knowledge held among the Gumay is bilateral and does not usually include generations above grandparents. The expression *nenek empat, puyang delapan* (meaning 'four grandparents and eight great-grandparents') defines the scope of genealogical knowledge held among the Gumay. Parents of grandparents and ascending generations are all referred to as ancestors, known as *puyang*. To distinguish sex, *puyang lanang* is used for male ancestors and *puyang betine* is used for female ancestors.

The Gumay select either a particular pair of ancestors or a single ancestor as the Puyang Ketunggalan Keluarge, or the sole family ancestor from whom all descendants have derived. Puyang Ketunggalan Keluarge is the highest or most distant ancestor remembered among these descendants. The selection of the Puyang Ketunggalan Keluarge is rather contingent, determined by the genealogical knowledge shared among descendants. Therefore, who is a descendant of one particular ancestor is not easy to define; rather, it is an individual point of view that determines the ultimate ancestor for each person.[5] The third ascending generation of *puyang* is the Puyang Ketunggalan Keluarge, but who is chosen for this position is determined by an individual's genealogical knowledge,[6] or possibly by a figurative adoption.

---

5   The contingency of origin group membership among the Austronesians is shown by various ethnographic findings. Waterson (1995), for instance, shows how actual membership of a *rapu*—an origin group among the Sa'dan Toraja of South Sulawesi—can only be manifested through the contribution made to the reconstruction of origin houses.

6   In other parts of Indonesia, a kin group is often formed through relationship to a house. For instance, Waterson (1995: 197) illustrates a case of *pa'rapuan* of the Sa'dan Toraja of South Sulawesi. People trace their descent from a particular house, which was made by a particular pair of ancestors. The boundaries of membership of *pa'rapuan* are contingent on the situation and individuals.

Adoption is widely practised among the Gumay. There are two types of adoption: the first is *angkat anak*, adoption of a child between genealogically related relatives. In this case, it is usually a childless uncle or aunt who adopts one of their nieces or nephews. The second type, which is equally common, is *angkat-angkatan* or figurative adoption between strangers. This can take place when two individuals share a strong friendship or affinity, and is often formalised after they have shared a loss of family members. The deceased family members may sometimes share the same name, traits or gender. For example, during my fieldwork between 1994 and 1996, I encountered the following case from Gumay Talang. SA, a woman in her 70s in Darmo village, adopted Y, a trader in her late 30s who came from Pagar Agung, in Lahat, to sell vegetables in Gumay Talang every day. Y was married and had four children, but she had lost one of her daughters, Tri, a few years earlier. In 1990, SA lost her daughter, Nur, who also had four children, one of whom was named Tri. When SA met Y, SA felt that her daughter was alive and, later, the two women discovered the coincidence of having a daughter named Tri. As a result of this adoption, Y became a daughter of SA and replaced her deceased daughter. In return, Y was able to regain Tri, her lost daughter, in the newly adopted kinship relation. In summary, both women were able to find a replacement for their deceased daughter through this figurative kinship relation.

My own adoption into two Gumay families also involved a death in both families. First, prior to my arrival, the second daughter of the Jurai Kebali'an, Ayuk Oli, had died of cancer. Before her death, she visited Japan with her husband and children and loved the country. I came from Japan and was almost the same age as Oli and became very close to Yulia, who had been close to Oli. My close relations with the family of the Jurai Kebali'an were witnessed when I went to see the last moment of the Jurai Kebali'an in a Jakarta hospital and attended his funeral in his house. As a result, I was invited to announce my adopted position in 2001 at the monthly ritual. Second, Haji Hasan Basri had lost his second daughter, who died when she was 19 years old. Her death had occurred long before my appearance in their house in the 1990s. My long stay in their family invoked memories of their lost daughter. Without undertaking any official ritual of adoption, I was often introduced as an adopted daughter from his family, and both my parents declared that I had replaced their lost daughter and my relations with them continue.

There are several reasons adoption is commonly practised, relating to the notion of remembering origins. First, the Gumay dislike not having descendants. If a Gumay dies childless, their life is regarded as unhappy because they do not have a successor in genealogical terms. Having no children is extremely undesirable among the Gumay. To avoid this, childless couples engage in both modern and traditional fertility treatments. If none of the treatments proves effective, the Gumay appoint a nephew or niece as *anak angkat* (adopted child), their genealogical successor. This adoption does not require the adopted person to cut ties physically or genealogically with his or her native place or genealogy. It aims to establish that the adopted person acknowledges origins to the adopter.

In my research site, many adult men and women had been adopted by relatives to be their successors. The adoption is normally announced at the time of a *sedekah*, or a special *sedekah* is organised to publicise it. After this, the adopted child declares that he or she is a descendant of the adopter. Thereafter, it is his/her duty to remember and make a visit to the *dusun laman* associated with the adopter.

Thus, it is evident that kinship relations are living representations of affinity to *dusun laman*, which also has close links with Gumay ancestors. There are a number of ways links with the Gumay ancestors are represented, such as through buildings or ancestral shrines.[7] One of the most important physical structures in a Gumay village is the graveyard (Sakai 2009: 56–7). However, I have noted that, due to multiple relocations of a particular village, some Gumay villages retain their dedicated graveyard at the original village site. It is common for a Gumay person to be buried in their origin village even though they had long lived elsewhere, because there is a strong desire to maintain a close relationship with their *dusun laman*.

Reflecting on this discussion, it is essential to note that the ultimate Gumay origins are represented in the notion of *dusun laman* in three ways: first, a *dusun laman* is the hamlet or village where a person is born; second, it is the place associated with one of that person's parents or a place from which ancestors originated; third, a *dusun laman* is the imagined place to which they will return for their afterlife—an abode of the soul

---

7   See Collins's (1979, 1998) and Barendregt's (2008) work on South Sumatran traditional houses.

of human beings (*roh*). The Gumay's neighbouring ethnic group the Besemah also use the concept of *dusun laman* as a place as well as a kin group (Barendregt 2008: 435).

Dreams, visions and feelings: Fostering links to the *dusun laman*

I will now present several ethnographic accounts that illustrate how dreams (*mimipi*), visions (*ginaan*) and feelings (*rase*) are used as a medium to maintain, revive or invent relations with origins or *dusun laman*. Overall, the most important concept to connect the living and the dead is *roh*, the soul of human beings. The closeness between the *roh* is considered to create strong affinity. *Roh* is distinguished from *kundu*, which determines a person's resilience and personality.

The appointment of the Jurai Kebali'an

The Jurai Kebali'an is the most important ritual role among the Gumay, and is strongly associated with his house. In other words, the Jurai Kebali'an can function best when he is within his home compound. Particularly important is the link between his bedroom and ancestral spirits. By tradition, the Jurai Kebali'an sleeps alone in his room, where the offerings are presented at the time of Sedekah Malam Empat Belas. His wife has her own room beside his bedroom; she is responsible for preparing the offerings for the rituals and enters his room only at the time of the rituals or when needed. It is a room kept for him as the Jurai Kebali'an, and should not be used for domestic or family matters. It is believed that ancestral spirits will visit the Jurai Kebali'an during his sleep to convey important messages. Gumay believe the spirits of human beings (*roh*) can travel during their sleep and, as a result, living spirits and those of the deceased can meet. Dreams therefore convey messages from the ancestors or deceased family members. One of the most important messages for the Jurai Kebali'an is who will succeed him.

It is expected the position will be inherited by one of the sons born to the Jurai Kebali'an's first wife. Where there is more than one son, it is expected the succession will be revealed by a dream or feeling experienced by the Jurai Kebali'an or his wife. In addition, a birthmark behind either ear, similar to the father's, is taken as evidence that a child is the successor. The succession is predetermined and not up to the individual to decide. For example, the previous Jurai Kebali'an, Pak Rumsyah, was not so interested in Gumay rituals or customary affairs when he was young. His elder brother, Wak Rustam Effendy, was much closer to their father and was very interested in knowing the history and customs of the Gumay people. However, their father announced that Rumsyah was going to succeed to the position of the Jurai Kebali'an, as he had a dream that showed this to be the case. Taking over his father's position was not what Rumsyah wished and he deliberately moved to Bandung after his marriage to look for a new life. During my frequent meetings with him between 1994 and 1996, he often told me that he had been plagued with illnesses and fevers while in Bandung and the doctors could not cure him. One day, out of desperation and hoping to get better, he vowed that he would go back to Lahat to take over his father's position. He later recovered from his illnesses and returned to Lahat with his wife.

Before his death in November 1999, Rumsyah did not clearly declare in public who would succeed him. There was speculation that his eldest son, Erlan, would take on the role as he was mature and had a calm and responsible nature.[8] However, Rumsyah indicated that his youngest boy, Ical, was going to replace him—to the amazement of the Gumay community. This was because Ical was then still a junior high school student, while Erlan was in his mid-20s and married with a family. Rumsyah never declared that he had a dream nor did his wife; however, his wife vividly remembered that she had not been allowed to use contraceptives before Ical was born, as Rumsyah said she still had the responsibility to bear his replacement. Shortly after that, she became pregnant with Ical. While she was pregnant she was preparing to travel to Palembang and Rumsyah told her that she had to exercise caution as she was expecting his replacement. Such feelings were eventually taken as evidence that Ical would replace Pak Rumsyah. Before his sudden death in 1999, Rumsyah was asked to announce who was going to replace him. His brothers saw Rumsyah nodding when he was asked to confirm it would be Ical. The unclear circumstances surrounding the appointment of the incoming Jurai Kebali'an cast doubt on Ical, particularly because he was still a school-aged child. Ical remained single, so he played a de facto role as Jurali Kebali'an for nearly two decades, with his official inauguration on hold until he married. He was finally married in November 2015. A week after the wedding, the inauguration ceremony took place. Following this

---

8   Erlan was elected to be a Golkar Party member of the local parliament for two terms after the democratisation of Indonesia.

event, Gumay ritual specialists were asked to report whether they had a dream revealing a suitable title to be given to the Jurai Kebali'an. Several meetings were held, but no conclusions were reached immediately, so the discussions continued for a few months until a decision was made that Ical's title would be Raden Arif, meaning wise and capable. Initially, the emphasis was given to *mangkuk*, meaning a bowl, symbolising generous acceptance and accommodation of the whole community, but the discussions eventually emphasised Arif. In summary, dreams and feelings form the most credible medium for conveying messages from the Gumay ancestors regarding the succession of the Jurai Kebali'an. This incident shows that the concept of *roh*, the human soul, is believed to enable a person to stay in this world while *nyawe* (life-sustaining principle) lasts, but *roh* can also drift during sleep. A *roh* continues to exist after death and may convey messages to Gumay descendants during a dream.

The invention of the *dusun laman*

Ancestors also convey messages to ordinary Gumay people through dreams and visions. The common theme of such dreams is to remember origins, which means Gumay people have to acknowledge and visit their origin village(s). As explained previously, there is no particular way to decide how to trace one's origins genealogically. Links are traced bilaterally to a particular ancestor and the origin village. The next case will summarise how Gumay people revive a link with their *dusun laman* and use figurative kinships to support their continuing links. Dreams and visions also play an important role, as outlined in an incident that took place in 1995 during my fieldwork.

Ali Asin knew he had a great-grandfather from Gumay; however, he had never visited any Gumay area in his life. He was married to Ross and they both lived in a village 130 km from Endikat Ilir. During 1995, they lost three grandchildren to illness. Following these deaths, Ross also became sick and fell unconscious, during which time she had a dream and spoke out loud that she acknowledged their origins in Gumay Talang. She promised she would visit and hold a *sedekah* in Gumay Talang. She also said that the medicine for her illness would be found 1 km from her home. The family later found some benzoin in a hut. In South Sumatra, benzoin is usually burnt to invoke ancestral spirits. The couple visited Gumay Talang 10 days later, but they could not find any relatives or genealogical connections with anyone and could not determine where to hold a gathering. Eventually, they went to the house of their son's best friend in Muara Tandi village. As their friendship was close, they formed an adopted sibling relationship (*saudara angkat*). Thus, it was logical to hold a gathering in Muara Tandi village, which the couple declared as their *dusun laman* at the time of the gathering.

Dreams of returning to *dusun laman*

It is reasonable to question whether interest in *dusun laman* has decreased under the increasing influence of Islam in contemporary Indonesian society. As explained earlier, the influence of Islam was strongly felt in wealthy regions of the South Sumatran highlands such as Pagar Alam, the heartland of Basemah region, as the number of pilgrims and the impact of modernist Islam (*kaum muda*) spread (Collins 1998: 13–14). I argue that the influence and importance of the *dusun laman* and ritual practice continue to dominate the everyday lives of the Gumay. Dreams and feelings continue to serve as an important medium for communication, as I outline below.

Although two families adopted me as a daughter, since 2008, I had not had a chance to visit Gumay Talang, and only maintained some communication via mobile phone calls and Facebook. One night in June 2015 while I was sleeping in Canberra, Mey, the daughter of my adopted sister Yulia, texted me from Gumay Talang. I had never received a text from her directly, but was aware she had married and had given birth to a baby boy. In my reply, I congratulated her and asked about her family. She immediately replied that her mother, Yulia, was being treated in hospital in Jakarta and had been calling my name during her sleep. Ical, Yulia's younger brother and now the de facto Jurai Kebali'an, was beside her bed and suggested that I should be contacted regarding Yulia's illness. For a month, I had some phone conversations with Yulia and her daughter regarding her illness. I later learnt that Yulia always displayed a photo of me with my son and husband in her room and explained to visitors that I was her 'sister' who lived overseas.

As her condition worsened rapidly, from late July to August 2015, I made a visit to see her in hospital—our first meeting for seven years—and saw Mey and her husband and son in Jakarta. The hospital did not provide much information about Yulia's condition, but seeing her indicated that her illness was terminal. While I was asking about Yulia's illness, Mey told me a story that indicated spirits of deceased relatives had visited her mother. It was in late June when Yulia was sitting on her bed after her bath in the early evening, with her legs swinging. Mey asked her mother what she was doing. Yulia responded that she had been invited to go somewhere far away by her elder sister Ayuk Oli and her father, Pak Rumsyah—both deceased close family members. Because Mey suggested that she should not join them, Yulia nodded, saying, 'Ok, it won't eventuate then' (*tidak jadi, ya*).

Another dream story was revealed the next day while I was at the hospital. I met Yulia's younger sister Novy and her husband, Andi, and their children. They had been visiting Yulia regularly as they lived in Jakarta. Fatigued, Andi decided to have a nap in the carers' rest room outside the ward.

While Andi was having a nap, I was alone with Yulia, who seemed to be sleeping, and I told her that I was going to Gumay Talang to see her (and my adopted) mother. I understood that she was getting old and her illness prevented her from leaving her house. I also learnt through my conversation with Novy's family that the most respected Jurai Tue of Mandi Angin village, Waq Mim, who was one of my discussants in Gumay Talang, was also unable to walk and remained confined to his house.

Later, I saw Andi sitting outside Yulia's ward chatting about various things. When I told him that I would visit Endikat Ilir to see our mother, he told me, with a surprised look, he had just had a dream during his nap in which Yulia had woken up to whisper into his ear that she wanted to go back to her house to see her mother and to visit her father's grave. It was taken as an indication of Yulia's strong wish to return to her *dusun laman*, which also could be interpreted as meaning her death was imminent and they endorsed the idea that I should visit the *dusun laman* on Yulia's behalf.

I left Jakarta the next day, as I learnt I could attend the Sedekah Malam Empat Belas in two nights. At the time of the monthly ritual, I was able to see the ritual specialists from the Gumay area who were also attending. My sudden return to Gumay Talang did not seem to cause surprise after nearly seven years of absence. I was showered with the same question: 'When did you return here?' On the night of the ritual, one of the Jurai Tue told me he had a feeling I was coming back to Gumay Talang and he told me a story related to the illness of Waq Mim. Earlier that year, he had become very ill with a high fever and fell unconscious. He was heard uttering unfamiliar words, which sounded like Japanese. People started to recite the Qur'an, as they thought Waq Mim might die at any moment. He later regained consciousness and recovered from his illness, although he had continuing problems with his leg. When he was asked to whom he was talking in his dream, he mentioned that I was visiting him. This incident was then taken as an indication that I would return to my *dusun laman* before long and people were expecting me.

Also important was the fact that this was the time it was announced in public that Ical would be married in November 2015 and would be inaugurated as the Jurai Kebali'an one week after the wedding. As an adopted member of the family, I was officially invited to attend Ical's wedding by one of the village elders because this ceremony would mark the most important event in the succession of Gumay customs. Yulia's family therefore thought she had wanted to see me before she died to inform me that her brother would finally be inaugurated in the coming November.

Yulia's close family members did not seem surprised by the fact that Yulia had become fatally ill after leaving her house the previous February. As her mother was ill and had lost her mobility, Yulia, as one of the daughters living in Endikat Ilir, had been responsible for preparing offerings at the time of the monthly Sedekah Malam Empat Belas ritual for the previous few years. However, when Mey was about to give birth, Yulia decided to move to Jakarta to look after her grandchild. To enable her to be away from her house in Endikat Ilir, Yulia had trained her half-sister and her brother's wife in how to prepare the offerings. She was heard to say that she would not be able to come back to Endikat Ilir after her grandchild was born, which was why she was teaching her sisters. It turned out that she was not able to return to Endikat Ilir at all after her grandson was born, due to her terminal illness. Her sister-in-law and her half-sister thought Yulia had experienced feelings that she would not return to her *dusun laman* to continue her ritual role, so she seemed to have prepared caretakers.

When Yulia died in early August 2015, her daughter informed me on the phone that her mother had 'returned'. Although *wafat* is increasingly the preferred Islamic expression among Muslims to refer to a death, *pulang* was used to refer to Yulia's death. Although Muslims prefer an immediate burial, her body was carried to Endikat Ilir village over 20 hours to be buried in her *dusun laman*, in the same graveyard as her father, in accordance with Gumay customs, followed by Qur'anic recitations at night. Yulia's soul (*roh*) is believed to visit her close family members, as she feels close and affectionate with them. Her daughter, in particular, feels much comfort as her mother continues to visit her during her sleep, indicating that she continues to care for her daughter's young family.

Longing for a home

Another death I experienced through my adopted family relationship was that of a younger sister, Ferry, in 2006. She was the daughter of Haji Hasan Basri, whose family I had lived with for two years in the town of Lahat. She became terminally ill with cancer while she was working in Jakarta. Her family wanted her to receive advanced cancer treatment in a hospital in Jakarta, but she was adamant she wanted to return to Lahat. Although she returned to her house, Ferry repeatedly said she did not feel she was at home and insisted that she still had to return home. Her house had undergone some renovations and, in an effort to help her feel at home, her family moved her bed between three different rooms. Despite these efforts, she continued to say she was not feeling at home right up to her death. Her family members, who had little involvement in Gumay *adat*, later felt that 'returning home' did not necessarily refer to the physical house or the town itself, but returning to the *dusun laman* to which both the living and the dead *roh* belong. Returning to the origin is the most cherished and comforting emotion for the Gumay.

Feeling, ancestors and Islamisation

The recent ethnographic examples of the Gumay I have presented show that strong affinity between a person and their ancestors as their origin is expressed through diverse feelings and revealed in dreams and visions. It is believed that the person's soul can travel and meet ancestral spirits during their sleep and important messages can be conveyed from ancestors to their descendants or among close family members in the form of a dream. Romantic and passionate feelings may be subdued or even discontinued if the person feels that ancestors do not approve of their intended marriage. Indeed, individuals may revoke an engagement that was based on romantic feelings (*rasan muda*) if either of the pair has a dream that indicates ancestors' disapproval of their marriage.

It is also believed ancestors send messages to their descendants if there is a breach in observing Gumay *adat* matters. Thus, people are inclined to undertake rituals to seek forgiveness on behalf of their family members (*jurai*) if they suspect wrongdoing. Such wrongdoing could involve sexual relations outside marriage or not returning to their *dusun laman* for an extended time. Rare but not uncommon is someone going into a semi-unconscious state, illustrated by the case of Ross, and conveying ancestral messages to their descendants.

A semi-unconscious state usually happens while someone is suffering from an illness, but can occur while someone is in the forest. Forests are believed to be the abode of natural guardian spirits who may feel invaded or disturbed for some reason. Such a transcendental state is expressed by terms such as *ada yang masuk* ('someone has possessed him'), *kesurupan* ('in a trance') or *orang halus* ('invisible being'), and people usually receive visions in which ancestors convey specific messages to their descendants to which the latter must adhere. For example, in August 1989, a ceremony to cleanse Gumay heirlooms, including weapons, was held in Lubuk Sepang village of Gumay Lembak, which resulted in the death of one participant and several others being injured. The procedures for the event were apparently modified from the original plan to accommodate the larger-than-expected crowd that had gathered to watch the ceremony. The venue was moved from a room in the house to the backyard, which was believed to be in breach of Gumay *adat*, and, in subsequent years, the event was returned indoors.[9] During the 1989 event, one man had stabbed several participants, killing one, but he faced no criminal charges as he was deemed out of his mind and was sent to hospital for treatment. In 1995, when I interviewed the man in his home in Bunga Melur village of South Bengkulu, he said the only thing he remembered from the incident was seeing an *orang halus* wearing white clothes and gold bracelets descending from the sky. The Gumay ritual specialists interpreted the *orang halus* as an invisible ancestral spirit that had come to condemn the breach in the ritual's procedures.[10]

---

9   Other Gumay ritual specialists take the view that weapons should only be taken out into a yard at times of war, and the cleaning of weapons should be conducted indoors with the roof slightly ajar.

10   This incident can be considered an example of *amuk* or *amok* among Malay males, which involves a loss of self-control and an outburst of violent behaviour.

Although dreams and visions are important for Gumay to communicate and express their connections with ancestors, references to visions and dreams are increasingly expressed privately while references to Islamic terms are chosen for use in public. As Indonesian Islam is becoming more orthodox (Sakai and Fauzia 2014), there is an increasing reluctance to admit openly that ancestral spirits determine the descendants' wellbeing and convey messages to descendants via dreams or feelings (Sakai 2017b), because such interpretations go against Islamic monotheism. Alternative, Islamic expressions such as *ilham* ('God's divine inspiration') and a general term such as *sugesti* ('feelings') have been used in public gatherings, while, in private conversation, people continue to maintain the importance of ancestral messages sent through visions in dreams.

A comparative analysis of ethnographic accounts of dreams among the Austronesians faces a significant difficulty as the Islamisation of contemporary society in South-East Asia has progressed to such a great extent and has decreased the use of expressions relating to connections with spirits and deities, particularly among Muslims in the public sphere. Thus, syncretic practices of religions well noted among the Javanese, as observed by Geertz (1960), have been marginalised in contemporary Indonesia (Hefner 2011). In Malaysia, reformist Islam spread with the strong backing of the state and swept away Malay shamanistic performances, which were deemed to be un-Islamic (Laderman 1991: 16–20). It is therefore no surprise that ethnographic accounts exploring the function of dreams, visions and feelings have received little attention to date in regions where the influence of Islam or Christianity is penetrating ever deeper. As a result, the importance of feelings communicated via dreams has continued to dominate life among indigenous populations such as the Temiar (Roseman 1991), is practised as part of local traditions of *ziarah* (a visit to various sacred sites or the graveyards of Islamic saints or ancestors) (Christomy 2008; Hellman 2013) or is carried on through spirit mediums (Bubandt 2009; Steadly 1993), while increasingly being contested by fundamentalist religious interpretations.

Conclusions

This chapter has analysed how Gumay people express their emotions, particularly their affinity with their origins, through the use of figurative kinship relations, visits to their *dusun laman* and ritual feast practices.

The ethnographic accounts I have presented show that dreams and feelings are frequently used as mediums to convey important messages from a Gumay person, living or deceased, to their loved ones. While the living often use dreams as a medium to communicate with the spirits of the deceased in other Austronesian-speaking societies,[11] the examples of Gumay show that dreams and feelings confirm and reinforce affinity between individuals while they are alive and also encourage Gumay people to remember their ancestral origins widely associated with a *dusun laman*. The Gumay commonly use the local word *balik* to express the return to origins, which can be translated into the standard Indonesian *pulang*. The meaning of this idea, however, refers not only to a return to the actual place of origin, but also to the notion of *dusun laman*—closely related kin members, living and deceased, as I have illustrated with Gumay examples. The Gumay therefore experience the closest affinity and affection when their soul can connect to places and incidents related to their ancestors. Thus, the Gumay continue to conduct monthly visits to the house of the Jurai Kebali'an and other rituals to celebrate and express their affinity to their origins.

References

Barendregt, Bart. 2008. 'The house that was built overnight. Guidelines on the construction and use of the southern Sumatran rumah uluan'. In Reimar Schefold, P. Nas and Gaudenz Domenig (eds) *Indonesian Houses: Survey of vernacular architecture in western Indonesia*, pp. 429–64. Leiden: KITLV Press. doi.org/10.1163/9789004253988_015.

Beatty, Andrew. 1999. *Varieties of Javanese Religion: An anthropological account*. Cambridge: Cambridge University Press. doi.org/10.1017/CBO9780511612497.

Bubandt, Nils. 2009. 'Interview with an ancestor: Spirits as informants and the politics of possession in North Maluku'. *Ethnography* 10(3): 291–316. doi.org/10.1177/1466138109339044.

Christomy, Tommy. 2008. *Signs of the Wali: Narratives at the sacred sites in Pamijahan, West Java*. Canberra: ANU E Press.

---

11   See Beatty (1999: 222–33) on how dreams are used to interpret the spirits of the deceased among Muslim Javanese.

Collins, William. 1979. 'Besemah concepts: A study of the culture of people of South Sumatra'. PhD dissertation. University of California, Berkeley, CA.

Collins, William. 1998. *The Guritan of Radin Sune: A study of the Besemah oral epic from South Sumatra*. Leiden: KITLV Press.

Geertz, Clifford. 1960. *The Religion of Java*. Chicago: University of Chicago Press.

Hefner, Robert W. 2011. 'Where have all the *abangan* gone? Religionization and the decline of non-standard Islam in contemporary Indonesia'. In Michel Picard and Rémy Madinier (eds) *The Politics of Religion in Indonesia: Syncretism, orthodoxy, and religious contention in Java and Bali*, pp. 71–91. London: Routledge.

Hellman, Jörgen. 2013. 'Meeting with ancestors: Contesting borders in Indonesian religion and politics'. *Anthropological Forum* 23(2): 178–97. doi.org.10.1080/00664677.2013.780964.

Laderman, Carol. 1991. *Taming the Wind of Desire: Psychology, medicine and aesthetics in Malay shamanistic performance*. Berkeley, CA: University of California Press. doi.org/10.1525/california/9780520069169.001.0001.

Roseman, Marina. 1991. *Healing Sounds from the Malaysian Rainforest: Temiar music and medicine*. Berkeley, CA: University of California Press.

Sakai, Minako. 1997. 'Remembering origins: Ancestors and places in the Gumai society of South Sumatra'. In James J. Fox (ed.) *The Poetic Power of Place: Comparative perspectives on Austronesian ideas of locality*, pp. 42–62. Canberra: The Australian National University.

Sakai, Minako. 2002. 'Modernising sacred sites in South Sumatra? Islamisation and institutionalisation of ancestral places among the Gumai, Indonesia'. In Anthony J. S. Reid and Henri Chambert Loir (eds) *The Potent Dead: Ancestors, saints and heroes in contemporary Indonesia*, pp. 103–16. ASAA Southeast Asia Publication Series. Honolulu: University of Hawai'i Press.

Sakai, Minako. 2003. 'Publicising rituals and privatising meanings: Gumai ritual practice in South Sumatra'. In Nicola Tannenbaum and Cornelia Kammerer (eds) *Founder's Cults in Southeast Asia*, pp. 159–83. New Haven, CT: Yale University Press.

Sakai, Minako. 2006. 'The origin structure of kute among the Gumai: An analysis of an indigenous territorial institution in the highlands of South Sumatra'. In Thomas Reuter (ed.) *Sharing the Earth, Dividing the Land*, pp. 39–64. Canberra: ANU E Press.

Sakai, Minako. 2009. 'From Bukit Seguntang to Lahat: Challenge facing Gumay ritual practice in the highlands of South Sumatra'. In Dominik Bonatz, John Miksic, J. David Neidel and Mai Lin Tjoa-Bonatz (eds) *From Distant Tales: Archaeology and ethnohistory in the highlands of Sumatra*, pp. 485–500. Cambridge: Cambridge Scholars Publications.

Sakai, Minako. 2017a. *Kacant Tidak Lupa Kulitnya: Identitas Gumay, Islam, dan Merantau di Sumatra Selatan*. Jakarta: Yayasan Pustaka Obor Indonesia.

Sakai, Minako. 2017b. 'Still remembering the origins: The continuity of syncretic Islamic practice among the Gumay (Gumai) in South Sumatra, Indonesia'. *Indonesia and the Malay World* 45: 44–65. doi.org/10.1080/13639811.2017.1274561.

Sakai, Minako and Amelia Fauzia. 2014. 'Islamic orientations in contemporary Indonesia: Islamism on the rise?'. *Asian Ethnicity* 15: 41–61. doi.org/10.1080/14631369.2013.784513.

Steadly, Mary Margaret. 1993. *Hanging Without a Rope: Narrative experience in colonial and postcolonial Karoland*. Princeton, NJ: Princeton University Press.

Waterson, Roxana. 1995. 'Houses, graves and the limits of kinship groupings among the Sa'dan Toraja'. *Bijdragen tot de Taal-, Land- en Volkenkunde* 15(2): 194–217.

3

A work of love: Awareness and expressions of emotion in a Borneo healing ritual

Clifford Sather

Andrew Beatty (2014: 546) is no doubt right in asserting that '[f]or most of our discipline's brief history … emotion has not been a theoretical focus', emotions being, as he puts it, 'just too imponderable for functional methodology' (p. 548). Recent decades, however, have dramatically altered this picture, and studies of emotion have emerged as a significant topic of anthropological theorising (Beatty 2005, 2010; Kapferer 1979; Levy 1973, 1984; Lutz 1988; Lutz and White 1986; Rosaldo 1984; Shweder and LeVine 1984; Wilce 2004). My purpose in this chapter is to explore the role of emotion in an Iban rite of healing, focusing in particular on what is arguably the most imponderable of all human emotions, love, looking at how this is understood by the Iban and how 'love' was made to serve, in a distinctively Iban ritual setting, as an instrument of healing.

First, however, it is useful to outline Iban notions of 'love' and briefly touch on the role that emotions associated with these notions traditionally played in Iban society, particularly in practices related to healing, illness and wellbeing.[1]

---

1   The Iban are the most populous Dayak, or indigenous, non-Muslim group of western Borneo. Tracing their origins to the Kapuas River basin of present-day Kalimantan Barat, the great majority of Iban now live in the Malaysian state of Sarawak, where, in 2010, they numbered over 700,000

The Iban vocabulary of love

There is no single term in Iban that, by itself, approximates the Western concept of 'love'. Instead, there exists a set of terms that, taken together, capture the concept's central range of meaning. Each of these terms denotes what we might call a different variety of Iban love. In Iban–English dictionaries, the two words that are most frequently glossed as love are *rindu'* and *kasih* (cf. Bruggeman 1985: 65; Richards 1981: 141, 309; Scott 1956: 154; Sutlive and Sutlive 1994: 642). The most common meanings of *rindu'* are 'like', 'love', 'be pleased by' or 'made glad by' (Richards 1981: 309). For example, *iya rindu' nginti* means 'he likes to fish [with a hook and line]'. When used to describe an emotional state—that is, as in *rindu' ati* or *pengerindu' ati*—the term *rindu'* refers to a feeling of 'joy', 'pleasure' or 'gratitude' such as a person experiences when in the presence of someone whose company they find pleasurable. *Kasih*, on the other hand, refers to love in the sense of 'caring for', 'supporting' or 'fulfilling the needs of [another]'. Hence, *kasih* is often translated, in addition to 'love', as 'kindness', 'sympathy' or 'compassion'. For example, *minta' kasih* means 'to ask a favour', while the transitive verb form, *kasihka*, means 'to pity', 'feel sorry for' or 'be kind to'. Another Iban term with a very similar meaning is *sayau*. Although more often translated as 'pity', *sayau* also connotes 'love' in the overlapping sense of 'sympathy'. Together, these three terms are regularly used by the Iban to describe the feelings that prompt a person to perform acts of kindness, such as caring for those who are ill. All three are what Catherine Lutz (1988: 145) has called 'emotions of strength', meaning that those who experience them are 'empowered' by the experience and so see themselves as capable of 'fulfilling the needs of others'. *Rindu'*, however, focuses more on mutuality, the ability of partners to satisfy each other's needs,[2] while *kasih* and *sayau* focus more on the unequal capacity of one person to gratify the needs of others.

(Department of Statistics Malaysia 2012). A smaller number, estimated at 14,000, continue to live in West Kalimantan, chiefly along the low-lying border region known in Iban as the Emperan or 'Flat Land' (Wadley 2004; Wadley and Kuyah 2001: 716–19). During the past century, Iban have also migrated northward from Sarawak to Sabah and the independent Borneo state of Brunei Darussalam (Sather 2004: 623).

2   In this sense, *rindu'* resembles the Hawaiian term *le'a*, famously discussed by Sahlins (1985: 3–4) in *Islands of History*, except that, unlike *le'a*, its meaning does not extend to sexual gratification.

Reflecting an interactive sense of selfhood, in which persons define themselves primarily by their relationships with others, the Iban tend to associate the needs to which feelings of *kasih* and *sayau* are associated with bonds of kinship, social support, health and care-giving. Thus, love, especially in the sense conveyed by these two terms, is seen as a highly positive emotion, one that motivates persons to offer social support and provide care to others. While those who provide care are highly respected, Iban society is also notably competitive. Individuals and families seek to advance their status relative to others by virtue of their material achievements and, in so doing, they regularly evoke love in a very different sense—one related more closely to notions of erotic or sexual love.

The terms *rindu'*, *kasih* and *sayau* are rarely used in connection with romantic love, sexual attraction or desire. Instead, separate terms are used to describe emotions associated with sexual love. These terms rarely find their way into Iban–English dictionaries, very likely because they lack the qualities of idealisation that English speakers generally associate with romantic love (see, for a discussion of the latter, Averill 1985). Instead, the connotation of these terms is notably physical and body-centred. To have sex with another is to 'mingle', 'cohabit' (*gulai*) or 'lie down together' (*gali*). During intercourse, sexual partners are said to become *setubuh*, a 'single body'. The most common term used in Iban to describe sexual love as an emotional state is *ka'*, a shortened form of *deka'*, meaning, literally, 'to want' or 'desire'. Thus, *ka'* is commonly used, in a shorthand way, to refer to an agreement to marry (Richards 1981: 71). An even stronger term is *keran* (or *pengeran*, n.f.), meaning 'urge' or 'craving'. Unlike *rindu'*, *kasih* and *sayau*, *ka'* and *keran* are socially ambiguous. Although sexual gratification is seen as a source of pleasure, sexual desire, when translated into action, represents a potential source of personal danger,[3] and, in the form of adultery, is regarded as a cause of almost certain social disruption (Sather 1994). Erotic love is also associated metaphorically with warfare and headhunting—formerly sources of male prestige. Consequently, sex is also often described using a language of combat or is referred to euphemistically as *ngelaban*, meaning, literally, 'to fight' or 'do battle [with]' (Sather 1994: 11). At the same time, erotic love is culturally valued

---

3   For example, it is considered mortally dangerous for a widow or widower to continue to pine for a deceased spouse after the final rites of mourning have taken place (Sather 1978: 317–18). Similarly, spirit assailants often appear to their victims as irresistibly attractive human beings of the opposite sex and their illness-causing attack is frequently experienced as a form of sexual seduction (see Freeman 1967; Sather 1978).

as a pleasurable pursuit in itself. Thus, traditional storytelling, wordplay and most song genres and forms of verbal entertainment centre on themes of sexual love, longing and flirtation.

Love and visibility: To see and be seen

The Iban tend to be highly sensitive to the interpersonal, as opposed to the purely subjective, dimensions of emotions. This is particularly so in the case of the emotional states that we have identified here with 'love'. What is particularly notable in this regard is that the varied senses of love conveyed by the terms *rindu'*, *kasih*, *sayau*, *ka'* and *keran*, as emotions experienced or expressed within a context of interpersonal relationships, are all similarly perceived by the Iban as sources of potential attraction. To be activated, however, love—whether as sympathy, gladness, compassion or sexual longing—requires that the object of this love be visible to the other. 'Visibility' (*pandang*) is thus the key that unites these different varieties of Iban love. Visibility reveals and so—when matched with perceptions of need, beauty, pleasure or feelings of physiological arousal—activates love as a source of interpersonal attraction. To see and to be visible to others are, in Iban cultural terms, preconditions for love's operation. Hence, love in whatever form it takes is associated with the acts of seeing, of making oneself seen and of being seen by others. The central concept here, *pandang*, means not only 'visible', but also 'show', 'display', 'exhibit', 'reveal' or, literally, 'shine forth' (cf. Richards 1981: 248). To display or show oneself means to make oneself visible—a condition that causes others to take notice and so, potentially at least, be attracted to us. In this sense, *pandang* also refers to a condition of power, as in the cognate term *pemandang*, referring to 'love charms', objects that are imbued with the power to compel others to see and so to admire those who possess them.

Love in this visually related sense—as a set of emotions activated by the sight of, or working through the gaze of, the other—applies not only to relations of care-giving, sexual liaisons and marriages, but also to political relations and ties of mutual obligation. Traditional Iban society, although competitive, was relatively egalitarian, lacking formal institutions of prescriptive ranking and clearly defined lines of chiefly power (Freeman 1981; Sather 1996). Instead, individuals, families and kindred groups actively competed with one another for prestige, influence and authority.

Leaders were essentially self-made men of prowess who attracted followers by virtue of their personal accomplishments, generosity and outward signs of spiritual favour. Renown, like love, was similarly associated, not with formal duty or inherited right, but with visibility. Each person was said to be the 'source' (*pun*) of his or her own renown (*nama*). To gain recognition required, in this visual idiom, that a person, literally, 'show himself' (*mandangka diri*)[4]—that is, that he demonstrate his worth through his actions and demeanour. For men, the traditional zenith of achieved status was represented by the *orang tau' serang, tau' pandang*—war leaders whose achievements in the past were made 'visible' (*pandang*) by a lifetime of 'showing themselves'[5] by repeatedly demonstrating their worth in ways that were overtly visible to others. Thus, competitive advantage, whether in love, politics or war, went to those who made themselves noticed.

While visibility activates love as a force of attraction, by contrast, illness, ageing and death are associated with its inverse—invisibility—and so threaten all that love represents.

The *Sugi Sakit*

The healing ritual that concerns us in this chapter was called the *Sugi Sakit* and was performed until its demise, some 25 years ago, by Iban priest bards in the Betong division of western Sarawak.[6] The ritual was performed primarily for the elderly, those nearing the end of their lives who were chronically ill or whose afflictions were considered beyond the scope of shamanic healing. Until the recent, and now all-but-complete, conversion of the Saribas Iban to Christianity, ritual life in Saribas was largely the work of ritual specialists, most notably priest bards (*lemambang*), shamans (*manang*) and soul guides (*tukang sabak*) (see Sather 2001: 5–13). Of these specialists, shamans were the primary healers. However, particularly severe forms of affliction were thought to be treatable only by the direct

---

4   *Mandangka*, like *pemandang*, derives from the same root, *pandang* (v.f., *mandang*), meaning 'visible'.
5   *Serang* means, literally, 'attack' (Richards 1981: 342). In the late eighteenth and early nineteenth centuries, the *orang tau' serang, tau' pandang* were regional war leaders who led their followers on raids and were responsible for defending the territorial boundaries of the regions within which their leadership was recognised (see Sather 1996: 79–80). They were, in Wolters's terms (1999: 18–21), classic 'men of prowess'.
6   As far as we know, the *Sugi Sakit* was never performed outside this area by Iban priest bards, either in other parts of Sarawak or in the neighbouring Indonesian province of Kalimantan Barat.

intervention of the gods (*petara*), and so were the special domain of the priest bards whose primary ritual function was that of invoking the gods and bringing them into direct contact with their human clients.

I first witnessed a performance of the *Sugi Sakit* in June 1977, during my first days of fieldwork in the Saribas. Although it made a deep impression, nearly 30 years passed before I was able to begin a serious study of the ritual. In June 2003, with support from the Tun Jugah Foundation,[7] I began field recording the ritual with my wife, Louise, and our Iban co-worker, Jantan Umbat.[8] In the late 1970s, when I began fieldwork, many families living along the Paku tributary of the main Saribas River identified themselves as Christian. However, longhouse ritual life was still little affected by Christianity and the *Sugi Sakit* and other forms of traditional healing remained very much alive. All of that was beginning to change, however, and, over the next 20 years, much of what I describe in this chapter ceased to exist, including, by the 1990s, the *Sugi Sakit* itself. Meramat anak Empong, the famous priest bard who had performed the *Sugi Sakit* I witnessed in 1977, died in December 1988. By 2003, when I began this study, more than a decade had passed since the *Sugi Sakit* was last performed. To carry out our work, it was therefore necessary to find a priest bard who had regularly performed the ritual in the past and commission a new performance. Fortunately, the son of one of my past informants, Renang anak Jabing, had become a priest bard like his father, and, when I first met him in the early 1980s, he was already a regular performer of the *Sugi Sakit*. In June 2003, Louise, Jantan and I arranged to work with Renang at his home in Tarum longhouse, near Debak. There, over six nights, we recorded a complete two-night version of the *Sugi Sakit* with detailed commentary. The following year, we visited Dit longhouse, the former home of Lemambang Meramat, and there recorded a second version of the *Sugi Sakit*, sung by two men who, although not priest bards themselves, had studied with Meramat. Most of the material contained in this chapter comes, however, from our work with Lemambang Renang.[9]

7   I am grateful to the Tun Jugah Foundation and, in particular, to its founding director, Tan Sri Datuk Amar Leonard Linggi Jugah, for the generous support that made this study possible.
8   Jantan Umbat, who played a crucial part in this study, is a retired Iban educator, novelist and scholar, and was at the time a senior member of the Tun Jugah Foundation research staff. At present, he is Research Officer and Officer-in-Charge of the Ethnic Culture Unit in the Sarawak Ministry of Social Development. I am grateful to Jantan, Louise, Oliver Venz, Bob Blust and Jim Fox for their comments on earlier drafts of this chapter.
9   Our working sessions are documented in some 40 hours of tape recordings, with extensive conversational commentaries. These have been deposited and are available in the Tun Jugah Foundation archives in Kuching, plus digital copies and a full transcription of our recording sessions with Renang (Sather and Umbat 2004).

Ritual as work, narrative and drama

Iban describe social performances such as the *Sugi Sakit* as *pengawa'*, a term that derives from the root word *gawa'*, meaning, literally, 'work', 'business' or, more generally, 'anything important or serious that has to be done' (see Richards 1981: 96). Farm work, for example, is *pengawa'* (Sather 1992: 108), but so, too, are what we would call 'rituals' in English.[10] As a kind of work, the *Sugi Sakit* was the exclusive province of Saribas Iban priest bards, although other participants, including the ritual's sponsors and a lay audience, were also essential in carrying it out. In performing this work, priest bards, like other ritual specialists, did so primarily by using words to create what the Iban call a *main*, meaning, literally, a 'play', 'drama' or 'entertainment'. Like the English word 'play', *main* connotes, in particular, a dramatic enactment or entertainment composed primarily in words. As Lemambang Renang observed, in performing the *Sugi Sakit*, priest bards 'treat the sick by means of [our] voice' (*ngubat orang ke sakit ngena' nyawa*).[11]

Compared with other rituals performed by Saribas priest bards, the *Sugi Sakit* was unique in two important respects. First, it incorporated within its *main* the singing of a long narrative epic. This epic, in varying forms, was also told as a longhouse entertainment on non-ritual occasions, often by lay storytellers. Second, the narrative itself was essentially a love story or epic romance. Hence, the singing of a love story was an integral part of the *Sugi Sakit*. By incorporating it directly into the ritual's *main*, a love story thus became, the Iban say, not 'merely an entertainment' (*main aja'*) or 'diversion' (*merindang*), but a purposeful act, something serious that *had to be done* if the *Sugi Sakit* were to succeed as a work of healing.

A healing romance: The Bujang Sugi epic

For a priest bard, Renang explained, performing the *Sugi Sakit* meant both *bemain* (lit., 'enacting a drama') and *becherita* ('telling a story [*cherita*]').

The principal characters in the *Sugi* story are not ordinary human beings but Orang Panggau (lit., 'people of Panggau')—culture heroes and heroines who inhabit a raised world known as Panggau, or Panggau Libau,

---

10 For more on Saribas Iban notions of ritual, see Sather (forthcoming).
11 In Iban, *nyawa* means, literally, 'mouth', but also 'voice', 'breathe' and even 'life'.

located between 'this world' (*dunya tu'*), the visible world of everyday human existence, and the 'sky' (*langit*), the upper realm of the most powerful of the Iban gods. While described as 'people' (*orang*), the Orang Panggau are also referred to as *bunsu antu*, benevolent spirits (*antu*), who are believed to have once lived together with the ancestors of the Iban in this world. Displaying all of the physical and psychological characteristics of human beings, the Orang Panggau also possess superhuman powers, including immortality and, for some, like Keling, the leader of the Orang Panggau, the power to transform their appearance at will. Bujang Sugi, the hero of the *Sugi* epic, is, in actuality, Keling. As Keling, he represents the embodiment of masculine prowess and physical perfection. Unlike the upper world of the gods, the Panggau world interpenetrates with this world, so that human beings sometimes encounter the Orang Panggau, particularly at mountain springs or waterfalls. Moreover, Keling at times enters this world, often appearing as a cobra, and here in the past he acted as a spirit-patron of Iban warriors and leaders, as did the heroines, Kumang and Lulung. In the Iban oral epics (*ensera*), Keling appears as a wanderer, who, in the course of his travels, assumes many disguises, but whose magical powers, appearance and bearing are such that men everywhere recognised him at once as a leader, while women fell instantly in love with him. His powers of attraction transcend different orders of being. Thus, his lovers (*ambai*) included not only women of the Orang Panggau world, but also female animal spirits, and, throughout the *Sugi* story, these various spirit-lovers appear at crucial times, providing the hero with timely warnings or with charms of invulnerability.

According to Renang, the serious work of the *Sugi* story occurs at the beginning and end of the narrative, while the middle episodes were highly variable and sung primarily for entertainment. Thus, the opening of the story recreates the predicament of the priest bard's patient and members of the sick person's longhouse. As with illness, infirmity and prospects of death, here, there is an absence of visibility. The longhouse in which the story is set is unable to attract visitors. No newcomers cross the top of its entry ladders, its betel nuts go unharvested and its cooked rice spoils because there are no visitors to feed and entertain. There are no young men coming to court the young women of the longhouse and the community's ageing leader, Father of Rimbu', has no young successor to whom he can impart his knowledge. To rectify this situation, his wife, Mother of Rimbu', calls together the eligible young women of the longhouse and gathers from them their love charms. These charms, called *pemandang*, embody the power of *pandang*—literally, 'visibility', but here, more fittingly, 'the power of attraction'. This first episode Renang called *ngayunka pemandang* ('to arouse [or, lit., "fan"] the power of attraction'). As it concludes, Mother of Rimbu' activates the young women's love charms and, from the rooftop of the longhouse, releases their power into the air. Erotic love thus serves as the primary means of supplication that draws the hero, Bujang Sugi, into his own narrative.

As the next episode opens, the hero, at home in his own longhouse, is overcome with longing (*pengusang ati*). And so, he departs for the longhouse of Mother and Father of Rimbu'. Here, disguising his appearance, he presents himself as a stranger and is adopted by Mother and Father of Rimbu'. As he is nameless, the couple name him Bujang ('Bachelor'/'Young Man') Sugi. In actuality, however, he is Keling. In telling Keling's story, the priest bard maintains the hero's deception and never explicitly identifies him as such; however, as the story progresses, he increasingly hints at his true identity. The story itself, in its basic outline, represents a version of the classic Austronesian myth of the stranger-king, telling of a visitor from abroad whose arrival transforms the society he visits (see Fox 1995: 217–19, 2008; Sahlins 1981, 2008, 2012). In this case, however, unlike most versions of the myth, the hero does not institute a new line of kingship, or otherwise alter the structure of his hosts' society, but, instead, serves as a temporary link between those who commission the telling of his story and the upper-world gods, making it possible for the latter to intervene directly in the this-world rite of healing the priest bard is in the process of performing.

A characteristic feature of stranger-king myths is that the transformative power of the stranger—being foreign to the society he visits—must be captured and in some way incorporated into the society of his hosts (Fox 2008). Typically, this capture comes about by means of a sexual union between the male visitor and a local woman (or women). The transformative power of the foreign thus complements the reproductive power of the autochthonous.[12] In the *Sugi* story, as soon as the hero enters Father of Rimbu's longhouse, he begins at once to court the longhouse beauty, Endu Dara ('Maiden'/'Young Woman') Semanjan. Semanjan, however,

---

12 This is an element of the *Sugi* story as well. After the priest bard completes singing the main epic, concluding with Sugi's descent into this world, he typically sings a brief epilogue, called *Anak Bujang Sugi*, in which he describes the birth of a son to Sugi and Sedinang, Sugi's departure and his eventual reunion with his son.

is literally a femme fatale. All who attempt to court her perish because she is in mourning for a husband who has recently disappeared and is presumed dead. This husband, however, is none other than Keling, who appeared once before, similarly as a stranger. Sugi is therefore what Fox (2008: 202) has called a 'returning outsider'. He came as a stranger before to Father of Rimbu's longhouse and in his earlier appearance he married Semanjan and so is immune to her lethal powers. Keling's object this time, however, is not Semanjan, but, rather, Sedinang, the most beautiful of all the Orang Panggau women. As Renang explained, Sedinang is, in reality, Kumang, Keling's wife in Iban epic tradition, while Semanjan is her cousin and rival, Lulung. In the *Sugi* story, she appears as the daughter of Father of Rimbu's brother, Sentukan 'The White-Haired', and, on their adopted son's behalf, Father and Mother of Rimbu' travel to Sentukan's longhouse to arrange the couple's marriage.

This marriage takes place in Father of Rimbu's longhouse. Here, however, Semanjan, in a jealous rage, challenges her rival, Sedinang, to a series of contests to determine which of them is the most comely. Although Sedinang easily wins these contests, Sugi refuses to cease his nocturnal visits to Semanjan's sleeping place, so Sedinang decides to return to her parents' longhouse. Sugi follows in pursuit and their journey turns into a contest of wills. In the meantime, enemies of the Orang Panggau, learning of the couple's journey, prepare an ambush. Forewarned, Sugi single-handedly takes on the enemy warriors, defeats them all and takes the heads of their leaders. The couple, now reconciled, arrive at Sentukan's longhouse, where Sugi is welcomed as a victorious warrior. What occurs next depends on the length of the performance commissioned by the sponsors. If the performance is to continue over a second night, the story is now temporarily suspended. The following night, it begins with a series of additional adventures and battles. After the last of these battles is fought, or, in the case of a one-night performance, immediately following the couple's arrival at Sentukan's longhouse, Bujang Sugi calls a meeting of his father-in-law's followers and announces his intention to hold a ritual celebration (*gawai*) to honour the gods for making his victories possible, inviting as his guests Selempandai, Biku Bunsu Petara and other upper-world gods associated with healing.

At the conclusion of the *Sugi* epic, as it is sung during the *Sugi Sakit*, Bujang Sugi leaves the narrative world in which it is set and, together with his Orang Panggau followers, and accompanied by Selempandai and the other Iban gods of healing who have come to attend his *gawai*, he enters the visible world in which the ritual is being performed, and here, in the words of the priest bard's *main*, he and the others intervene directly in the ritual by treating the patient with their medicines and special healing powers. All of this happens at the conclusion of the hero's *gawai*. Before his guests return home, Sugi informs them that they are now invited by human beings to participate in a work of healing that is taking place in the human world below. And so, now as the invited guests of the sponsors of the *Sugi Sakit*, the gods and spirit heroes accompany Bujang Sugi as he descends to this world. Here, in the words of the priest bard's *main*, they treat the patient with their medicines and chants. In this way, a narrated ritual is merged momentarily with the actual ritual, and the two become for a brief moment one and the same.

As soon as he finishes singing of Bujang Sugi's descent, the priest bard briefly leaves his swing and goes to where the patient is installed at the centre of the longhouse gallery. There he briefly re-enacts what Bujang Sugi and the gods have just done by treating the patient himself. His role as a storyteller thus anticipates his actions as a healer, and, in the end, both roles merge, as the priest bard briefly assumes the part of the principal actors in the story he has just related.

The role of emotions, thought and awareness in the *Sugi Sakit*

The *main Sugi Sakit* was intended not only to compel the gods and spirit heroes to make themselves present as unseen healers; its performance, as a dramatic entertainment, also acted on the emotions and, through the emotions, on the awareness and behaviour of those who participated in the ritual.

'The Iban', as the late Robert Barrett (2012: 114) asserted, 'feel emotions in their body'—and not only emotions, but also, one might add, desires and intentions. For the Iban, the 'body' (*tubuh*), while outwardly visible, is said to contain within it invisible interior spaces. These spaces, particularly those 'inside the chest' (*di dalam dada*), are the location of bodily organs that are believed to be the seat of emotions, feelings, thoughts and intentions, hence of the faculties that most fully define a person in everyday social and psychological terms (Sather 2001: 48–9).

James Matisoff, in a pioneering essay entitled 'Hearts and minds in South-East Asian languages and English' (1986: 8), notes that in most European languages expressions referring to emotional states and other psychological phenomena usually make no explicit reference to the locale within which these phenomena unfold. In contrast, many languages of East and South-East Asia treat psychological phenomena as an 'overt class' by means of what Matisoff calls 'psycho-collocations'—morphologically complex expressions, one constituent of which is a morpheme that refers specifically to the locale within which psychological processes occur (1986: 8). Not only are 'psycho-collocations' abundant in East and South-East Asian languages, but also this locale, when arrayed across a 'mind–body continuum', tends to be situated towards the 'body' end of the spectrum—that is, it refers less to 'mind', 'soul' or 'spirit' than it does to 'visceral organs' of the body (Matisoff 1986: 14). While Matisoff's essay concerns primarily Sino-Tibetan languages, Goddard (2001: 167) has suggested that the same general feature also holds for the Austronesian languages of peninsular and island South-East Asia. More recently, Robert Blust has surveyed Austronesian expressions relating to emotions, particularly those that are similarly constructed as metaphorical extensions of body-part terms (2013: 321–7). Among the most prevalent of these expressions are those based on reflexes of the Proto-Malayo-Polynesian (PMP) morphemes *qatay* ('liver') and *qapeju* ('gall bladder'). Expressions based on the first of these terms are particularly numerous and tend to be associated with emotions generally, while the second tend to be associated more specifically with judgement, commonsense and courage (Blust 2013: 325–6). Both terms figure significantly in Iban, particularly the first of the two.

Thus, in Iban, most expressions associated with feelings and other psychological phenomena make use of the morpheme *ati*, a reflex of the PMP *qatay*, which the Iban explicitly identify with the heart–liver region of the body. More specifically, the term *ati* derives from the word *atau*, which, strictly speaking, refers to the 'liver'. By extension, however, *ati* also encompasses the heart, which in Iban is generally described as the *tungkul atau* (lit., 'the flower bud of the liver'), which, as a physical organ, the heart closely resembles. As Barrett (2012: 115–16) notes, Iban speakers typically use the word *ati* in a way that encompasses both the heart and the liver, as well as, at times, other organs contained within the chest (*di dalam dada*) or upper interior of the body.[13] In everyday speech, virtually all emotions, desires and states of feeling are expressed through the use of the term *ati*. For example, *gaga ati* means 'happy'; *pengerindu'* (*rindu'*) *ati*, 'glad'; *penenguk* (*tenguk*) *ati*, 'desire', 'yearn for'; *pengusang* (*kusang*) *ati*, 'long for', 'be infatuated by'; *tusah ati*, 'sad'; *sinu' ati*, 'pity'; *penakut* (*takut*) *ati*, 'frightened'; *pengerawan* (*rawan*) *ati*, 'nervous', 'fearful'; *pengirau* (*irau*) *ati*, 'worried', 'anxious'; *pemerani* (*berani*) *ati*, 'courageous'; *tembu' ati*, 'contented'; *penaluk* (*taluk*) *ati*, 'obedient'; *pengangkun* (*angkun*) *ati*, 'steadfast', 'loyal'; *chemuru ati*, 'jealous'; *pengaru'* (*garu'*) *ati*, 'suspicious'; *bebulu ati*, 'ill-natured'; *begedi'* (*gedi'*) *ati*, 'hate'; *ensiban ati*, 'resentful', 'bearing a grudge'; *panas ati*, 'hot-tempered'; and *pedis ati*, 'angry'. Iban is a Malayic language and, semantically, the Iban term *ati* parallels in many ways its Malay cognate, *hati*.[14] Anatomically, most Malay writers identify *hati* with the liver, which Karim (1990: 26), for example, describes as 'a mysterious organ … believed to control the moods and emotions of humans and … command their psyche'. While Goddard similarly identifies *hati* with the liver, metaphorically, he glosses it as 'heart'. However, as he observes, *hati* is not semantically identical, being 'significantly more active, and more cognitive' (Goddard 2001: 167). Like the Iban term *ati*, it is used particularly in expressions referring to emotions aroused or activated within the context of interpersonal relationships. In contrast to the metaphoric use of 'heart' in English, it is also more 'dynamic', being, as Goddard (2001: 178–9) puts it, a place where 'things happen'. Hence, like *ati* in Iban, it is the primary seat not only of feelings, but also of cognition and awareness, and so is used, like *ati*, in many contexts where 'mind' would be a more appropriate English gloss than 'heart' (Goddard 2001: 179).

---

13   This is consistent with the derivation of *ati* from *atau*. While the term's connection with 'liver' is clear, in Proto-Malayo-Polynesian, as Blust notes, the word for heart was not an independent body-part term, but also had a botanical referent (2013: 325). Barrett (2012: 116) has proposed 'heart/ liver' or 'heart/liver complex' as a translation of *ati*. Here, for the sake of convenience, I gloss the term simply as 'heart'. *Atau*, on the other hand, is culturally significant for the Iban primarily in the context of divination (*senaga*). For a concise, but detailed, account of the meaning of *ati/atau* in Iban, see Ensiring et al. (2011: 47–8).

14   In Iban, the phoneme /h/ never occurs in an initial position. While a number of metaphorical expressions in Malay based on the term *hati* have *ati* counterparts in Iban, others do not. For example, *ambil hati* (fetch + heart) in Malay and *ngambi' ati* (fetch + heart) in Iban have roughly the same meaning: 'to attract' or 'win the affections of'. Similarly, *bakar hati* (burn + heart) in Malay and *panas ati* (hot + heart) in Iban both mean 'hot-tempered'; *busok hati* (rotten + heart) in Malay and *jai ati* (bad + heart) in Iban both mean 'quick to take offence', 'ill-natured'; and *sakit hati* (sick + heart) in Malay and *pedis ati* (hurt + heart) in Iban both mean 'annoyed', 'angry'. On the other hand, *besar hati* (big + heart) in Malay has a slightly different meaning to *besai ati* (big + heart) in Iban. In Iban, there are no precise counterparts of the Malay *kecil hati* (small + heart) or of *puteh hati* (white + heart), while there are no apparent counterparts in Malay of the Iban expressions *pengaru' ati* (scratchy + heart), *bebulu ati* (to have hair + heart) or *ensiban ati* (splinter/thorn in the flesh + heart).

In addition to *ati*, other parts of the body are also identified with feelings, especially in the poetic language register (*leka main*) used by Iban ritual specialists in composing their ritual *main*. One of these is *empedu*, a reflex of PMP **qapeju*, meaning, literally, 'gall' or 'gall bladder'. In compound expressions, *empedu* represents the locale of feelings of shame or embarrassment (*malu*). In contrast to a number of other Austronesian languages, in Iban, *empedu* is not directly associated with courage or judgement, except, in the latter case, in a negative sense. Thus, *radai empedu malu* (not + gall bladder + shame) means to do what is shameless—that is, to act without common sense or respect for social convention. Another term frequently used in metaphorical extensions is *tulang* ('bone/s'). *Tulang* is associated in particular with feelings of strength, energy or resolve, or, inversely, of weakness, exhaustion or idleness. Thus, *tulang aku lembut* (lit., 'my bones are soft') means to feel weak or exhausted. Feelings may also be linked to the lungs (*lempuang*), spleen (*tekura'*) and stomach (*perut*). The recessive, or 'interior' (*di dalam*), nature of these organs of feeling is often reinforced in the poetic language of the *main* by additional expressions that describe them as 'enclosed' or 'fenced in' (*kandang*)—for example, by the 'lungs' (*lempuang*), 'chest' (*dada*) or 'ribs' (*kerigai*).[15]

In the special language register (*leka main*) used in the composition of ritual *main*, lines and stanzas are structured primarily through the recurrent use of final-syllable rhyme (see Sather 2001: 163–5). Thus, in this register, expressions relating to the emotions often occur in the form of rhyming pairs. For example, *malu* ('embarrassment') is regularly paired with *empedu* ('gall bladder'), *irau* ('worry') with *atau* ('liver'), *tekenyit* ('surprise') with *kulit* ('skin'), *kusang* ('longing') with *lempuang* ('lungs'), *nari* ('quarrelsomeness') with *lepi'* ('folds') plus *tandan lempuang* ('stem of the lungs'), *kesal* ('startled') with *jungkal* ('flower bulb') plus *kandang dada* ('heart'; lit., 'flower bulb enclosed by the chest') and *sinu'* ('pity') with *leku'* ('coils') plus *perut* ('intestines'; lit., 'coils of the stomach').

The active verb form of *ati*, *beati*, means 'to feel', 'sense' or 'experience [feelings]', while the expression *beati-ati* means 'to be aware', 'conscious' or 'mindful'. To experience conflicting or divided feelings is to have, literally, 'two hearts' (*dua ati*), while persons who share the same feelings

---

15 The recessive nature of the *ati* and other organs of feeling contributes to their ambiguous status. On the one hand, these organs are indisputably parts of the body; on the other hand, they are not directly visible from outside the body, and hence they are also allied with the unseen.

or intentions are said to be of 'one heart' (*seati*). A 'complete' or 'finished heart' (*tembu' ati*) signifies contentment; a 'bad heart' (*jai ati*), ill will; a 'hurt heart' (*pedis ati*), anger; a 'hot heart' (*panas ati*), a hot temper; a blocked heart (*pengalit ati*), puzzlement; a 'scratchy heart' (*pengaru' ati*), suspiciousness; a 'hairy heart' (*bebulu ati*), hatred; a 'splinter' or 'thorn in the flesh heart' (*ensiban ati*), resentment, holding a grudge; a 'disturbed heart' (*pengirau ati*), anxiety; and a 'big heart' (*besai ati*), 'boastfulness'.

To be *gerai* (in 'good health') as opposed to *sakit* ('sick') is to feel energetic, clear-headed and strong. These feelings make themselves known through the bodily senses and so are registered chiefly in the *ati* as the principal seat of sentient awareness—that is, they are made manifest through a work of *beati-ati*. But, not only are the symptoms of illness and good health experienced within the body, they also are apprehended and acted on by the body. Thus, for the Iban, feelings are described as experienced not within a disembodied 'mind', but directly in various parts of the body, chiefly in the *ati*, but also in other parts. Indeed, as Barrett (2012: 114) has noted, the Iban language has no term specifically for 'mind', or for its adjectival form, 'mental'. This has important implications in terms of how the Iban explain the effectiveness of healing rituals such as the *Sugi Sakit*. While traditional anthropological explanations of how healing rituals work have typically relied on a mind/body duality, seeing rituals as working on the mind in ways that effect physical changes in the body,[16] Iban explanations, by contrast, typically focus on a seen/unseen duality (see Barrett 1993; Sather 2012a: xxiii–iv). While states of good or ill health are experienced by the body, and apprehended by the *ati*, their source is potentially far more complex, reflecting not only conditions internal to the body, but also relationships between unseen components of the self, such as the 'soul' (*semengat*), and other beings and powers, both seen and unseen, that are thought to be at work outside the body (Sather 2001: 48–74).

For the Iban, the body is also the site of intentionality. The usual way of saying 'I want to' in Iban is *ati aku deka'*, literally, 'my heart wants to'. Again, however, intentions are similarly diffuse, and may derive not only from the *ati*, but also from other parts of the body, especially those associated with particular actions, such as the eyes (*mata*) with seeing and the mouth

---

16   There are, of course, exceptions. In recent years, many anthropologists have embraced the concept of 'embodiment' and so have explicitly rejected explanation framed in terms of mind/body dualities (see, for example, Csordas 1990, 1996).

(*nyawa*) with speaking. For example, a newly recovered patient, who has just regained a sense of wellbeing, is described as one whose 'mouth now wants to eat, [whose] legs now want to walk' (*nyau benyawa deka' makai, bekaki deka' bejalai*). Like intent, hesitancy or reluctance (*lembau*) is also experienced in the body, typically in the liver (*atau*), while failure to execute an intended action may be attributed to a conflict between the *ati* and the particular body part responsible for the action. For example, 'my heart wanted to, but my bones were weary' (*ati aku deka', tang tulang aku lelak*) means 'I wanted to go, but was too tired'.

Thoughts likewise are said to arise within the body. In Iban, the verb *berunding* means 'to think', and, in everyday speech, the usual way of saying 'I think' is *ba runding aku*, literally, 'according to my thoughts' (*runding*). However, in conversational Iban, thought and speech are often conflated. The common expression *ku' aku* (lit., 'says I') also means 'according to me', 'in my opinion' or, simply, 'I think'. Consequently, the term *jaku'*, or its shortened form, *ku'*, means not only 'speak', but also 'think'. By contrast, *ku' ati aku* (lit., 'says my heart') or *ba ati aku* ('according to my heart') means, more reflectively, 'I thought to myself'. In this connection, *berunding* means not only 'to think', but also, more collectively, 'to deliberate', 'discuss' or 'talk [things] over [with others]'. Barrett thus argues that the Iban see thinking, because of its links to speech, more 'as a social rather than [an] introspective process' (2012: 117).

While Western concepts of personhood tend to privilege the internal mental life of an individual, which is seen as disembodied, taking this disembodied mentality to be a defining feature of a person, for the Iban, the body itself is 'mentalised'—that is, it is seen as the field in which mental life operates. Consequently, personhood is defined less in terms of the uniqueness of an individual's internal mental life and more in terms of his or her interactions with other persons, with the body, as seen from without, serving as its visible representation.[17] Thus, the body, unmediated by any notion of a disembodied mind, is seen as the field in which feelings, emotions and volition are experienced, apprehended and acted on. While the heart/liver is the principal locale in which all of this occurs, it is not the sole source of cognition and action. Other parts of the body are also involved. Speech, touch, turning the eyes and moving within

---

17 The term *tubuh* ('body') is thus used by Iban speakers in much the same way that English speakers use the term 'person'. For example, *berapa iku' tubuh dia* means 'how many persons are there [over there]?'.

the environment all require other parts of the body, such as the mouth, teeth, fingertips, arms, legs and bones; in short, one's entire corporeal being is involved in taking in and acting on the world—a perspective clearly reflected in Iban ethno-semantics.

This kind of highly embodied sense of feeling, thought and action has been described for other Austronesian societies as well. Robert Levy, for example, writes of Tahitians (1984: 221):

> [W]hen asked to describe such matters as anger, desire, fear, and so on, villagers say that their 'place' is in the 'intestines' … These feelings can arise spontaneously in the intestines or they may be stirred up by some thought from the head, or by something that is seen by the eyes or heard by the ears … The feeling can lead to action directly, but this usually produces a bad result. It should first be thought over in the head, the seat of proper judgment, prior to taking action.

In contrast to the Tahitians, for the Iban, the process of 'thinking' is not the work of the 'head',[18] but occurs both in the *ati* and outside the body in the interactive realm of speech. Ideally, feelings and intentions should be subject to verbal deliberation before they are translated into action, particularly if this action is likely to affect others.

As Bruce Kapferer (1995: 134) reminds us, no matter how embodied our awareness may be, it is never limited to processes internal to the body alone. 'All human beings are oriented within a life-world of other human beings', their actions directed towards the horizons of the various life worlds they and others share (Kapferer 1995: 134–5). This sharing of life worlds is crucial to understanding how the emotions, intentions and awareness work in processes of healing.

The body, ageing and illness

Despite its centrality, the body tends to disappear from awareness when functioning unproblematically. It is mainly at times of dysfunction that it tends to seize our attention. Illness, pain and other forms of bodily

---

18   However, as Barrett (2012: 116) notes, in addition to the heart/liver, many Iban, particularly younger, educated Iban, also identify thinking with the 'brain' (*untak*), especially in regard to forms of thinking associated with formal education. In contrast to the Iban, the people with whom I did earlier fieldwork, the Sama Dilaut, like the Tahitians, similarly associate thinking with the head (see Sather 1997: 296).

affliction not only call attention to the body, they also direct our attention to particular parts of the body—for example, to an injured ankle or a chest in pain (see Leder 1987: 173). In this way, pain interrupts our links to the external world and to the life worlds we share with one another. As Elaine Scarry (1985: 33) writes: 'As in dying and death, so in serious pain the claims of the body utterly nullify the claims of the world.' Thus, intense pain, like the process of dying, is 'world destroying' (Scarry 1985: 29). Bodily affliction 'tends to induce ... isolation' and brings about what Drew Leder has called 'a spatio-temporal constriction' of the self (1987: 181). However, although 'it disrupts our intentionalities', it:

> never leads to a complete collapse of the world. It is our nature, as beings-in-the-world, to inhabit a significant continuum of space and time, projects and goals. However, the new world into which we are thrust by pain has a constricted aspect ... We are no longer dispersed out *there* in the world, but suddenly congeal right *here*. (Leder 1987: 181–2)

This inwardness of pain places it, Leder argues, always 'a little behind what can be seen or touched. It takes over our perceptual field and yet eludes us' (1987: 182). Much of Iban healing is about overcoming this elusiveness. Shamans, for example, by focusing directly on the body, overcome this inwardness by palpating their patients, feeling their bodies with their fingertips for invisible pain or illness-causing objects lodged beneath the surface of the skin. By removing these objects, they make them visible, often as tiny stones (Sather 2001: 124–5), and so they not only disclose them visually, but also remove them from the body. Because of the inwardness of pain, space, too:

> loses its normal directionality. Physical suffering constricts not only the spatial, but also the temporal sphere. It pulls us back to the *here* but also calls us back to the *now*. Pain thus exerts a 'centripetal' force, gathering space and time inward to the center. (Leder 1987: 182–3)

Serious illness and infirmity also tend to restrict the mobility of the sufferer's body, possibly rendering it no longer capable of acting in the world. As a result, '[t]he body, immobilized and restrained', becomes, Kapferer (1995: 139) argues:

> no longer vital in the production of consciousness. It becomes the boundary of a consciousness given up to itself in virtual reverie ... that projects back into itself ... within the closure of the body. Not only does it exhaust meaning within itself, but also such a confined consciousness attacks its prison, the body itself.

Curing thus becomes a process that Kapferer describes as an 'intentional re-extension' of embodied awareness back into the life worlds the sick person formerly shared with others (1995: 137). The narrative and staging of the *Sugi Sakit* worked to produce just such a re-extension, re-establishing the directionality of space and time, and so refocused the patient's awareness outward, beyond the boundaries of their body, on a shared life world evoked by the priest bard's *main*. Everything in the *Sugi* narrative drew the listener into this external world and its attractions. Mountains soar into the heavens and longhouses stretch across the horizon. War boats miraculously skim over the water or even fly. The priest bard's use of hyperbole and extravagant imagery in the *Sugi Sakit* aroused the listeners' interest and drew them into an idealised and seemingly timeless world of heroic adventures and romance. The story and the larger verbal drama in which it was set thus worked on the emotions as a powerful counteragent to the constrictive, world-obliterating effects of illness and infirmity.

The *Sugi Sakit* as a work of love: The aesthetics of pleasure and beauty

In talking with Iban elders about the *Sugi Sakit*, many of them said that participating in the ritual 'made them feel joy' (*ke ngasuh rindu'*)—that is, it literally 'made [them] feel love' (*rindu'*). Dari anak Alen, Lemambang Meramat's sister, for example, told us:[19]

> For me, I don't know about others [*aku, orang enda' mih nemu*]—I don't know what others experienced in [their] hearts [*enda' nemu ati orang*]— but, for myself, when he [the priest bard] performed it, I couldn't sleep [*enggi' aku nama sida' iya (lemambang) bemain, aku endang enda' tinduk*]. I truly loved it [*rindu' endar ati*]. That's why I couldn't sleep [*nya' alai ke enda' tinduk*].

Not only the *Sugi* story, but also the spectacle of the ritual itself aroused love:

> The bard singing, the people taking part in the procession to welcome the gods, to welcome the shaman [gods] [*orang bemain, orang ngalu petara, ngalu manang*]. Oh, the women really looked magnificent wearing all their gear [*oh balat ngepan indu' kau*]! They really dressed up [*endang*

---

19   Interview, Rumah Dit, 4 August 2004.

bengepan manah-manah]. It was a truly beautiful sight [*mata pan rindu' ga* (lit., 'the eyes were also made glad')]. I really loved it [*ati pan rindu ga'*]. It made me want to be young again [*tetenguk ka biak baru*].

As a ritual drama, the *main Sugi* was intended to both cure the sick and bring pleasure to those who took part in the ritual. Participating 'helped the sick person get well' (*nulung ngeraika orang ke sakit*), but also caused those taking part 'to feel love' (*ke ngasuh rindu'*). Indeed, some described the *Sugi Sakit* as a 'ritual/work of love' (*pengawa' rindu'*).

'Love', in contrast to pain, Scarry writes, affirms our capacity 'to move out beyond the boundaries of our body into an external, sharable world' (1985: 5). In contrast to sickness and ageing, love and perceptions of beauty not only maintain, but also intensify, our intentional links to the external world and to other human beings.

The aesthetic emphasis in the *Sugi Sakit* on entertainment, pleasure and beauty not only worked on the feelings of those taking part in the ritual, but also transformed the longhouse setting where the ritual took place. The gallery became a public gathering place. At its centre, the ritual's sponsors constructed a raised platform (*panggau*),[20] partially encircling it with an enclosure of finely woven ritual cloth (*pua' kumbu'*). This construction, in the special language of the priest bards, was called the *meligai*. The beauty of the cloth that formed the walls of this enclosure was said to attract the notice of the gods and spirits, while the structure itself was a sign to these unseen observers that human beings were holding a curing ritual to which they, too, were invited as 'guests' (*pengabang*). The *meligai* thus served as both a visual invitation and a sign of welcome. Its construction was followed by an offering ceremony (*biau*), after which offerings were placed in and around the structure and at the entrance to the outdoor platform (*tanju'*), where a divining pig was tethered for slaughter at the conclusion of the ritual. These offerings demarcated the stage on which the *Sugi* drama was enacted and served as primary points of contact between the gods and the ritual's human participants. They also provided the gods and spirits, in the words of the priest bard's *main*, with a sumptuous feast. As soon as this offering ceremony was over, the priest bard left the gallery and entered the sick person's family apartment. In so doing, he signalled the formal beginning of the *Sugi Sakit*. Inside the apartment, he began,

---

20 Note the semantic connection of *panggau* with the intermediating raised world of the Orang Panggau.

for the first time, to sing as family members escorted the patient out on to the gallery. This journey, accompanied by gong music and the priest bard's singing, was deliberately slowed to allow the observing gods and spirits time to witness and react with compassion to what was occurring. Inside the *meligai*, the patient was installed on the platform and made comfortable with bedding and cushions.

One side of the *meligai*, through which the party entered with the patient, was left open. This faced a swing (*tali wa*) on which the priest bard sat as he sang the *main Sugi Sakit*.

The struggle to stay alive is a struggle to maintain one's extension out into the world. As Scarry points out, not only states of feeling, but also speech is important in this struggle. Oftentimes, she writes, 'the voice becomes a final source of self-extension; so long as one is speaking, the self extends out beyond the boundaries of the body' (Scarry 1985: 33). 'Verbal virtuosity' thus becomes, Scarry writes, 'a mode of survival' (1988: 33).

Speech, however, works the other way as well, as a source of self-extension not only for the speaker, but also for the listener. In the *Sugi Sakit*, verbal virtuosity was the special gift of the priest bard, not of the patient. It was the patient as a listener, however, who benefited. The *main Sugi* was not only poetically composed, it was also sung and enacted. Hence, the priest bard's *main* was made available to the senses through its theatrical presentation and the melodic qualities of the priest bard's singing, and so became an object of direct experience (see Sather, forthcoming). The musicality, rhyme and other aesthetic features of the priest bard's use of language brought the sensory, perceptible qualities of ritual speech (*leka main*) to the awareness of his audience, thereby playing on the 'ability of the listener to focus alternatively on meanings and sounds' (Urban 1996: 182). The sound dimensions of speech were heightened and so distracted the audience from a tendency towards what Urban has called 'referential consciousness', opening them instead to 'experiences other than those permitted by the overt meaning of words' (1996: 185). At the same time, sound foregrounded 'nonreferential signs, embodied experience, [and an] immediate encounter with the world' (Urban 1996: 185), and so exercised a magnetic pull, drawing the listener directly into the verbal drama that the priest bard created as he sang. Physical sound also points to the contrast between the seen and the unseen: between the here-and-now realm of the senses and the reality beyond this realm contained in verbal imagery and poetic language. The aesthetic emphasis on beauty, entertainment and pleasure was not incidental to the purpose of the *Sugi Sakit*, but, rather, contributed directly to the ritual's effectiveness and to that of the priest bards who in the past performed it.

Compassion and visibility

While love in the sense of gladness played a central role in the *Sugi Sakit*, it was love primarily in the sense of compassion that brought together the ritual's human audience and motivated them in carrying out the ritual as a work of healing. To love in the sense of *kasih* and *sayau* was to intervene, to respond to the needs of the patient by making oneself present.

For the Iban, the struggle to maintain life and recover a sense of wellbeing is understood, above all, as a struggle to see and remain visible. Hence, illness, infirmity and dying are the inverse of love and so are associated, as we have said, with invisibility and a severing of visual connections. The patient and, perhaps, their whole longhouse are no longer visible to the gods. Invisibility becomes both the cause and a consequence of bodily affliction. While the patient loses their awareness of the external world, others lose sight of the patient. Illness causes the sick person to withdraw from active involvement in the everyday life of the longhouse, oftentimes confining them to a sickbed. Although physically present, they become invisible to others. A major object of the *Sugi Sakit* was to reverse this diminished visibility by making the sick person a central focus of visual scrutiny. Consequently, the opening stage of the *Sugi Sakit* involved removing the patient from the relative seclusion of their family's apartment and installing them at the centre of the longhouse gallery. Here, the patient was ceremonially placed inside the *meligai*. Although enclosed on three sides by walls of ritual cloth, with upright spears forming its four corners, this enclosure was meant to safeguard the ailing patient, not to separate them from the rest of the community or to render them invisible. On the contrary, the walls of cloth were intended to attract notice, to arrest the eyes of all who beheld the structure, signalling to observers that, inside, it was a loved one, dangerously ill and in need of their care. Moreover, the *meligai* was not fully enclosed, but was open on one side. Its open side not only faced the priest bard's swing, but also was oriented towards what the Iban call the *ujung ramu* ('tip of the beams'). This orientation, relative to the long axis of the longhouse (see Sather 1993: 76–8), ensured the gods and spirit heroes would have to come completely inside the longhouse to gaze into the *meligai*, rather than merely 'peep in' from the nearest entrance, and that the priest bard would not have his back to them when they first entered. Thus, the structure was oriented in a way that was welcoming and not only invited visitors to approach the *meligai*, but also encouraged them to enter the enclosure itself and there attend to the patient inside.

The greater part of Iban healing—particularly that which was the work of the priest bards—was concerned with counteracting the centripetal effects of pain, ageing and illness. Pain and illness brought about an alienation from the body. Experiencing them not only made the body an object of awareness, but also distanced it (Leder 1987: 189). The ailing body, now distanced, became the focus of an interpretative quest. In the *Sugi Sakit*, this quest involved 'viewing' or 'inspecting' (*ngabas*) the sick person and a gradual extension of the process of inspection to include ever more distant observers. The act of inspection aroused feelings of compassion and sympathy so that the patient's body became not only an object of inspection, but also a focus of action. To care for a patient was to be present, so that the sick person was never allowed to lapse into a disconnected state of personal isolation. Initially, when someone fell ill, those who responded first were typically neighbours and members of the sick person's family. To respond meant to intervene so as, literally, 'to view' or 'inspect the sick person' (*ngabas orang ke sakit*). In this visual language, the sick person's caregivers were said to respond by becoming *ngintai*, meaning 'watchful' or 'on the lookout'.[21] Being watchful meant to enter a state of heightened vigilance. In this state, caregivers sought, for example, dreams—particularly dreams favourable to the sick person's prospects for recovery—or they went into the forest to seek omens or collect special foods favoured by the sick person to coax them back into eating.[22] Outside the immediate family, for others, to demonstrate compassion meant *bejalai*, literally, 'to walk' or 'go on a journey', even if this journey was only to the neighbouring *bilik* (apartment). When other families learned that someone in the community had fallen ill, they typically responded by walking to the sick person's apartment 'to inspect' the patient. If the illness persisted, or appeared to be serious from

---

21   From the root *intai*, meaning 'wait' or 'watch for [an opportunity]' (Richards 1981: 117).
22   Loss of appetite is seen as both a symptom of illness and a sign that the patient may have lost their will to live. Hence, every effort is made to encourage the patient to resume eating.

the outset, family members were generally dispatched to surrounding longhouses to inform close relatives and friends. In this way, the circle of visitors typically expanded.

At first, a person was often unsure as to the cause of their illness or how to deal with it. Other family members and even the longhouse elders might also be uncertain. As an ever-expanding circle of visitors arrived to 'inspect' the sick person, their visits prompted an increasingly public discussion of the symptoms and circumstances of the patient's illness. In this way, the sick person's personal plight quickly became a matter of shared concern and discussion. The patient's illness, its possible causes and how it might be treated became topics of an ever-widening conversation. If, out of these visits, the sick person's family decided to summon a priest bard, the decision itself was preceded by a general meeting of longhouse members (*aum*), the major purpose of which was to achieve a further level of shared consensus and clarity.

In this way, the familiar institutions of travelling, visiting and hospitality became the basis on which the *Sugi Sakit* was socially organised. During the ritual, relationships between visitors and hosts assumed an increasingly formalised character, undergoing what Bell (1997: 81) has called a process of 'ritualisation'. To begin the process, the arrival of the priest bard on the day of the ritual signalled the appearance of a person of recognised ritual authority. Priest bards in the Saribas were generally revered figures and were welcomed by their hosts as honoured guests. Their relationship with the sponsoring families—'those who owned the work' (*sida' ke empuka pengawa'*)—was based on a division of labour in which the priest bard, using his *main*, invoked a participating audience of unseen visitors, while the sponsors, for their part, assembled a corresponding audience of invited human guests. The human participants in the *Sugi Sakit* were divided, again, into hosts and guests. The hosts included the families of those who 'owned' the ritual, their kindred (*kaban belayan*) who came, sometimes from other communities, to assist them and other members of the sick person's longhouse. The most important guests were the owners' *pengabang* ('invited guests') coming from other longhouses. At the beginning of the ritual, the welcoming of the human *pengabang* formed a prelude to the welcoming of the unseen guests. Their reception typically began in the early afternoon and ended at sundown. The invocation of unseen *pengabang* began soon after dark and ended with the arrival of Bujang Sugi and his unseen *pengabang* from beyond the human world just before sunrise.

Eros and ritual storytelling

Following the offering ceremony mentioned earlier, the *Sugi Sakit* was temporarily suspended for an evening meal, served by the sponsoring families to their guests along the outer gallery (*pantar*). As soon as the meal was over, the priest bard resumed his work, first singing a prologue called the *sempalai*.[23] The *sempalai* was a playful interlude meant to capture his audience's attention. It also served as a transition to the more serious work that followed. In this prologue, the priest bard described his *sempalai* as a praise song sung in honour of the *meligai*. But here, he referred to this structure, not in the special language of a priest bard, but by its common language meaning, to refer to the traditional sleeping place of young unmarried women. It now became in his *main* the bed of a maiden and its walls of ritual cloth became a mosquito curtain.

Traditionally, in coming of age, young women ceased to sleep in the family apartment and moved to a raised sleeping platform immediately above it in the loft. This was partially enclosed for privacy. Here, late at night, after everyone in the longhouse was assumed to have gone to sleep, young women were free to receive male suitors and engage in nightly courting. Young unmarried men also moved from the family apartment and slept on the outer section of the gallery, which, in the distant past and in the stories of the Orang Panggau, was also elevated and so was called the *panggau*.[24] The Iban described courting as a form of 'visiting' (v.f., *nguang*, *guang*, n.f.). 'Courting bachelors' (*bujang nguang*) visiting from other longhouses also slept on the *panggau* and from there it was relatively easy to climb to the lofts without disturbing those asleep in the family apartment. Traditionally, courting was conducted in the dark. Hence, the common term used to describe it was *ngayap*, meaning, literally, 'to grope in the dark'. If a young woman wished to be left undisturbed, she left a small oil lamp burning by her bedside, indicating that she did not wish to be courted. On the surface, the fact that courting took place in the dark would seem to contradict the notion that visibility activates love. On the contrary, however, it was a direct reflection of this notion. For young people of both sexes, one of the objectives of visiting was 'to inspect' and 'be seen' by possible romantic partners. In initiating a night-time

---

23   The term *sempalai* derives from the root word *empalai*, meaning, literally, 'a fenced garden' (Richards 1981: 380).
24   In a modern Iban longhouse, this part of the gallery, which is no longer raised, is called the *pantar* or *penyurai*.

romance, a young man initially presented himself as a stranger, much like Pujang Sugi in the *Sugi* epic. For a young woman, a primary object was to overcome the initial anonymity of her suitor, so that, if he were serious and the relationship seemed likely to deepen, he was compelled to reveal his identity and so make himself visible, ultimately, not only to the young woman herself, but also to her family, through a proposal of marriage.

In his *sempalai*, the priest bard, in addition to praising the *meligai*, described in poetic language the immediate setting. Night had fallen and surrounding him on the gallery were throngs of handsome bachelors and beautiful maidens. The latter urged him to sing a love song, which he was compelled to do at the request of his clients. Without a break, he shifted from the prologue to a new song called the *ngadingka lemambang* (to introduce the priest bard) in which he summoned his spirit helpers. As he sang, he shifted the perspective of his *main* from the here-and-now setting of the longhouse, the plight of his patient and the mood of his audience, to the unseen world, where, as he sang, the gods and spirits were described as gazing down from above and so taking note of the *meligai* and the activities unfolding on the gallery. He then called for the descent of the shaman gods (*petara manang*) and, as soon as they had finished treating the patient, he returned to his swing and began to sing the story of Sugi and Sedinang. As indicated by Dari and the other elders, the telling of this story was, for the priest bard's audience, the high point of the ritual.

Storytelling (*becherita*) was thus a central feature of the *Sugi Sakit*. It was also critical to the ritual's emotional impact. 'Emotions', as Andrew Beatty asserts, 'implicate narrative, and vice versa' (2014: 558). Narratives provide the time dimension needed for the development and playing out of emotions, while emotion-eliciting situations are the primary subject matter of narratives (Beatty 2010). The principal hero of the *Sugi* story is portrayed as a miraculous healer, who is able to bring back to life even the enemies he has decapitated in battle. He and Maiden Sedinang, as Keling and Kumang, represent the epitome of masculine and feminine beauty, their very perfection itself acting in the story as a source of healing power. Like love charms, they embody *pemandang*; to behold them is to be drawn to them. The effect of the *Sugi* story was thus to reawaken the listeners' attachment to the living world and to the physical pleasures and experiences that made life in this world worth living. The aesthetic beauty of the story, the hyperbole and the dramatic, vivid way in which it was performed caused listeners to 'feel' or 'experience love' (*asai rindu'*) directly as an emotional response to what they were hearing and seeing. For the patient, the *Sugi* story opened their awareness to an imaginary world, beyond pain, fear or the infirmities of the body, while, at the same time, it restored their connections with the past, evoking memories of youth, and with a possible future free of bodily affliction. The *Sugi Sakit* brought about an emotional transformation in both the patient and the social community who assembled to take part in it. From an initial state of worry and grieving, the community was mobilised, united in a common purpose and motivated by shared feelings of compassion and gladness evoked by the priest bard's *main*, greetings and rites of hospitality, and by the spectacle of the ritual itself. The patient, too, was transformed. Brought into the ritual as an ageing, and often very ill, patient, he or she became, through identification with the heroes and heroines of the *Sugi* epic, a young man or woman in the prime of life, a victorious warrior or a maiden being courted.

Here, the aesthetics of beauty, the capacity of persons or things to give pleasure, was bound up with the embodied experience of what it meant to be alive, in good health and actively engaged in the external world. In her book *On Beauty and Being Just* (1999), Elaine Scarry attempts to define what occurs when someone sees or hears something they experience as beautiful. While beauty itself is beyond definition, the perceiver, in encountering it, experiences it immediately as such. One common metaphor compares the response to a greeting. Beauty, when we encounter it, whether in a person or an object, causes 'unease and indifference [to] drop away [so that] the world of existence loses its capacity to harm'. When we stand in the presence of something beautiful, 'it makes life more vivid, animated, worth living' (Scarry 1999: 24–5). Beauty, moreover, has a 'forward momentum'—it engages us with the world and incites us to contemplation and to bringing new things into being. It thus reinforces the inherent tendency of the healthy, lived-in embodied self to project itself into the world and to seek to apprehend and act on whatever the bodily senses perceive to be present there. When one beholds a beautiful person, or a beautiful object, even if this object is inanimate, the beholder, Scarry tells us, confers on it a 'surfeit of aliveness' (1999: 89). This conferral involves 'a reciprocal pact'. The perceiver confers the gift of life on what he or she experiences as beautiful, while the beautiful thing or person confers the gift of life on the perceiver.

During the *Sugi Sakit*, all of this was reinforced by the physical setting in which the ritual took place, represented, in particular, by the *meligai*. For males, the platform inside this structure represented the *panggau*, the raised sleeping platform of visitors and of the bachelor heroes of the *Sugi* epic, while, for women, it symbolised the sleeping place of the maiden heroines, the site of courtship and love affairs. As the ritual's visible focus, it evoked the life-restoring powers of love in all the varied forms described here, from gladness to eros.

References

Averill, James R. 1985. 'The social construction of emotion: With special reference to love'. In Kenneth J. Gergen and Keith E. Davis (eds) *The Social Construction of the Person*, pp. 89–109. New York: Springer-Verlag. doi.org/10.1007/978-1-4612-5076-0_5.

Barrett, Robert J. 1993. 'Performance, effectiveness and the Iban manang'. In Robert L. Winzeler (ed.) *The Seen and the Unseen: Shamanism, mediumship and possession in Borneo*, pp. 235–79. Monograph 2. Williamsburg, VA: Borneo Research Council.

Barrett, Robert J. 2012. *Psychiatric Research among the Iban: Collected papers of Robert J. Barrett*. Monograph Series No. 13. Anna Chur-Hansen and George N. Appell (eds). Phillips, ME: Borneo Research Council.

Beatty, Andrew. 2005. 'Emotions in the field: What are we talking about?' *Journal of the Royal Anthropological Institute* 11: 17–37. doi.org/10.1111/j.1467-9655.2005.00224.x.

Beatty, Andrew. 2010. 'How did it feel for you? Emotion, narrative, and the limits of ethnography'. *American Anthropologist* 112: 430–43. doi.org/10.1111/j.1548-1433.2010.01250.x.

Beatty, Andrew. 2014. 'Anthropology and emotion'. *Journal of the Royal Anthropological Institute* 20: 545–63. doi.org/10.1111/1467-9655.12114.

Bell, Catherine. 1997. *Ritual: Perspectives and dimensions*. New York: Oxford University Press.

Blust, Robert. 2013. *The Austronesian Languages*. Rev. edn. Canberra: Asia-Pacific Linguistics.

Bruggeman, G. 1985. *English–Iban Vocabulary*. Kuching: Persatuan Kesusasteraan Sarawak.

Csordas, Thomas J. 1990. 'Embodiment as a paradigm for anthropology'. *Ethos* 18: 5–47. doi.org/10.1525/eth.1990.18.1.02a00010.

Csordas, Thomas J. (ed.). 1996. *Embodiment and Experience: The existential ground of culture and self*. Cambridge: Cambridge University Press.

Department of Statistics Malaysia. 2012. *Population Distribution and Basic Demographic Characteristic Report 2010*. Kuala Lumpur: Department of Statistics Malaysia. Available from: www.dosm.gov. my/v1/index.php?r=column/cthemeByCat&cat=117&bul_id=MDM xdHZjWTk1SjFzTzNkRXYzcVZjdz09&menu_id=L0pheU43NWJ wRWVSZklWdzQ4TlhUUT09 (accessed 25 September 2017).

Ensiring, Janang anak, Jantan Umbat and Robert Menua Saleh (compilers). 2011. *Bup Sereba Reti Jaku Iban*. [In Iban]. Kuching: Tun Jugah Foundation.

Fox, James J. 1995. 'Austronesian societies and their transformations'. In Peter Bellwood, James J. Fox and Darrell Tryon (eds) *The Austronesians: Historical and comparative perspectives*, pp. 214–28. Canberra: The Australian National University.

Fox, James J. 2008. 'Installing the "outsider" inside: The exploration of an epistemic Austronesian cultural theme and its social significance'. *Indonesia and the Malay World* 36(105): 201–18. doi.org/ 10.1080/13639810802267942.

Freeman, Derek. 1967. 'Shaman and incubus'. *Psychoanalytic Study of Society* 4: 315–44.

Freeman, Derek. 1981. *Some reflections on the nature of Iban society*. Occasional Papers, Department of Anthropology, Research School of Pacific Studies. Canberra: The Australian National University.

Goddard, Cliff. 1995. '"Cognitive mapping" or "verbal explication"? Understanding love on the Malay Archipelago'. *Semiotica* 106(3–4): 323–54.

Goddard, Cliff. 2001. 'Hati: A key word in the Malay vocabulary of emotion'. In Jean Harkins and Anna Wierzbicka (eds) *Emotions in Crosslinguistic Perspective*, pp. 167–96. New York: Mouton de Gruyter. doi.org/10.1515/9783110880168.167.

Howell, William and D. J. S. Bailey. 1900. *A Sea Dyak Dictionary*. Singapore: The American Mission Press.

Kapferer, Bruce. 1979. 'Emotion and feeling in Sinhalese healing rites'. *Social Analysis* 1: 153–76.

Kapferer, Bruce. 1995. 'From the edge of death: Sorcery and the motion of consciousness'. In Anthony P. Cohen and Nigel Rapport (eds) *Questions of Consciousness*, pp. 134–52. New York: Routledge. doi.org/ 10.4324/9780203449486_chapter_7.

Karim, Wazir Jahan (ed.). 1990. *Emotions of Culture: A Malay perspective*. Singapore: Oxford University Press.

Leder, Drew Lance. 1987. 'The absent body: A phenomenological anatomy'. PhD dissertation. State University of New York at Stony Brook, NY.

Levy, Robert. 1973. *Tahitians: Mind and experience in the Society Islands*. Chicago: University of Chicago Press.

Levy, Robert. 1984. 'Emotion, knowing, and culture'. In Richard A. Shweder and Robert A. LeVine (eds) *Culture Theory: Essays on mind, self and emotion*, pp. 214–37. Cambridge: Cambridge University Press.

Lutz, Catherine A. 1988. *Unnatural Emotions: Everyday sentiments on a Micronesian atoll and their challenge to Western theory*. Chicago: University of Chicago Press.

Lutz, Catherine A. and Geoffrey M. White. 1986. 'The anthropology of emotions'. *Annual Review of Anthropology* 15: 405–36. doi.org/ 10.1146/annurev.an.15.100186.002201.

Matisoff, James. 1986. 'Hearts and minds in South-East Asian languages and English: An essay in the comparative lexical semantics of psycho-collocations'. *Cahiers de linguistique-Asie Orientale* 15(1): 5–57. doi.org/10.3406/clao.1986.1191.

Richards, Anthony. 1981. *An Iban–English Dictionary*. Oxford: Oxford University Press.

Rosaldo, Michelle. 1984. 'Toward an anthropology of self and feeling'. In Richard A. Shweder and Robert A. LeVine (eds) *Culture Theory: Essays on mind, self and emotion*, pp. 137–57. Cambridge: Cambridge University Press.

Sahlins, Marshall. 1981. 'The stranger king: Or Dumézil among the Fijians'. *Journal of Pacific History* 16: 107–32. doi.org/10.1080/00223348108572419.

Sahlins, Marshall. 1985. *Islands of History*. Chicago: University of Chicago Press.

Sahlins, Marshall. 2008. 'The stranger-king: Or, elementary forms of the politics of life'. *Indonesia and the Malay World* 36(105): 177–99. doi.org/10.1080/13639810802267918.

Sahlins, Marshall. 2012. 'Alterity and autochthony: Austronesian cosmologies of the marvelous'. *HAU: Journal of Ethnographic Theory* 2(1): 131–60. doi.org/10.14318/hau2.1.008.

Sather, Clifford. 1978. 'The malevolent koklir: Iban concepts of sexual peril and the dangers of childbirth'. *Bijdragen tot de Taal-, Land- en Volkenkunde* 134: 310–55. doi.org/10.1163/22134379-90002590.

Sather, Clifford. 1992. 'The rites of manggol: Work and ritual in Paku Iban agriculture'. *Sarawak Museum Journal* 40: 107–34.

Sather, Clifford. 1993. 'Posts, hearths and thresholds: The Iban longhouse as a ritual structure'. In James J. Fox (ed.) *Inside Austronesian Houses: Perspectives on domestic designs for living*, pp. 65–115. Canberra: The Australian National University.

Sather, Clifford. 1994. 'Wooden weapons: Constrained violence and the evolution of adat in a nineteenth-century Iban society'. *ASSESS Journal* 1: 5–23.

Sather, Clifford. 1996. '"All threads are white": Iban egalitarianism reconsidered'. In James J. Fox and Clifford Sather (eds) *Origins, Ancestry and Alliance*, pp. 70–110. Canberra: The Australian National University.

Sather, Clifford. 1997. *The Bajau Laut: Adaptation, history, and fate in a maritime fishing society of south-eastern Sabah*. Kuala Lumpur: Oxford University Press.

Sather, Clifford. 2001. *Seeds of Play, Words of Power: An ethnographic study of Iban shamanic chants*. Kuching: Tun Jugah Foundation and Borneo Research Council.

Sather, Clifford. 2004. 'The Iban'. In Ooi Keat Gin (ed.) *Southeast Asia: A Historical Encyclopedia. Volume 2*, pp. 623–5. Santa Barbara, CA: ABC Clio Press.

Sather, Clifford. 2012a. 'Introduction'. In Anna Chur-Hansen and George N. Appell (eds) *Psychiatric Research among the Iban: Collected papers of Robert J. Barrett*, pp. x–xxxvi. Monograph Series No. 13. Phillips, ME: Borneo Research Council.

Sather, Clifford. 2012b. 'Recalling the dead, revering the ancestors: Multiple forms of ancestorship in Saribas Iban society'. In Pascal Couderc and Kenneth Sillander (eds) *Ancestors in Borneo Societies: Death, transformation, and social immortality*, pp. 114–52. Copenhagen: NIAS Press.

Sather, Clifford. 2017. *A Borneo Healing Romance: Ritual Storytelling and the Sugi Sakit, A Saribas Iban Rite of Healing*. Phillips, ME/Sarawak, Malaysia: Borneo Research Council/The Tun Jugah Foundation.

Sather, Clifford and Jantan Umbat. 2004. Ripih Pengawa' Besugi Sakit. Unpublished transcription of the *Sugi Sakit* performed by Lemambang Renang anak Jabing. Iban Archives Collection. Tun Jugah Foundation, Kuching.

Scarry, Elaine. 1985. *The Body in Pain: The Making and Unmaking of the World*. New York: Oxford University Press.

Scarry, Elaine. 1999. *On Beauty and Being Just*. Princeton, NJ: Princeton University Press.

Scott, N. C. 1956. *A Dictionary of Sea Dayak*. London: School of Oriental and African Studies, University of London.

Shweder, Richard A. and Robert A. LeVine (eds). 1984. *Culture Theory: Essays on mind, self and emotion*. Cambridge: Cambridge University Press.

Sutlive, Vinson and Joanne Sutlive (eds). 1994. *A Handy Reference Dictionary of Iban and English*. Kuching: Tun Jugah Foundation.

Urban, Greg. 1996. *Metaphysical Community: The interplay of the senses and the intellect*. Austin: University of Texas Press.

Wadley, Reed L. 2004. 'Punitive expeditions and divine revenge: Oral and colonial histories of rebellion and pacification in western Borneo, 1886–1902'. *Ethnohistory* 51(3): 609–36. doi.org/10.1215/00141801-51-3-609.

Wadley, Reed L. and Fredrik Kuyah. 2001. 'Iban communities in West Kalimantan'. In Vinson Sutlive and Joanne Sutlive (eds) *The Encyclopaedia of Iban Studies. Volume 2*, pp. 716–34. Kuching: Tun Jugah Foundation.

Wilce, J. M. 2004. 'Passionate scholarship: Recent anthropologies of emotion'. *Reviews in Anthropology* 33: 1–7.

Wolters, O. W. 1999. *History, culture, and region in Southeast Asian perspectives*. Studies on Southeast Asia No. 26. Ithaca, NY: Cornell Southeast Asia Program Publications.

4

Learning to share emotions through ritual participation among the Toraja of Sulawesi

Roxana Waterson

Introduction: The anthropology of the emotions and the concept of empathy

Anthropology has always been about two big questions—simply expressed: what makes humans everywhere the same and what makes us different? Just like comparative studies of language and rationality, the anthropology of emotions has been an important testing ground for the exploration of these always interrelated questions. Austronesian ethnography has played a significant role in the development of anthropological thinking about the emotions (see, for example, Geertz 1974; Heider 1991; Levy 1973; Lutz 1988; Lutz and White 1986; M. Rosaldo 1980; R. Rosaldo 1984; White 1993; White and Kirkpatrick 1985, to mention only a few). In these works, there is a strong focus on indigenous discourse about emotions, their acceptable expression and the socially patterned intentions that shape them, while some outstanding studies, such as those by the Rosaldos on Ilongot *liget* or by Lutz on Ifaluk *fago*, have presented detailed analyses of culturally unique emotional concepts or complexes of ideas.

Much less has been written to date about the comparative ethnography of an ethos of empathy or on the question of how children, as subjects actively involved in the reproduction of culture, learn what is expected of them in the realm of shared emotions. The idea of ethos was notably employed by Gregory Bateson (1958: 32–3) in his highly original study of Iatmul society to talk about 'the emotional emphases of [a] culture' (as distinct from eidos, which he defined as the standardised cognitive aspects involved in the premises of a particular culture). Ethnographers working both within and beyond the Austronesian world have noted that culturally salient ideas about emotions help to establish particular concepts of personhood and 'modes of relationship' (Levy 1973: 271), and ultimately the moral order itself. Children, it has been argued, absorb a particular cultural ethos, not only through what they hear adults say about emotions, but also, and perhaps more importantly, through direct experience of social interactions or participation in collective activities in which local theories of the emotions are implicitly embedded (Myers 1979). Toren's studies in Fiji (1990, 1999, 2006) have made pathbreaking contributions in examining how children form their own ideas about how their culture works. The ideas of these authors provide a starting point for this chapter, which examines the emotional content of Toraja children's accounts of what they have learned from attendance at rituals.

Any discussion of the contributions made to the study of emotions by ethnographers of Austronesian societies would be incomplete without reference to the substantial body of work by Douglas Hollan and Jane Wellenkamp on the Toraja of Sulawesi (Hollan 1988, 1990, 1992a, 1992b, 2008, 2011; Hollan and Wellenkamp 1994, 1996; Wellenkamp 1984, 1988, 1991, 1992). Wellenkamp in particular has focused on emotions associated with death and grieving, which have a special importance for the Toraja given the salience they accord to funerary rituals as social occasions—I shall say more about this in a moment. Hollan and Wellenkamp's research was based largely on life-history interviews with adults. Since the study I am going to discuss was done with children, I hope to be able to extend their insights by seeing what can be learned from this still much neglected constituency of research participants. I should say at the outset that exploring empathy or emotional expression was not the original intention of the investigation. Seeking to discover what Toraja children think about the complex ceremonial system in which as adults they will be expected to participate, at great financial cost, it was quite by chance that I found many of the children had written about a felt need or duty to share in the feelings of others. I am encouraged to explore this further by the fact that Hollan, in collaboration with Jason Throop (Hollan and Throop 2008, 2011), has recently turned his attention to the cross-cultural study of empathy, a concept that is currently of consuming interest also to neuroscientists and evolutionary biologists. In what follows, I hope to pick up on some threads of their discussion, while adding a new perspective to the already extensive ethnography of ritual among the Toraja.

The discovery of mirror neurons has triggered intense and still vexed debate in the biological sciences about their possible role in providing a neurological basis for empathy and theory of mind—capabilities that, while not totally unique to humans, are clearly developed in our species to a quite remarkable degree.[1] Not all social scientists, however, keep up with the rapid developments taking place in biology, or they may explicitly reject the possibility that these could have the slightest relevance to what we are doing. Hollan and Throop (2008), in their introduction to a special issue of *Ethos* on the problem of empathy in anthropology, note that 'empathy has remained muted in anthropological discussion to the extent that it is often oddly absent from even the most relevant of studies' (p. 386), although related issues to do with intentionality and theory of mind may possibly have been serving 'as a means to bring empathy back into anthropology through the back door' (p. 385).[2] Anthropological aversion to a consideration of empathy, Hollan and Throop suggest, may be laid at the door of Clifford Geertz (1984), who famously dismissed the concept in his oft-cited essay 'From the native's point of view: On the nature of anthropological understanding'. But the content of that essay, in fact, has nothing to do with efforts to understand empathy from an evolutionary perspective or its role in enabling complex sociality in humans. Geertz was simply having a dig at Malinowski's own claims to special anthropological gifts of empathic understanding—claims that could be put in perspective following the posthumous publication of the latter's diaries. These revealed—to much declared shock in anthropological

---

1   To review these debates is beyond the scope of this chapter, but, on mirror neurons and empathy, see Bastiaansen et al. (2009); Decety and Ickes (2009); Decety and Jackson (2004); Gallese (2001, 2007); Iacoboni (2008); Iacoboni et al. (2005); Preston and de Waal (2002); Rizzolatti and Craighero (2004); Stamenov and Gallese (2002). For evolutionary and developmental perspectives on empathy, see Baron-Cohen (2011); Eisenberg and Strayer (1987); Frith (2007); Gallagher (2012); Hoffman (2000); Young (2012).
2   For a recent comparative contribution in this field, with a focus on Pacific societies, see Wassmann et al. (2013).

quarters at the time—that he had not unfailingly enjoyed his fieldwork and, when having an off day, was not above recording embarrassing comments about his Trobriand acquaintances in the putatively private space of his personal journal. In their recent book *The Anthropology of Empathy* (2011: 2), which focuses on Pacific societies, Hollan and Throop note that empathy 'remains a woefully understudied and unanalysed form of behaviour' in anthropology. This did not stop a reviewer of the book from dismissing the concept as unworthy of serious anthropological investigation (Rollason 2012). Dwelling on the difficulties of definition, and the obvious limitations of using English as the language of discussion for issues of comparative ethnography, Rollason (2012: 707) concludes: 'Empathy, one feels reading this collection, is too flimsy a notion to accommodate the excellent ethnographic work that the individual essayists have produced.' This easy dismissal might be due to the reviewer not having considered any of the neurological literature painstakingly referenced by the authors or it might indicate the adoption of a certain postmodernist position of extreme cultural relativism, from which the according of any special precedence to the findings of natural scientists is discounted as yet another hegemonic manoeuvre. That attitude is regrettable, however, since, as Ingold (1985: 16) passionately argued long ago, it cuts us off from asking questions about what makes us human, and risks leaving 'a vacuum that the more bigoted practitioners of other disciplines are only too eager to fill'.[3] What is more to the point now, in today's 'postgenomic' age, is that we should not inadvertently continue to adhere to an outdated image of biology as 'fixed', just when biological theorising itself is experiencing a radical 'social turn' that opens up the possibility for a rapprochement across the great divide between the social and the natural sciences (Meloni 2014).

It is instructive to compare the very different histories of the two, apparently closely related, words 'sympathy' and 'empathy'. Sympathy is an ancient word that has had a place in philosophical discussion since the time of the Greek philosophers. It has been variously deployed over the centuries, giving rise to an accumulation of meanings, some of which are by now strange to us. Prior to an understanding of gravitational forces, medieval astronomers speculated that the planets were kept in their orbits by a force of mutual attraction, which they labelled 'sympathy'. In the eighteenth century, the concept was central to the moral philosophy

---

3   For an inspired analysis of the problems with this position, see also Latour (1993).

of Hume (1739–40, 1751) and Smith (1759) (Stueber 2006: 29–31). Empathy, on the other hand, is a relatively modern word. It first appears in English in 1909, as the psychologist E. B. Tichener's chosen translation of the German *Einfühlung*, literally, a 'feeling into'. Stueber (2006: 5–19) provides an excellent summary of the term's conceptual history in Germany. It was first employed as a technical concept in the philosophical aesthetics of Robert Vischer in 1873 (Vischer 1994), although it already had a longer history within the tradition of German Romanticism, where it was generally used to describe a poetic and spiritual identification with nature. A more direct influence on Tichener, however, was the work of Theodor Lipps (1903–06) on aesthetics. Lipps was concerned to give a psychological account of naturally occurring human tendencies towards aesthetic experience and the making of judgements about the beauty of objects. He argued for an essentially kinetic appreciation of the human body in movement, and of external objects in general, linked to an innate tendency to motor mimicry. Most crucially for present purposes, he further drew a connection between the mimicry phenomenon and our ability to theorise about the minds of others. He thus saw empathy as a necessary and fundamental category of sociology and psychology (Stueber 2006: 7–8).

From the evolutionary point of view, empathy—or the ability to put ourselves in another person's place and thus interpret the minds and moods of others—can be seen as fundamental to the complexity of human sociability (Hoffman 2000). Most recent contributors to the empathy debate agree that it is a complex and multilayered phenomenon. The original insight about mirror neurons was that similar brain activity occurs in observers as well as performers of an action. There is now evidence that mirror systems are involved not only in observing an action, but also in emotional simulation, the observing and generating of facial expressions and shared emotions. Simulation is 'a highly integrated process' involving networks connecting various brain regions to produce a synthesis (Bastiaansen et al. 2009: 2398). But beyond its probable grounding in these neurological mechanisms, which facilitate an initial attunement to others' emotional states, empathy is generally seen to require both affective and cognitive aspects (Baron-Cohen 2011: 12; Gallagher 2012: 356; Stueber 2006: 20–1). Stueber (2006: 20–1), for instance, gives the term 'basic empathy' to 'the theoretically unmediated quasi-perceptual ability to recognize other creatures directly as minded creatures and to recognize them implicitly as creatures that are fundamentally like us'.

While he sees this as neurologically grounded, he notes that 'we also have to be able to explain a person's subsequent behaviour in a complex social situation' (Stueber 2006: 20–1). He calls the cognitive and deliberative capacities brought to bear to re-enact or imitate in our own mind the thought processes of another person 'reenactive empathy'. Given this interactive and socially situated quality, Gallagher (2012) goes further and proposes that narrative must also play a key role in empathy. This proposition can usefully be integrated into developmental perspectives, since the ability to tell and understand stories, like the development of theory of mind, is also a fundamental human capacity, one that follows a predictable developmental pathway in small children in tandem with the emergence of language. If we accept a definition of empathy as also involving a dimension of caring, Gallagher (2012: 376) states, then for this to happen, the context must be understood: 'empathy depends on A having the right story about B's situation'. At this point, we are back on anthropological terra firma: the study of social context. As Hollan (2008: 484) puts it:

> We need to recognize that the kinds of problems and situations people want recognized and understood and the ways in which they seek that recognition will be socially and culturally specific.[4]

Thus, while we may well agree that 'sympathy' is too amorphous and historically polysemous a term to be analytically useful to the social sciences, 'empathy', on the contrary, is a concept that currently has powerful interdisciplinary traction and analytic potential. This would seem to be a promising moment for anthropologists to contribute their own perspectives to the debate, using comparative ethnography to illuminate how other societies theorise about sociality, as well as how they practise empathy or cooperation, and how children actively learn about any such culturally distinctive ethos. The evidence suggests considerable cross-cultural variation in how empathy is expressed (or suppressed), and to whom. Cultural beliefs differ about the essential legibility or opacity of other minds, and hence the possibility of empathising in the first place (Lohmann 2011; Robins and Rumsey 2008), the degree to which ideals of secrecy and concealment may affect the expression of emotions (Throop 2011) or whether individuals may fear that others may abuse empathic knowledge of their vulnerabilities (Hollan 2008, 2011).

---

4   Clearly, this is variable over time as well as space. On historical shifts in emotional ethos and norms, see Elias (1994) and Stearns and Stearns (1994).

Hollan, writing of the dialectical aspects of empathy, notes that, among the Toraja, a person may try to hide their emotions for fear that empathic understanding will be used by others to harm them; alternatively, they may beg, cajole or appeal for empathy from the other according to the norms of a socially established 'discourse of persuasion' (2008: 486). Just as humans everywhere share the same neurological potential for language use yet speak different languages, such variation in discourses about empathy and caring for others should hardly come as a surprise.

Learning through ritual

How do children learn about the ethos of their society? I want to argue here that rituals provide a crucial arena for the absorption of emotional lessons and moral values, not necessarily through explicit instruction but, even more importantly, in a tacit manner, as they observe and gradually join in the activities of adults or become the focus of ritual attention themselves. Besides eventual competence in practical tasks, a great deal of social learning takes place in the ritual context, about kin relations, personhood and morality. Read (1955), for instance, provides vivid descriptions of how, among the Gahuku-Gama of Papua New Guinea (PNG), children learn through the experience of ritual how to 'make their skin good'. This occurs partly in the context of their own initiation rites (which, for boys especially, build to a highly emotional climax in which they are the centre of attention for the whole day). But they also learn through participation in adult rites such as pig feasts, which feature elaborate self-decoration, boasting and oratory. In daily life, too, they are constantly being encouraged to show off, absorbing messages about self-worth and self-expression, as well as about desired physical contact with others who constantly hug and kiss them. The culture thus fosters a certain style of personal expression, one that allows considerable leeway for individual foibles and eccentric behaviour. By contrast, Mageo (2011) provides a nuanced analysis of Samoan children's experiences of empathy (or the lack of it) at the interpersonal level, as those become interwoven with their experiences of ceremonial obligations and the generation of a cultural ideal of collective empathy through ritual. Mageo translates as 'empathy' the Samoan term *alofa*, standing for 'love', 'affection', but also 'compassion', 'pity' and 'kindness'. Having been showered with *alofa* by adults as an infant, the small child experiences an abrupt separation by the age of two as it is taught respect for elders and may be rebuked for showing off or even seeking physical or eye contact with its betters (Mageo 2011: 75). Children then learn to show *alofa* by performing service to others, especially within the extended family. Finally, young people experience the extension of *alofa* to the community level, as they take part in the hosting of travelling parties from other villages (*malaga*), to whom it is compulsory to offer hospitality. The ceremonial exchanges that take place on these occasions, in Mageo's words, 'flooded participants with what Victor Turner calls communitas—a word I take to mean empathy between groups' (2011: 79). These events, more than anything else, represent a social ideal of shared feelings in action, even if people may sometimes weary of the effort involved or revert to vicious rivalries once the party is over. Another Samoan term relating to empathy (and one of comparative interest in this chapter) is *fa'alavelave*—the moral imperative to help the extended family, especially in the context of contributing to ceremonial obligations, notably funerals (Mageo 2011: 78). In short, Samoan moral ideals of empathy, Mageo suggests, are much more collectively based than, say, American ones, which tend to be imagined primarily in the context of dyadic relationships.

A collective ethos is especially likely, perhaps, to find expression in funerary ritual. Durkheim, in his *Elementary Forms of the Religious Life* (1982: 397), wrote of mourning—which he carefully distinguished from individual feelings of 'sadness'—as a collective emotion expressed through organised ritual work. Barbalet (1994: 114), in a more recent discussion, puts it thus: 'Indeed, mourning may be thought of as an organisational emotion that could only be experienced in human society through the application of social means.' Jakoby (2012) contrasts the medical model of grief as an illness from which the individual should recover with its actual occurrence (even in supposedly individualist Euro-American societies) within the framework of family and community relations, where it is also being shaped by cultural and gendered expectations. She draws on Hochschild's conceptualisation of 'emotion work' as 'a gesture of social exchange that is not to be misunderstood as a facet of personality' (Jakoby 2012: 693). In Fiji, as in Samoa, funerals are vital occasions for communal activity. Toren (2006), who elicited Fijian children's accounts of funerals they had attended, considers the effects for them of being exposed to collective norms regarding grieving by adults (which is very public and dramatic) and, further, the more implicit messages absorbed from these performances regarding kinship solidarity. Regarding the formative power of this sort of situated learning, she observes:

our engagement in the peopled world is always an emotional one, and all our long-held ideas and practices are imbued with a feeling of rightness that goes well beyond any mere rationalization. (Toren 2006: 187)

Weeping and the expression of grief on the occasion of a death are such powerful and binding cultural expectations that they were the most salient feature in the accounts children (aged seven to 13) wrote for her about funerals (Toren 2006: 205–8).

In what follows, that same 'feeling of rightness' can be discerned in Toraja children's assertions about the need to support kin, to feel what others are feeling and to continue traditional practices. These feelings appear to grow directly out of their repeated attendance at rituals, where they witness adult cooperation and, sooner or later, have the opportunity to join in themselves. Some children in my study well expressed the resulting unselfconscious absorption of knowledge about ritual that occurs simply by being present:

I learn from other people by watching those around me when they are carrying out the rite. (Girl, aged 16)

I've seen the way the ceremony is done so I don't need to go to a lot of bother learning what to do, because when the time comes, God willing, I will have further opportunities to take part and I'll be able to do it easily. (Boy, aged 14)

This mode of learning through participation is, after all, how most cultural knowledge has been passed on, in most times and places. While I had imagined that the children in my study would tell me what they had learned about the practicalities of ritual organisation, I discovered instead that many of them had written about the moral necessity of sharing emotions, whether happiness or sorrow. A more general discussion of my findings is presented elsewhere (Waterson 2015), but in what follows I will focus specifically on themes relating to the emotions, and particularly that of the sharing of feelings as a sort of collective duty. The ideas that were expressed serve to illuminate the process by which Toraja children, through their own experiences in a ritual setting, learn about the wider ethos of their own society and begin to form their own opinions about the responsibilities the system entails, and about their own cultural identity. At the same time, a substantial proportion of children wrote about the anxieties created by the obligations of ceremonial exchange, which create a heavy burden of debt, especially among the poor. Their own hopes of pursuing their education are constantly at risk as parental funds are inescapably siphoned towards ceremonial expenditure, and thus they are already in a position to have strong opinions on this matter.

The context of the study

The Sa'dan Toraja people are a population of around 450,000 living in the highlands of South Sulawesi. The sense of a unitary ethnic identity as 'Toraja' grew partly out of the experience of Dutch colonisation; this part of the highlands became known only in the 1930s as the Kabupaten or regency of Tana Toraja ('Land of the Toraja'). Devolutionary policy in Indonesia since the fall of President Suharto in 1998 has led here, as in many other parts of Indonesia, to a subdivision of previous administrative entities. In 2008, the regency was split into two parts, such that the name Tana Toraja now refers to the southern part, with its main town of Ma'kale, while the northern part, centred on the town of Rantepao, is now known as Toraja Utara (North Toraja). Most Toraja will still insist, however, that in spite of local variations they share the same culture.

The Toraja have long been known for their rich and dramatic ritual life. Mortuary rites, in particular, are famed for their expense and complexity, being celebrated on a spectacular scale, especially by wealthy aristocrats, whose ceremonies may be accompanied by sacrifices of hundreds of buffaloes and pigs. Today, the great majority of Toraja are Christian, leaving perhaps only 5 per cent of the population (mostly older people in remote areas) still adhering to the indigenous religion known as *Aluk To Dolo* or 'Way of the Ancestors'. While some types of ritual have, as a consequence, become very rare, certain parts of the formerly complex cycle of rites continue to be vigorously celebrated, notably funerals and the rites for inauguration of newly restored or rebuilt origin houses (*tongkonan*).

In the indigenous cosmology of the Toraja, rituals are divided into two main categories, depending on whether they have to do with the living or the dead. Communal rites designed to enhance fertility and wellbeing, to ward off sickness or to celebrate the renewal of origin houses, as well as those that formerly accompanied the rice-growing cycle, are referred to as *Aluk Rambu Tuka'* or 'Rites of the Smoke of the Rising [Sun]' and are associated with the east and the deities (*deata*). Mortuary rites, by contrast, are called *Aluk Rambu Solo'* or 'Smoke of the Setting [Sun]', and are associated with the west and the ancestors. Certain rites fall in between these two categories, enabling a transition from west to east that was intended to end the work of mourning, and, in some areas, was considered to effect a deification of aristocratic ancestors. The Dutch Reformed Church mission, which commenced work in Toraja in 1913, was particularly opposed to the Rites of the East, especially those that involved trancing. At present, with the exception of house inauguration rites (*mangrara banua*), most of these rites have almost disappeared, while weddings—formerly very modest occasions—have become greatly elaborated as a result of Christian influence. The Toraja proved very much more resistant to the mission's attempts to curtail and modify the perceived 'extravagance' of mortuary rites. Funeral rituals today have been Christianised and continue to be performed on an ever more lavish scale. They are undeniably the most conspicuous and salient social events in Toraja life.

In fact, new sources of wealth have been funnelled into the ceremonial economy, causing an escalation of funeral expenditure and a dramatic inflation of livestock prices, which continued unabated even during the Asian monetary crisis of 1997. In my fieldwork with the Toraja, which began in 1978, indigenous religion and ritual life were, not surprisingly, a major focus of interest, and it was impossible not to be aware of the importance of mortuary ritual in social life. Most ethnographers of the region, in fact, have written about funerals, sometimes at great length, and I am no exception.[5] While my colleagues have tended to focus on the details of the rites themselves or on their ability to attract foreign tourists, I was curious about the organisational complexity of such demanding rites (Waterson 1993). How were decisions made about the numbers of buffaloes to be sacrificed? How exactly did the ceremonial prestation of animals for sacrifice (generally from affines to the children of the deceased person—gifts that must be repaid at a later date) contribute to the maintenance and enhancement of rank and prestige? Historically, it was clear that, in spite of Dutch missionary and administrative disapproval in the early twentieth century, the ceremonial prestation and sacrifice of buffaloes and pigs were so embedded a part of kinship, social and political relations that nothing could persuade people to give them

---

5   See Adams (1997); Donzelli (2003); Koubi (1982); Nooy-Palm (1986); Rappoport (1999, 2009); Volkman (1979, 1985, 1987); Waterson (1984, 1993, 2009); and Yamashita (1997). Wellenkamp (1984, 1988, 1991) has focused on emotional aspects of death and grieving, while de Jong (2008, 2013) has undertaken the most concentrated study to date of the economics of funerals.

up. As I continued making regular return trips to Toraja, I tracked the continuing escalation of livestock prices and found myself still pondering the reasons for this extraordinary expenditure, which inevitably places great stress on individual families and often drives people into debt. What has happened in Toraja shows many striking points of comparison with studies of ceremonial economies in PNG societies. Not only do we see the same efflorescence of ceremonial expenditure as money enters the system, but we can also observe that such systems are able to survive wrenching changes in cosmology brought about by conversion to Christianity—something that has radically transformed many PNG societies since the 1960s (Akin and Robbins 1999; Gregory 1980; Stewart and Strathern 2009).

In my conversations with adults about the meanings that ritual performance has for them, they have offered many kinds of insight into the emotional commitments involved and how ritual is bound up with their perceptions of a distinctively Toraja sociality.[6] What I had never done was to ask children how they learned about the ritual duties they would soon have to assume as adults, and what they thought of this complex and competitive system. Realising that this was a constituency I had wrongly neglected, in 2007, with the help of friends who are retired teachers, I approached the heads of eight middle and high schools in different parts of Toraja and asked permission to carry out a study with some of their pupils.[7] A total of 451 children agreed to share with me, through writing and drawing, their ideas and experiences of ritual life.

The research followed well-established participatory methods for ethical research with children (Alderson and Morrow 2004; Beazley et al. 2009; Boyden and Ennew 1997; Christensen and James 2008; Ennew 2009). Although children's capacities as informants have often been overlooked or underestimated, they can make excellent research participants and are very capable of expressing useful opinions on matters that concern them. Christina Toren (1993) has argued with particular eloquence that a failure to take children seriously, not just as research subjects but also as human subjects, impairs not only our broader conceptualisations of agency, but also our deeper theoretical understandings of what it means to be human.

---

6   For a fuller discussion of the Toraja ceremonial economy and its emotional entailments, see Waterson (2009: 395–430).

7   I would like to express my gratitude to Pak Banti (Nene'na Regina) in Rantepao, and to Pak Frans Dengen in Ma'kale, for their help in facilitating the study.

Children are not just passive recipients in the socialisation process, but are themselves actively producing culture in their social interactions with others. Besides Toren's work in Fiji, Laurence Goldman's (1998) innovative study of children's play among the Huli and Lyn Parker's research on children and schooling in Bali (1997, 2002) provide further excellent examples of how children's own developing cultural perspectives can yield vital insights into cultural processes in general.

Children's perceptions of ritual

With the permission of principals and teachers, I visited classrooms and elicited children's participation in answering my questions. The schools visited were a middle school (Sekolah Menengah Pertama, SMP) and a high school (Sekolah Mengah Atas, SMA) in each of four areas: two rural locations, Sa'dan in the north and Mengkendek in the south, whose pupils tend to be drawn from the immediate vicinity; and the two towns that form the administrative centres of the regencies, Rantepao (North Toraja) and Ma'kale (Tana Toraja). The town schools have generally higher standards than those of outlying areas and accept pupils from many different districts. There was a preponderance of girls in the sample (278 of 451, representing 61 per cent of middle schoolers and 62 per cent of high schoolers). This is due to the fact that more boys than girls opt to attend the parallel technical schools at each level, rather than the mainstream schools. The ages of the middle schoolers ranged from 10 to 16, the majority being 14, while the high schoolers' ages ranged from 15 to 19, the majority being 17 years old.

All the responses were written in Indonesian, the language the children are accustomed to using in school, although Toraja is still spoken at home by most families. Regrettably, this means that the study failed to shed light on specifically Toraja vocabulary for the ideas the children expressed, although there is no doubt that some of these ideas are distinctively Toraja in character.[8] I did not ask children to state their religious affiliations, but, given the dramatic decline of Aluk To Dolo in the areas studied, and the

8   A key Toraja term for mutual caring is *sikaboro'*, which is often used by adults in the western part of Toraja where I lived during my fieldwork to explain why, in that area, they prefer to refrain from driving each other to ruin through competitive excess in funeral sacrificing. Another term for love, with an emphasis on its compassionate aspect, is *mamase*, while *mali'* ('to want, desire'), when used in the phrase *mamali' lako*, carries the sense of longing or 'yearning towards' another person, sometimes specifically by an inferior to a superior (Donzelli 2003).

fact that schools have long been a major locus of Christianisation, it can be safely assumed that all the children in my study are at least nominally Christian. Another difficulty in interpreting the results is to know precisely how far the responses are influenced by the children's exposure to Christianity, although this influence is obviously present in some of their responses and reflects the current situation in which, for a majority of the population, Toraja identity is already bound up with being 'modern' and Christian, while the indigenous religion is perceived as old-fashioned, in spite of people's continuing investment in the performance of Christianised rituals. It is noteworthy that only five children voiced religious objections to rituals per se (see Appendix Figure A4.4).[9]

Age distribution of children

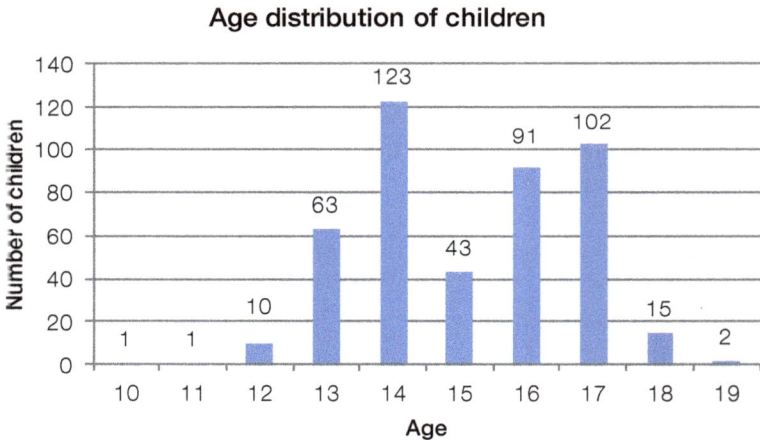

Figure 4.1 Age distribution of participants
Note: n = 451.
Source: Author's data.

A simple and graphic consent form was given to each child and it was made clear that participation was voluntary. Drawing paper, crayons and felt pens were provided for those who wished to draw pictures related to their experiences at rituals. Before beginning, I explained my own long-term research interest in Toraja ritual life and my awareness that adults

---

9   It is conceivable that some of these children were Pentecostalists, since this sect forbids participation in funeral sacrifices, but, if so, none of them mentioned the fact. Only one child in my study mentioned the existence of this Pentecostal prohibition in general terms. Pentecostal churches (of which up to 20 are now represented in the highlands) have won the most converts in southern districts, where the status system is most rigid, since they offer a way out of the ceremonial system to those who can least afford its demands (de Jong 2013: 205–9).

held a range of opinions about the ceremonial system. I emphasised that there were no 'correct' answers, but that I valued their opinions and they were free to write whatever they wanted. The questions I asked them to write about were the following:

1. What ceremonies have you attended?
2. Whom did you go with?
3. Describe a ceremony you have attended and what was done there.
4. What is the purpose of that ceremony?
5. What did you learn from attending the ceremony?
6. What will you do when you are grown up if someone in your family is having a ceremony?
7. Is there anything else you would like to tell me about ceremonies in Tana Toraja?

The children's responses to these questions were coded for emergent themes, which were then consolidated into a smaller number of categories and analysed using SPSS Statistics. Tabulated results are shown in Appendix 4.1. In what follows, I discuss certain themes that revealed emotional content and examine more closely the content of selected individual responses. I was interested to see how far the content or elaboration of answers might differ between the two age groups. It transpired that only one 10-year-old, one 11-year-old and ten 12-year-olds participated in the study, so I am unable to say anything conclusive about how the ideas of pre-teenagers might differ from those of teenagers in the study. But, in general, while some of the middle-schoolers (including these youngest participants) gave very brief and simple answers to my questions, the responses of others were just as articulate as those of the older teenagers, and the themes they expressed turned out to be very similar across both groups.

Reviewing the data, the first thing that leaps to attention is the extraordinary salience of funerals compared with any other ritual event. In stating what rituals they had attended, most children named rites of both east and west; but, when asked in Question 3 to choose one of them to write about, an overwhelming majority elected to write about funerals. Slightly more girls than boys selected a Rite of the East (house ceremonies, weddings and, once or twice, a birthday party—a very recent innovation), but, in all, 401 of 451 children, or 89 per cent, elected to write about funerals and only 33, or 7 per cent, about other rituals. A further 12 of

451, or 3 per cent, wrote of their attendance at rituals of both the east and the west, while five (1 per cent) gave no answer. We can assume that not only had all the participants attended funerals multiple times, but also the rite was taken by many respondents to be the most distinctive feature of their culture—one they wrote about with considerable pride. House ceremonies (*mangrara banua*) are celebrated only by families of noble rank and they take place at much longer intervals; but funerals happen all too frequently, and it is a compelling social duty to attend them. What the children's responses chance to reveal, then, about the emotional dimensions of ritual has to do chiefly with their understandings of mortuary ritual.

The purposes of funerals: Shared feelings and the theme of consolation

In response to Question 4, regarding the purpose of the ceremony they had chosen to write about, most children offered multiple answers. Various ideas were put forward to explain the purpose of funerals. Most prominent was the idea of duty to one's kin and, more specifically, to show respect to the deceased person themselves (mentioned by 41.9 per cent of children), followed by the need to uphold tradition, culture or *adat* ('custom') (30.7 per cent). Rituals provided occasions for kin to gather together, according to 24.1 per cent. Another frequently mentioned the idea was that sacrifices help the deceased to reach the afterlife (28.9 per cent). This is a noteworthy finding, in the face of the apparently drastic changes of cosmology that have been entailed in the conversion to Christianity. According to the Aluk To Dolo, when a person dies, an aspect of their soul, called *bombo*, travels to Puya, an afterlife far away in the south-west, where life continues to be lived in much the same way as on Earth, but without fire. Animals also have *bombo*, and those of the buffaloes and pigs slaughtered at the funeral are supposed to follow the dead person to Puya to provide for their needs in the afterlife. Thus, those who are wealthy on Earth and have many descendants to sacrifice for them will continue to enjoy a comfortable life in the hereafter. The Dutch Reformed Church preached a quite different vision of life after death, yet the socially binding requirement to sacrifice has survived and, to some extent, so has the cosmological rationale for it. Somehow, sacrifice is still seen as assisting the soul's transition. The blending of cosmologies is reflected in what children wrote, for some of them used the traditional

Toraja name for the afterlife, Puya, while others used the Indonesian term *surga* to refer to the Christian 'heaven', or said the deceased would be 'received at the right hand of God', would 'rejoin their Creator' or would be helped by the sacrifices to 'get to the Almighty [*Yang Maha Kuasa*] quickly and safely'. Others used the more neutral term *alam baka* to refer to 'the afterlife' or even described the soul's destination as 'nirvana'. Taken together, their answers indicate considerable ingenuity in integrating the various opinions they may have heard from adults about the reasons for mortuary sacrifice. Indeed, 12.6 per cent named sacrifice of livestock as being in itself the chief purpose of the funeral rites, while an almost equal proportion (11 per cent) also mentioned the status dimension of sacrifice (which by adults is seen as the culmination of the deceased's career) with answers such as the following:

> Sacrificing buffaloes is part of Toraja culture because it represents the final duty [*bakhti terakhir*] towards our parents, and if someone gives us a buffalo or pig that becomes a debt of honour [*utang budi*] that we owe to that person. (Girl, aged 14)

> The buffaloes that are sacrificed indicate the rank of the person who has died. For instance, if the buffaloes killed are many, and among them is a spotted buffalo [*tedong bonga*], that means that the deceased is a prominent [*terpandang*] person in their area. And the converse also applies. (Girl, aged 14)

A distinctive set of answers expressed the cultural requirement to share the grief of those who have been bereaved or described the funeral rites as providing consolation or entertainment for those involved. The need to 'share sorrow' was mentioned by 14 per cent of children. Some used conventional Indonesian turns of phrase for the expression of condolences, while others chose imagery that is more characteristically Toraja:

> The point of the ceremony is to share each other's sorrow [*saling membagi kedukaan*]. (Girl, aged 14)

> The purpose of the ceremony is so that people can join in expressing their condolences [*turut mengungkapkan bela sungkawa mereka*]. (Girl, aged 14)

> It's to strengthen kin ties, and also we can meet our relatives and share in the grief they are feeling [*saling merasakan duka*]. (Girl, aged 14)

> The point of the ceremony is to share in the sorrow over the death of a family member and besides that, the family also wants to share whatever they have even though they are in a state of mourning. (Girl, aged 16)

The purpose of the ceremony is to uphold our customs and traditions so the young people nowadays won't forget them, and maybe also to cast away all sadness by sacrificing buffaloes [*menghempaskan semua kesedihan dengan cara memotong kerbau*]. (Girl, aged 14)

The purpose of the ceremony is so that the person who has died will see how sad all their family and friends are when they recall the person's life story. (Girl, aged 14)

In the last three examples, we see that the sharing of feelings is conjoined with the sharing of material goods in staging the rituals and engaging in the expected ceremonial exchanges. The idea that sacrificing enables the casting away of sadness' echoes adult ideology. It is an explanation often given by adults, and a distinctively Toraja cultural trope, that sacrifice serves to 'take the place of our sorrow' (*ussondai pa'di'ki*) at a bereavement and relieves feelings of grief (Waterson 1993). The idea that the deceased person is still present, able to watch the actions of their kin and witness their grief is also in accord with traditional conceptions, while the mention of recalling the person's life story relates to the performance of the funeral chant, *ma'badong*. For the highest-ranking funerals, an effigy (*tau-tau*) of the deceased is made.[10] In the old days, the making of this effigy was accompanied by offerings and it was considered that the *bombo* inhabited the effigy until the completion of the rites. Only after the burial would the *bombo* set out on its journey to Puya; until then, it would be enjoying the festivities prepared for it. During the rituals, the *tau-tau* would be placed in the centre of the slowly rotating circle of dancers who, throughout the night, would perform the *ma'badong*. In part of the litany, the deceased's life story is related, improvised by the song leader, who draws on a stock of poetic imagery, expressed in paired lines of verse. Several other responses also mention the *ma'badong*, which remains an indispensible part of the proceedings. Its function is clearly stated here as entertainment, whether for the deceased or for the grieving relatives. Dana Rappoport (1999, 2009) has written searchingly of the significance of group vocal performances whose sensory effects serve to create the special atmosphere of rituals, whether of the west (*ma'badong*) or of the east (where a parallel kind of

---

10 The Toraja Church (Gereja Toraja) tried hard to ban the *tau-tau* as idolatrous, and, in the early 1980s, the controversy over this issue was extremely divisive. The bid failed, however, and, nowadays, the practice continues in a desacralised form. After some Toraja carvers went to Bali and studied with Balinese woodcarvers, there was a change in the style of *tau-tau*. Once highly stylised, the statues are now made as lifelike as possible. Instead of becoming a potent image of the dead as ancestor, it is rationalised that the statue is nothing more than a commemorative portrait, the equivalent of a photograph.

performance, with different words, is called *ma'simbong*). At larger events, it is common for several groups to perform, sometimes simultaneously but in competition rather than in concert with each other. The 'thick' melismatic aural texture produced by the singing creates its own peculiar, immersive atmosphere, both mournful and pleasing—an effect that is touched on in the last comment in the quotes below:

> Everything that is done in the funeral rite, the *ma'badong* dance among other things, has a purpose, which is to please and entertain the soul of the deceased. (Boy, aged 17)

> *Ma'badong* is like a lullaby to soothe the deceased so they will sleep peacefully. (Girl, aged 15)

> *Ma'badong* is a sad song to cheer the hearts of those who are in mourning. (Boy, aged 16)

> I can feel the sadness and loss of the person who has died through the waves of sound created by the *ma'badong* singers [*lewat alunan orang yang ma'badong*]. (Girl, aged 14)

Here we touch on a distinctively Toraja interpretation, emergent also from other responses, which holds that the point of the funeral proceedings is to provide entertainment or consolation (*penghiburan*). This applies not only to the *ma'badong*, but also to the more spectacular aspects of high-ranking funerals, such as making the buffaloes fight each other before they are sacrificed (*ma'pasilaga tedong*). Some 13.1 per cent of children wrote that the point of funerals (and, hence, the duty of those taking part in them) is to console or distract (*menghibur*) the bereaved family, the guests and/or the soul of the deceased. Although 'console' is in fact the primary meaning of this Indonesian verb, the noun *penghiburan* is more commonly used to mean 'distraction', 'recreation' or 'entertainment'. This borrowing from Indonesian is not a direct translation of any Toraja phrase, since in Toraja the more traditional expression would be *undampi pa'dinna*, 'to heal/provide medicine for their pain'—a reference to the heartache (*pa'di' penaa*) of bereavement. However, the idea that ritual represents a particular combination of 'work' and 'play', and that the playful part is actually intrinsic to the ritual's success, is a theme that is evident not only among the Toraja but also in many other Austronesian cultures. This is something about which I have written elsewhere (Waterson 1995); a comparative example will also be found in Sather's Chapter 3 in this volume, which describes the essential role of play, beauty, entertainment and pleasure in an Iban shamanic curing ritual, the *Sugi Sakit*. As he puts it, this aesthetic emphasis was 'not incidental to the purpose of the [rite], but, rather, contributed directly to the ritual's effectiveness'. He makes some searching comments about the potential importance of this aspect of entertainment even (or perhaps especially) in the context of illness or death, as a means of asserting the extension of the person out into the wider world. In the face of death, with its entailments of grief, loss and the reduction of ties, the mobilising of the community, 'motivated by shared feelings of compassion', works to counter that sense of loss by creating a spectacle in defiance of the social disruption that death entails.

On this note, some children further stated that the whole point of the event was to be festive, expressing the culturally salient idea that there is pleasure in seeing festive crowds gathered together. This is reflected in the positive associations of the Toraja word *marua'*, which corresponds to Indonesian *ramai* ('noisy, cheerful, crowded'). One person also wrote that the funeral rite ensures the family will be prosperous and well (*sejahtera*), reflecting a traditional belief that generous sacrificing brings blessing and long life to the sacrifier (Waterson 2009: 396).

> [The purpose is] to entertain the family of the deceased. (Boy, aged 17)
>
> [The purpose is] to entertain the Toraja people with buffalo fights. (Girl, aged 14)
>
> The point of the ceremony is to make the ceremony more festive [*memeriahkan pesta tersebut*]. (Girl, aged 14)
>
> Our reason for holding the ceremony is to see people being *ramai-ramai*. (Girl, aged 10)
>
> [The purpose is] to cheer us up so we won't be broken-hearted in our sadness. (Girl, aged 15)
>
> [The purpose is] to entertain the family that has been left behind so that they will not be overwhelmed by their grief [*tidak larut dalam kedukaan*; lit., 'will not dissolve in grief']. (Girl, aged 16)

The last two responses point to other culturally specific reasons for such a priority being placed on providing distractions for the grieving family, since excessive mourning is considered potentially dangerous to one's health (Hollan and Wellenkamp 1994: 200; Wellenkamp 1988, 1991: 129).

Learning through ritual participation

When asked what they had learned through participation in rituals (Question 5), the children's most common answers concerned not so much education in practical tasks, but kinship and the moral necessity to work together. Among the responses, 53.3 per cent spoke in general terms of learning about their 'culture' or 'the way things are done', while 38.5 per cent wrote of the importance of working together and 34.2 per cent of the strength and value of kin ties. The requirement to share the feelings of others was specifically expressed by 10.9 per cent, or 48 of the 451 children. Many children gave multiple answers, such that their placing of these features in combination builds up a picture of a moral universe of mutual support and shared feeling, leading naturally to the sharing of work and cooperation, which, in turn, serve to constitute kinship solidarity and, ultimately, the feeling of being Toraja:

> I've learned to urge myself to feel what the bereaved family is feeling [*mengajak diri untuk merasakan apa yg dirasakan oleh keluarga yang berduka*]. (Girl, aged 17)

> I've learned to share the grief of the bereaved [*turut berdukacita*]. (Girl, aged 14)

> I've learned to join in feeling the sorrow [*turut merasakan kesedihan*]. (Boy, aged 16)

> I've learned how strong and close the kin ties in our family are and also how to share sorrow [*saling membagi duka*]. (Girl, aged 14)

> What I've learned from going to funerals is to share in feeling the sorrow of the family who have been left behind [by the departed]. (Girl, aged 17)

> I've learned to join in feeling what others are feeling, so that we can help each other. (Girl, aged 17)

> There is a really great feeling of love for the family of the person who has died. This is shown in the relatives' willingness to lay out so much money to sacrifice pigs and buffaloes. (Boy, aged 14)

> One thing we can learn from ceremonies is the strength of family feeling between the bereaved family and the guests, because the guests usually bring buffaloes, pigs or cakes to express their shared sorrow with the bereaved. (Girl, aged 16)

> We must care for each other, whether at times of happiness or sadness. At these times, we can share the feelings that they are feeling, whether happiness or consoling those who are grieving [*menghibur yang berduka*]. (Girl, aged 16)

The theme of helping each other was repeatedly expressed. While some focused on empathy with the bereaved, others described learning to join in with specific tasks. This is described by some as helping to lighten the burden of sorrow and, by others, in terms of a broader social principle of cooperation:

> We learn from our parents how to serve the guests with food and drink. (Girl, aged 10)

> I learned how they slaughter buffaloes and roast pigs. (Boy, aged 12)

> I helped people wash dishes and they were very pleased because someone helped them. (Girl, aged 16)

> When there is a ceremony everyone works together without being forced, and all have different jobs to do … e.g. I have joined in helping to wash dishes and sweep the guest shelters, even when I was little. (Boy, aged 16)

> People cooperate to help the family in mourning, for instance by helping with the cooking or building guest shelters. (Boy, aged 18)

> I've learned that work gets done quickly when we work together. (Boy, aged 17)

> From funerals I've learned that we can help and work together to lighten the burden and share the grief. (Boy, aged 16)

> I've learned the feeling of togetherness and cooperation while doing heavy work, for instance in *ma'palao* [the procession that carries the corpse in its bier on its final journey to the tomb] we all pick up the body together to carry it out, so as to please the soul of the deceased. (Boy, aged 17)

This theme of cooperation as a cultural value or moral requirement was often expanded into more generalised statements, sometimes including mention of kinship bonds, but often expressed simply as a fundamental characteristic of Toraja society:

> If there is work to be done, it must be done cooperatively. (Boy, aged 13)

> By taking part I've learned that we must help each other in every task. (Girl, aged 14)

What I've learned is to urge myself to help others and in helping each other we come to know that this is our *adat* in Toraja. (Girl, aged 17)

I have learned about feelings of togetherness in the community and being friendly [*beramah-tamah*]. (Girl, aged 16)

We can develop the feelings of cooperation within the community and become aware that humans can't live without the help of others. (Girl, aged 15).

By taking part we can see how great is the feeling of mutual assistance, tolerance and sympathy [*gotong royong, toleransi dan simpati*] among the Toraja people. Besides that, the ceremony shows the togetherness and close kin feelings among members of the *tongkonan*. (Girl, aged 16)

I've learned that there is a very good feeling of cooperation in carrying out a ceremony because all the family whether close or distant relatives will come and help, in short the family feeling that Toraja people have is very strong, to pray that the soul will be saved. (Girl, aged 16)

And in the matter of participation, it's a very beautiful thing how if there is any organisation or activity going on, people will come and help even if they are not family, but they know about kinship in our beautiful and prosperous Tana Toraja. (Girl, aged 17)

In the following examples, the theme of the necessity of cooperation is touched on in relation to a more practical aspect—namely, the competitive nature of the ritual system within which a family's own performance will be judged. The challenge of organising such a complex and expensive event, and the difficulties it may pose to kin in marshalling the necessary resources, is particularly clear in the third statement:

The children of the deceased must try their utmost to sacrifice pigs and buffaloes, because the rank of the family can be seen from how many pigs or buffaloes are sacrificed. (Boy, aged 17)

I can see which families have profited and done well on the *rantau*, so much so that it becomes a motivation to me as well. (Girl, aged 17)

It's clear that funerals in Tana Toraja are considered so sacred ... and we must really prepare ourselves as well as we possibly can if we are to hold such a ceremony, and the family must stand shoulder-to-shoulder to support each other ... because this ceremony will really drain our strength and ingenuity [*sangat menguras tenaga dan pikiran kita*]. (Girl, aged 13)[11]

---

11 *Menguras* means, literally, 'to flush out a drain'.

Some children wrote of what they had learned about etiquette and politeness in social interaction—often expressed as paying attention to or showing respect for each other's feelings. They noted further that ceremonial occasions provided important opportunities to learn to know a wider circle of kin, including migrants who might be returning home from distant places:

> I learned how to receive the guests and how to behave when I meet other people. (Girl, aged 15)

> I have learned how to cooperate with others, to be polite and help those who are working. (Girl, aged 13)

> I have learned how we should respect those who are older than we are. (Girl, aged 14)

> I've been taught how to serve the guests nicely, and I've also learned the customs of my area such as that one must not turn one's back on people while eating. (Girl, aged 13)

> I've learned that there is an attitude of mutual respect between the guests and the hosts of the rite. (Girl, aged 16)

> We must take care of each other [*peduli kepada sesama*], and most especially of our kin. (Boy, aged 17)

> I've learned that there is an attitude of looking out for each other [*adanya sikap saling mengingatkan*]. (Boy, aged 16)

> What I have learned is that we must know all our kin so that the bonds of kinship will always remain strong and we shall maintain our closeness and unity. (Girl, aged 13)

> We can learn about other families [or family members] because during the rite the family's genealogy is often explained. (Girl, aged 17)

> I have got to know my distant relatives, and even the closer ones that I hadn't yet met. (Girl, aged 13)

> I have got to know family members coming from various cities. (Girl, aged 14)

> I have learned to know my kin, especially those we see rarely, because those who are away on the *rantau* [i.e. migrants living outside the homeland] will return, and we will meet them. (Girl, aged 17)

A few children also mentioned that taking part in these public occasions had in itself been an experience or had made them feel more socially confident. When asked with whom they had attended rituals, the majority named their immediate family (40 per cent), extended family (16 per cent) (often including long lists of categories of relatives in their answer), 'family and friends' (31 per cent) and 'family, friends and neighbours' (10 per cent). But some (2.7 per cent, mostly boys) mentioned going alone. This is not an innovation, since these are the social events par excellence; they were even more important traditionally in providing one of the few socially approved opportunities for young people to see and meet each other. The last comment below indicates that they may still be serving that function, even today when young people have many more opportunities to meet, at school and elsewhere:

[I have learned to] be more self-confident [*percaya diri*]. (Girl, aged 13)

I have learned about these ceremonies and that has also been an experience in my life. (Girl, aged 14)

We can take part in different places without having to have anyone accompany us. (Girl, aged 13)

Not surprisingly, some of the children's responses reflected newer ideas about attitudes to death and the purposes of the funeral ritual, some of them doubtless derived from listening to Christian sermons. Calvinist doctrine can hardly be said to have lightened the load when it comes to dealing with grief; perhaps it has even accentuated it by introducing worries over sin and salvation:

Even though the person we love is gone, we must still be steadfast [*tabah*], and continue to praise and give thanks to God. (Girl, aged 14)

I've learned to work together to pray for the relative who has died, so that they will be received at God's side. (Boy, aged 16)

I have learned that in this world it is certain that all people must die. Therefore we must use our time as well as we can, for instance by doing good to everyone, so that when we die there will surely be many people who will join in mourning us, and our good deeds will live on and be remembered for ever, and in the afterlife we shall get our reward. (Boy, aged 14)

We must be steadfast in facing everything and learn not to be too carefree [*tidak terlalu bersenang-senang*] because a moment will come when we will experience a sorrow we were not expecting. (Girl, aged 13)

In Question 6, children were asked what they expect to do as adults if someone in their family is holding a ceremony. I was seeking to learn more about their views of the ritual responsibilities that lie ahead of them, and how far they envisaged themselves becoming involved in the ceremonial system. I also expected that the question might shed light on whether any of them might, on the contrary, wish to limit their engagement with it. Their answers once again brought to the fore the importance of shared feelings, specifically within the family. The identification with the family and its reputation in some responses extended into the claim that this is a distinctively Toraja characteristic:

> I will try to join in attending every funeral as a sign that I share the sorrow [*turut berbela sungkawa*]. (Girl, aged 15)

> I will attend the ceremony from the first day to the last. (Boy, aged 14)

> I will share in happiness or in sorrow (join in feeling whatever the family is experiencing). (Girl, aged 19)

> I will join in sharing sorrow, I will join in sharing joy, and I will join in taking a role in the ceremony. (Girl, aged 14)

> I will join in with whatever the family is doing, feel whatever they are feeling, and help them in any way I can. (Girl, aged 18)

> We must help the family in all sorts of ways because who else will help us if not our close family? In my view, people can't live without the help of others, and if we ever suffer a misfortune, they are the ones who'll help us. Because in my opinion Toraja *adat* is strongly bound up with the ties formed by working together and helping each other. (Girl, aged 17)

> I will join in helping so that all the work of the ceremony will be done well and reflect our family feeling [*rasa kekeluargaan*]. (Girl, aged 17)

> I will participate because I am part of the family, so I must show an attitude of family feeling [*sikap kekeluargaan*] because family feeling is a special characteristic of Toraja people. (Girl, aged 17)

Many answers expressed formulaically the social compulsion to contribute to ceremonies, with phrases about helping 'materially and physically', 'materially and spiritually', 'with labour and goods' or 'with labour, time, thoughts and materials'. Thinking was mentioned often as a necessary contribution to planning, so that the complicated rite would go smoothly and bring credit to the family. These responses—categorised for purposes of analysis under the heading 'Help in any way I can'—accounted for 46.9 per cent of all responses. Some examples follow:

> If I am given a job to do, I will strive to ensure that whatever task has been entrusted to me is carried out properly. (Girl, aged 17)

> When I am grown up I will automatically do what's expected, for instance carrying pigs, serving cigarettes to the guests, killing pigs and joining in the *ma'badong*. (Boy, aged 17)

> I will do anything I can to help the family and ensure that the rite goes smoothly. (Girl, aged 17)

> I will help with: labour, time, thoughts and materials. (Girl, aged 14)

> I will contribute my time and labour; materials to prepare for the rite such as money, livestock such as pigs, and I shall help the women cook in the kitchen. (Girl, aged 14).

> I will help by contributing my thoughts [*sumbangan pikiran*] so far as I am able so that the ceremony will be well planned and carried out. (Girl, aged 15)

> I have to help others with whatever I have, whether we have goods or things or anything at all that we have, we have to give it to our kin, e.g. at funerals we can give either a buffalo or a pig. (Girl, aged 17) [It is noteworthy that this girl, in her response to Question 7, was also critical of excessive funeral expenditure.]

Besides helping in this generalised way, 37.7 per cent of children stated more specifically that they would try to contribute a pig or buffalo for sacrifice if they could afford it. The following examples strongly express the felt necessity to contribute to the ceremonial system, and some children even envisage migrating (*merantau*) to earn money for this purpose, while others express reservations about the risk of exceeding one's means:

> I will contribute pigs and buffaloes with a pure heart and without being forced to [*tanpa paksaan*]. If I have no livestock or money to contribute I will still attend; just attending is already sufficient to strengthen the bonds of kinship. (Boy, aged 15) [This answer expresses the cultural maxim that attendance in itself is already a virtue, and that it is better to attend, even with nothing to bring, than to stay away for fear of coming empty-handed.]

I will join in sacrificing buffaloes and pigs because this is my responsibility as a Toraja person and I must do it because this is the expressed wish of my deceased family members. (Boy, aged 16)

I will participate for instance by sacrificing buffaloes or pigs even though it's very expensive, but the thing is, family members must help each other. (Girl, aged 17)

I will take part without having to be forced, as far as my means allow. I will give whatever I can afford without interfering with my primary needs. (Boy, aged 17)

The help I shall give will not be in the shape of pigs or buffaloes, but money, because it will be more useful. (Boy, aged 16)

To follow the *adat* and sacrifice buffalo you need a lot of money. First of all I will look for work, then when I have earned lots of money I will come back to Toraja. (Girl, aged 15)

I will attend because whatever I may think, I am still a Toraja, so I must take part even if I think it's all a lot of fuss about nothing [*hura-hura belaka*: 'just noise']. From another point of view, this is our tradition passed down by our ancestors. So we must carry it on [lit.: 'these are their shoes, which we must put on and walk in them'], so long as we are able and can afford to. (Girl, aged 17)

The ritual dilemma: Debt, anxiety and the desire to lessen the ceremonial burden

The darker emotional side of Toraja mortuary ritual is the danger of being financially overstretched and driven into debt, and the resulting anxiety attendant upon trying to meet one's obligations. Children inherit land rights and property from their parents, but they also inherit any unpaid ceremonial debts, which thus pass down the generations. Added to this is the difficulty of refusing a gift of sacrificial livestock from an affine without causing serious offence and rupturing the relationship, so that every funeral creates a new round of debts to be met in future. Managing the ceremonial demands upon a family's resources certainly gives adults cause to worry; one woman friend told me that, in an entire lifetime spent raising pigs for the household, she had never been able to sell a single one, since as soon as she had one large enough to sell, it would inevitably be needed to repay some ceremonial debt or other. Children likewise showed that they are already aware of these problems, and some clearly hope to find ways to limit their expenditure:

Ceremonies in Toraja are so impressive, but there are some people who think otherwise, for instance, they say Toraja people are never sincere about giving; if they take a buffalo to a ceremony they even expect it to be repaid and then you'll be looking for money the whole year just to use it up in one moment at a ceremony. But it depends how you look at it. As for me, since I'm Toraja, I always support the holding of ceremonies in whatever form. (Girl, aged 14)

In my view Toraja ceremonies are pretty extravagant because we have to bring pigs or buffaloes. And if someone dies and a member of our family has ever been given a buffalo then we have to pay it back at the funeral by bringing them a buffalo too. And if we haven't enough money to buy one, we shall certainly go into debt to someone else in the process. (Girl, aged 14)

Everyone who is of Toraja descent is sure to want to carry out Toraja traditions/*adat* fully if they can afford it, and it's the same with me. I should like to take part in the *adat* for instance by bringing buffaloes or pigs, but I shan't cut too much, but in accordance with what I can afford. (Girl, aged 15)

I will refrain from giving buffaloes to a poor family because it will be burdensome for them—I will give them what they most need. (Boy, aged 16)

I will take part in accordance with what I can afford. I will not force myself to spend more than I can afford, because I am sure that even the person who has died would not agree with that. How much better it would be if those resources were spent on furthering one's education and saving for the future. (Girl, aged 17)

I will not force myself to buy pigs or buffaloes that I really can't afford. I don't want my children's education to be ruined because of our customs. I don't mean to disavow Toraja culture. But culture must be tailored to our means. (Boy, aged 17)

I will still participate, on the condition that I will not hold ceremonies that are extravagant. If someone in my family dies I will still strive to honour Toraja culture but I will also try not to be trapped in it [*terjebak di dalamnya*]. (Boy, aged 17)

When I am an adult I will keep to the *adat*. But I shall do my best to minimise the family's debts, so as not to burden the next generation. These debts can be passed down from generation to generation. So, in order that the next generation should not have to struggle to repay their debts, the older generation must reduce the debts they incur. (Girl, aged 16)

I value our *adat* which represents our cultural wealth which attracts tourists. But I think more about the future when it will be harder and harder to meet our needs, and I imagine how that will get even harder if we are involved in the business of reciprocal exchange and debt [*utang-piutang*]. I am determined not to create new debts except with very close family. And I intend to pay off my parents' remaining debts so that there won't be any more of them. This doesn't mean that I hate funerals, I still love the culture because besides the system of debts there are other things that we can be proud of in the mortuary rituals, and I shall still want to attend them, and I will help bring drinks to the guests and join in the *ma'badong*, or meat divisions, so as to perpetuate Toraja culture. (Girl, aged 15)

Question 7 was entirely open-ended, simply asking, 'Is there anything else you would like to tell me about ceremonies in Tana Toraja? In all, 282 of the 451 children (or 62.5 per cent) chose to answer this, providing further details and commentary on a number of aspects of ritual. The subjects on which they chose to elaborate revealed a certain amount of ambivalence about Toraja culture. Striking above all was the intense pride expressed in the 'uniqueness' of Toraja culture (mentioned in 128, or 45.4 per cent of, responses) and the necessity of preserving it (109, or 38.7 per cent of, responses). Again, the festive drama of rituals was stressed as an admirable and distinctive feature. Of the responses, 77 (or 27.3 per cent) explained various aspects of the funeral rituals as being manifestations of rank and status; and 17, or 6.2 per cent, also mentioned that their culture was sufficiently extraordinary as to attract international tourists. Some made the point that Toraja was a peaceful area (implicitly drawing a contrast with other regions that were afflicted with outbursts of ethnic violence in the years immediately following the fall of Suharto):

There are many fine things about our culture that are unique and sacred. (Girl, aged 14)

Toraja ceremonies are only for Toraja people, so they cannot be carried out in other areas. (Boy, aged 13)

In my opinion ceremonies in Tana Toraja are already pretty terrific as far as the Toraja people themselves are concerned [*pesta di Tana Toraja sudah cukup maksimal bagi masyarakat Toraja sendiri*]. (Boy, aged 16)

There is no ceremony more festive [*meriah*] than a Toraja funeral. (Boy, aged 14)

Ceremonies in Tana Toraja are very festive [*sangat ramai*] … whenever there is a ceremony, especially funerals, people are always sacrificing buffaloes and making them fight. Our ceremonies are really festive. (Girl, aged 13)

It's clear that ceremonies like this are not to be found in other places, only in Toraja. They are unique and different from everyone else's. That is why we must be proud of Toraja. (Girl, aged 14)

In my view ceremonies in Tana Toraja are very unique and extraordinary, such that they have become famous and attracted much attention from people of other countries, and also Toraja traditions and customs are not like those of other areas, hence our culture is more different. (Girl, aged 14)

In my opinion, Toraja *adat* is very unique and should be preserved [*diabadikan*]. Even though most rituals in Tana Toraja are very expensive. However that may be, I am extremely proud to live here and to be Toraja. I LOVE TANA TORAJA. *'Misa' kada dipotuo, Pantan kada dipomate.'*[12] (Girl, aged 14)

I hope you like Toraja ceremonies, whether of the West or of the East, because in them you can see a lot about Toraja culture which is unique and very impressive and different from other cultures. I hope Toraja culture will not be lost or fade away and will continue to attract tourists to come here. (Girl, aged 15)

TANA TORAJA is very, very beautiful, it has lovely landscapes, there is rarely any unrest, not like other areas, its people are friendly and help each other and they cooperate in everything. Another thing is that Toraja people always do their best to work hard so as to pay off their debts. I am proud to be a Toraja person. (Girl, aged 14)

---

12   A traditional saying meaning: 'Let agreement be upheld and discord be done away with.' This refers particularly to the ideal maintenance of harmony within the family (by no means always achieved in practice, since almost all disputes in Toraja are over land and inheritance issues, and occur between family members). Here, it is implicitly extended to characterise Toraja culture itself as peaceful and harmonious.

> The culture of TORAJA is very unique, and for this reason, TORAJA ceremonies whether of the West or of the East must continue to be preserved and perpetuated so that TORAJA will always possess its special culture which reflects the [cultural] richness of TORAJA. (Girl, aged 16)

These comments are remarkable for the extent to which they reveal a highly self-conscious sense of ethnic identity among the young. Although the very idea of a distinctively 'Toraja' ethnic identity has been a relatively recent process, set in motion in the twentieth century, and one that is still unfolding today, the writers clearly see themselves as carriers of a unique cultural identity, positioned within the modern Indonesian state and the wider world. One might ask whether the extent to which this identity is presented as being bound up with rituals, and funeral celebrations in particular, is an artefact of the kinds of questions I was asking, or whether the evident pride expressed in being Toraja was simply a response to having a foreign researcher in the classroom. But I do not think these factors can entirely account for the results. After all, children could have chosen to write about other kinds of ritual. On the contrary, the overwhelming consideration given to funerals only serves to confirm the general picture in which a former balance between rites of the east and of the west has been lost. Rites of the east have borne the brunt of Christian disapproval, as well as suffering a loss of plausibility in the face of other aspects of social change (Waterson 2009: 350–1), while mortuary rituals have retained their place of honour as quintessential social events, and have even become more grandiose. At the same time, however, some children expressed the view that some aspects of Toraja ceremonies should be changed. These comments show a certain degree of ambivalence: 38.7 per cent stated that ceremonial culture must be preserved, while 25.2 per cent spoke of changing it. But these conflicting thoughts were sometimes combined; 24 (8.5 per cent) who were in favour of moderating the expenditure incurred at funerals also said that their culture must be preserved.

A total of 67, or 23.8 per cent, of the children also chose to write their opinions about the burden of debt. High-schoolers in particular were likely to comment on the parental conflict between meeting ceremonial obligations and paying for their children's education; they are the ones most keenly aware of the obstacles in the way of their completing their schooling and, still more, pursuing higher education, which has become ever more expensive in the post-Suharto era. The following example from a middle-schooler provides a vivid visual image of the dilemma, clearly based on personal experience:

> Ceremonies in Tana Toraja need to be preserved so that what is special about our culture won't be lost, but parents with children who are still in school ought to put their needs first. For instance, if we ask our mother for money to buy school books she won't give it, but suddenly she gets news that there is a funeral that must be attended the next day. Well, the next morning the pig will be there in front of the house, ready to take to the funeral. Actually, she said there is no money to buy books, but she's quite well able to buy a pig, so here we can see that parents may be more concerned about going to funerals than about fulfilling the needs of their children. (Girl, aged 14)

Others echoed this girl's concerns, or pointed out that traditional rituals disrupt the rationalised calendar of the modern working week:

> What is most surprising is that parents say they haven't any money, but if a ritual comes around they are able to buy buffaloes and pigs and everything that is used in the ceremony. Maybe for this reason many Toraja children are unable to continue their education and don't finish high school or middle school. Their parents force them to migrate [*merantau*] to increase the family's income. (Girl, aged 16)

> At funerals the family members compete with each other to sacrifice pigs and buffaloes just to win praise or to pay their debts. Logically isn't this ruinous [*sangat merugikan*]? To tire ourselves out looking for money only to use it all up in a single day buying buffaloes worth hundreds of millions of rupiah? Yet no thought is given to the children who are still getting an education? But in this matter Toraja are still Toraja, their character is such that you could say they don't want to be outdone by others [*tidak mau kalah*]. (Girl, aged 17)

> Ceremonies that are held on week days (not in school holidays) interfere with getting an education, because they usually go on for a week or more. (Girl, aged 16)

Apart from their own interests, some children expressed concern about the burden caused to the poor, who may feel obliged to try to keep face, even if they cannot afford it. One girl even went so far as to suggest that people may be driven out of their minds with worry on this score:

I have noticed that many people are mad/not in their right minds [*gila/tidak waras*] and it has occurred to me that they have been driven mad through worrying about all the debts they owe at ceremonies all over the place. (Girl, aged 16)

It is all very well for the rich to hold extravagant ceremonies, but those who force themselves to join in even when they can't afford it end up selling their house after the ceremony is over and living miserably, because they are burdened with debts all over the place. So it would be better if funerals were only held by those who are better off. Those who can't afford it would be better off not holding them because it will cause them anxiety later. (Boy, aged 17)

In my view ceremonies in Toraja cause families to go into debt. However we can't just say we haven't got anything to contribute, the point is you have to have something. If the family isn't well off they still have to try and hold a funeral ceremony because that is our *adat* that has been passed down to us over the generations. (Girl, aged 17)

I think Toraja ceremonies, especially funerals, are a real torment [*sangat menyiksa*] for the poor, because they are sometimes forced to borrow money in order to meet funeral expenses. (Boy, aged 17)

Conclusion: The ceremonial economy and the enactment of empathy

Children's statements about rituals, and funerals in particular, reveal just how much they have observed and tacitly absorbed about an ethos that compels the sharing of emotions, work and resources among kin. The moral imperative to know one's kin, and to support them in their ritual endeavours, finds its most vivid expression in the organisation of mortuary ritual, and it is sufficiently strong for some children already to see themselves migrating in search of work as adults in order to contribute to their own family's ceremonial expenses. Why, one might wonder, is there so little here about shared happiness? A few children, admittedly, did mention the sharing of joy as a counterpart to sorrow, but hardly any of them chose to write about the thanksgiving rituals traditionally associated with the east, or even about newer rituals, such as Christian weddings. Partly, I believe, this is due to the relative decline in salience, already mentioned, of the eastern half of the ritual corpus and the fact that, in practice, children will have attended funerals far more frequently than any other type of ritual.

But partly this is doubtless also due to the stronger moral compulsion that exists to be present at, and contribute to, funeral rites. These are the events that activate the reciprocal duties of exchange between affines, who, as guests, must present their hosts with sacrificial livestock. I have argued elsewhere that these activities do not merely reflect, but rather are generative of, kinship relations (Waterson 2009). Family honour (*longko'*) is at stake—hence the statements regarding the impossibility of opting out of contributing. But it is for this reason that adults sometimes claim special powers for the Toraja kinship system, in binding people to their culture and keeping it vigorous. Some people express the opinion that it is precisely the bilateral character of the Toraja kinship system, embedding every individual in a network of links to houses of origin, and obliging spouses to work together to meet ritual obligations to both their families, that constitutes that strength. Others comment that the ceremonial system forces Toraja people to be industrious to meet their obligations. Children's experiences of the communal efforts put into organising funerals have clearly given them insights into not only family cooperation, but also the competitive nature of sacrificing and the emotional strains that can result from being caught up in this high-stakes game. They sometimes feel the impact of this directly when their own parents are forced to make choices between ritual and educational expenditure.

In various responses, the elevation of kinship morality to the level of the community and, further, to Toraja cultural identity in general, can be seen. Children learn in school to be Indonesian citizens, and one entailment of this process is a heightened sense of local distinctiveness in relation to the many other ethnic groups making up the nation. Events in Indonesian politics since 1998 may also have made some impression; there were many Toraja migrants living both in Maluku and in Central Sulawesi—two areas worst hit by outbreaks of ethnic violence between Muslims and Christians in 1999–2000—who had to flee their homes and who returned as refugees to the Toraja highlands at that time. Children may have relatives among this group of returnees or may have heard stories from their parents about that time. As inhabitants of the only Christian regency in the otherwise Muslim province of South Sulawesi, Toraja have also felt a heightened anxiety about the possible dangers of Islamic extremism since 11 September 2001 and the Bali bombings of 12 October 2002, as well as more recent attacks against churches in Java. A sense of connection to the wider world is enhanced by the increasing numbers of Toraja working overseas, as well as by tourist arrivals in the highlands. Tourism has suffered badly since 1999, but it still contributes to the local economy and Toraja people have long grown accustomed to foreign sightseers showing up at funerals. Children's repeated emphasis on the 'uniqueness' of their culture must be understood within this national and international context.

Turning to comparative Austronesian ethnography, the Polynesian examples discussed earlier suggest some interesting parallels. Toraja are not alone in claiming for themselves special moral virtues of empathy, as expressed through ritual. Nor are they unique in thus emphasising an image of empathy as a communal commitment, even if previous studies, such as those of Hollan, have largely focused on the dyadic dimensions of empathic involvement with others. Mageo's study of Samoa examines both intersubjective and group-focused styles of empathy, while proposing that the latter is the form that has primary cultural salience for Samoans. She suggests that a Samoan penchant for teasing contrasts with Hollan's account of a Toraja etiquette of politeness, which is designed to avoid shaming others and thus requiring that empathy be enacted all the time (Mageo 2011: 87–8). Hollan (2011: 204) notes that, among the Toraja, as among the Balinese, a contrasting cultural theme is that others, if offended, may seek revenge through black magic. Indeed, the inverse of the image of compassion and cooperation in the staging of rituals is the competitive streak that may putatively lead others to do magic to upset the smooth performance of a rite, by causing rain, upset stomachs among the guests or loss of voice in a competing *ma'badong* group (Rappoport 1999). Mageo also cautions that idealised cultural forms are not simply upheld without resistance; a variety of Samoan turns of phrase also describe the exhaustion brought on by hosting visitors and the efforts that may be made to avoid them. We must be alive to these nuances, and will do well to avoid overstressing a simplistic binary opposition between individualist and collectivist orientations in different cultures, since these are not mutually exclusive options, and individuals within any cultural grouping will also differ in their emotional style. Yet, Mageo makes an important point that Samoans set little store by mere statements of empathy; its collective expression must be demonstrated through actions. She goes further to suggest that 'enacted empathy is the constitutive practice of what Mauss calls "gift economies"' (Mageo 2011: 76). I find this idea worthy of further comparative exploration, since I have argued elsewhere (Waterson 2009: 395–430) that economies—particularly, but by no means only, those involving ceremonial exchange—cannot be understood without also delineating their emotional aspects. Toraja children's understandings of ritual, as revealed here, likewise point to a conviction that core cultural values must be expressed in action. Children learn these shared values most vividly through their direct participation in ritual events. My findings show them actively making sense of their experience and forming diverse opinions about it. Whatever their misgivings about the ceremonial burdens that their culture will shortly impose on them as adults, they are already poised to take up the challenge.

References

Adams, Kathleen. 1993. 'The discourse of souls in Tana Toraja (Indonesia): Indigenous notions and Christian conceptions'. *Ethnology* 32(1): 55–68. doi.org/10.2307/3773545.

Adams, Kathleen. 1997. 'Ethnic tourism and the renegotiation of tradition in Tana Toraja (Sulawesi, Indonesia)'. *Ethnology* 36(4): 309–20. doi.org/10.2307/3774040.

Akin, David and Joel Robbins (eds). 1999. *Money and Modernity: State and local currencies in Melanesia*. Pittsburgh: University of Pittsburgh Press.

Alderson, Priscilla and Virginia Morrow. 2004. *Ethics, Social Research and Consulting with Children and Young People*. Essex, UK: Barnado's.

Barbalet, J. M. 1994. 'Ritual emotion and body work: A note on the uses of Durkheim'. In David Franks, William Wentworth and John Ryan (eds) *Social Perspectives on Emotion. Volume 2*, pp. 111–23. Greenwich, CT: JAI Press.

Baron-Cohen, Simon. 2011. *Zero Degrees of Empathy: A new theory of human cruelty*. London: Allen Lane.

Bastiaansen, J., M. Thioux and C. Keysers. 2009. 'Evidence for mirror systems in emotions'. *Philosophical Transactions: Biological Sciences* 364(1528): 2391–404. doi.org/10.1098/rstb.2009.0058.

Bateson, Gregory. 1958. *Naven*. 2nd edn. London: Wildwood House.

Beazley, Harriott, Sharon Bessell, Judith Ennew and Roxana Waterson. 2009. 'The right to be properly researched: Research with children in a messy, real world'. *Children's Geographies* 7(4): 365–78. doi.org/10.1080/14733280903234428.

Boyden, Jo and Judith Ennew (eds). 1997. *Children in Focus: A manual for participatory research with children*. Stockholm: Radda Barnen.

Christensen, Pia and Alison James (eds). 2008. *Research with Children: Perspectives and practices*. 2nd edn. London: Falmer Press.

Decety, Jean and William Ickes. 2009. *The Social Neuroscience of Empathy*. Cambridge, MA: MIT Press. doi.org/10.7551/mitpress/9780262012973.001.0001.

Decety, Jean and Peter Jackson. 2004. 'The functional architecture of human empathy'. *Behavioral and Cognitive Neuroscieince Review* 3: 71–100. doi.org/10.1177/1534582304267187.

de Jong, Edwin. 2008. *Living with the Dead: The economics of culture in the Torajan highlands, Indonesia*. Nijmegen, Netherlands: Radboud University Nijmegen.

de Jong, Edwin. 2013. *Making a Living between Crises and Ceremonies in Tana Toraja: The practice of everyday life of a South Sulawesi highland community in Indonesia*. Leiden: Brill.

Donzelli, Aurora. 2003. '"Sang Buku Duang Buku Kada" (one or two words): Communicative practices and linguistic ideologies in the Toraja highlands of eastern Indonesia'. PhD thesis. University of Milano-Bicocca, Milan.

Durkheim, Emile. 1982 [1915]. *The Elementary Forms of the Religious Life*. 2nd edn. London: Allen & Unwin.

Eisenberg, Nancy and Janet Strayer (eds). 1987. *Empathy and its Development*. Cambridge: Cambridge University Press.

Elias, Norbert. 1994 [1939]. *The Civilizing Process*. Oxford: Blackwell.

Ennew, Judith. 2009. *The Right to be Properly Researched: How to do rights-based, scientific research with children*. Bangkok: Black on White Publications.

Fortes, Meyer. 1970 [1938]. 'Social and psychological aspects of education in Taleland'. In Meyer Fortes, *Time and Social Structure and Other Essays*, pp. 201–59. London: Athlone Press.

Frith, Chris. 2007. 'The social brain?' *Philosophical Transactions of the Royal Society B* 362: 671–8. doi.org/10.1098/rstb.2006.2003.

Gallagher, Shaun. 2012. 'Empathy, simulation, and narrative'. *Science in Context* 25(3): 355–81. doi.org/10.1017/S0269889712000117.

Gallese, Vittorio. 2001. 'The "shared manifold" hypothesis: From mirror neurons to empathy'. *Journal of Consciousness Studies* 8: 33–50.

Gallese, Vittorio. 2007. 'Embodied simulation: From mirror neuron systems to interpersonal relations'. In Greg Bock and Jamie Goode (eds) *Empathy and Fairness: Novartis Foundation Symposium 278*, pp. 3–19. Chichester, UK: John Wiley.

Geertz, Clifford. 1984 [1976]. 'From the native's point of view: On the nature of anthropological understanding'. In Richard A. Schweder and Robert A. LeVine (eds) *Culture Theory: Essays on Mind, Self and Emotion*, pp. 123–36. Cambridge: Cambridge University Press.

Geertz, Hildred. 1974 [1959]. 'The vocabulary of emotion: A study of Javanese socialization processes'. In Robert A. LeVine (ed.) *Culture and Personality: Contemporary Readings*. Chicago: Aldine.

Goldman, Laurence. 1998. *Child's Play: Myth, mimesis and make-believe*. Oxford: Berg.

Gregory, C. 1980. 'Gifts to men and gifts to god: Gift exchange and capital accumulation in contemporary Papua'. *Man* (NS)15(4): 626–52. doi.org/10.2307/2801537.

Heider, Karl. 1991. *Landscapes of Emotion: Mapping three cultures of emotion in Indonesia*. Cambridge: Cambridge University Press. doi.org/10.1017/CBO9780511527715.

Hoffman, Martin. 2000. *Empathy and Moral Development: Implications for caring and justice*. Cambridge: Cambridge University Press. doi.org/10.1017/CBO9780511805851.

Hollan, Douglas. 1988. 'Staying "cool" in Toraja: Informal strategies for the management of anger and hostility in a nonviolent society'. *Ethos* 16(1): 52–72. doi.org/10.1525/eth.1988.16.1.02a00030.

Hollan, Douglas. 1990. 'Indignant suicide in the Pacific: An example from the Toraja highlands of Indonesia'. *Culture, Medicine and Psychiatry* 14: 365–79. doi.org/10.1007/BF00117561.

Hollan, Douglas. 1992a. 'Cross-cultural differences in the self'. *Journal of Anthropological Research* 48(4): 283–300. doi.org/10.1086/jar.48.4. 3630440.

Hollan, Douglas. 1992b. 'Emotion work and the value of emotional equanimity among the Toraja'. *Ethnology* 31(1): 45–56. doi.org/ 10.2307/3773441.

Hollan, Douglas. 2008. 'Being there: On the imaginative aspects of understanding others and being understood'. *Ethos* 36(4): 475–89. doi.org/10.1111/j.1548-1352.2008.00028.x.

Hollan, Douglas. 2011. 'Vicissitudes of "empathy" in a rural Toraja village'. In Douglas W. Hollan and C. Jason Throop (eds) *The Anthropology of Empathy: Experiencing the lives of others in Pacific societies*, pp. 194–214. New York: Berghahn Books.

Hollan, Douglas and C. Jason Throop. 2008. 'Whatever happened to empathy? Introduction'. *Ethos* 36(4): 385–401. doi.org/10.1111/ j.1548-1352.2008.00023.x.

Hollan, Douglas W. and C. Jason Throop (eds). 2011. *The Anthropology of Empathy: Experiencing the lives of others in Pacific societies*. New York: Berghahn Books.

Hollan, Douglas and Jane Wellenkamp. 1994. *Contentment and Suffering: Culture and experience in Toraja*. New York: Columbia University Press.

Hollan, Douglas and Jane Wellenkamp. 1996. *The Thread of Life: Toraja reflections on the life cycle*. Honolulu: University of Hawai'i Press.

Hume, David. 1739–40. *A Treatise of Human Nature: Being an attempt to introduce the experimental method of reasoning into moral subjects*. London: John Noon.

Hume, David. 1751. *An Enquiry Concerning the Principles of Morals*. London: A. Millar.

Iacoboni, Marco. 2008. *Mirroring People: The new science of how we connect with others*. New York: Farrar, Straus & Giroux.

Iacoboni, Marco, Istvan Molnar-Szakacs, Vittorio Gallese, Giovanni Buccino, John C. Mazziotta and Giacomo Rizzolatti. 2005. 'Grasping the intentions of others with one's own mirror neuron system'. *PLoS Biology* 3(3): 529–35. doi.org/10.1371/journal.pbio.0030079.

Ingold, Tim. 1985. 'Who studies humanity? The scope of anthropology'. *Anthropology Today* 1(6): 15–16. doi.org/10.2307/3033249.

Jakoby, Nina. 2012. 'Grief as a social emotion: Theoretical perspectives'. *Death Studies* 36(8): 679–711. doi.org/10.1080/07481187.2011. 584013.

Koubi, Jeanine. 1982. *Rambu Solo', 'La Fumée Descend': Le Culte des Morts chez les Toradja du Sud* [*Rambu Solo' 'The Smoke Descends': The cult of the dead among the southern Toraja*]. [In French.] Paris: CNRS.

Latour, Bruno. 1993. *We Have Never Been Modern.* New York: Harvester Wheatsheaf.

Levy, Robert. 1973. *Tahitians: Mind and society in the Society Islands.* Chicago: University of Chicago Press.

Lipps, Theodor. 1903–06. *Ästhetik: Psychologie des Schönen und der Kunst* [*Aesthetics: The Psychology of Beauty and Art*]. 2 Vols. Hamburg and Leipzig: Leopold Voss.

Lohmann, Roger. 2011. 'Empathic perception and imagination among the Asabano: Lessons for anthropology'. In Douglas W. Hollan and C. Jason Throop (eds) *The Anthropology of Empathy: Experiencing the lives of others in Pacific societies*, pp. 94–116. New York: Berghahn Books.

Lutz, Catherine. 1988. *Unnatural Emotions: Everyday sentiments on a Micronesian atoll and their challenge to Western theory.* Chicago: University of Chicago Press.

Lutz, Catherine and Geoffrey White. 1986. 'The anthropology of emotions'. *Annual Review of Anthropology* 15: 405–36. doi.org/ 10.1146/annurev.an.15.100186.002201.

Mageo, Jeanette. 2011. 'Empathy and "as-if" attachment in Samoa'. In Douglas W. Hollan and C. Jason Throop (eds) *The Anthropology of Empathy: Experiencing the lives of others in Pacific societies*, pp. 68–93. New York: Berghahn Books.

Meloni, Maurizio. 2014. 'Biology without biologism: Social theory in a postgenomic age'. *Sociology* 48(4): 731–46. doi.org/10.1177/0038038513501944.

Myers, Fred. 1979. 'Emotions and the self: A theory of personhood and political order among Pintupi Aborigines'. *Ethos* 7(4): 343–70. doi.org/10.1525/eth.1979.7.4.02a00030.

Nooy-Palm, Hetty. 1986. *The Saʹdan Toraja: A study of their social life and religion. Volume II: Rituals of the east and west.* Dordrecht: Foris.

Parker, Lyn. 1997. 'Engendering school children in Bali'. *Journal of the Royal Anthropological Institute* 3(3): 497–516. doi.org/10.2307/3034764.

Parker, Lyn. 2002. 'The subjectification of citizenship: Student interpretations of school teachings in Bali'. *Asian Studies Review* 26(1): 3–37. doi.org/10.1080/10357820208713329.

Preston, Stephanie and Frans de Waal. 2002. 'Empathy: Its ultimate and proximate bases'. *Behavioral and Brain Sciences* 25: 1–72.

Rappoport, Dana. 1999. 'Chanter sans être Ensemble. Des Musiques Juxtaposées pour un Public Invisible [Singing without being together. Juxtaposed music for an invisible audience]'. [In French.] *L'Homme* 39(152): 143–62. doi.org/10.3406/hom.1999.453666.

Rappoport, Dana. 2009. *Songs from the Thrice-Blooded Land: Ritual music of the Toraja (Sulawesi, Indonesia). Volume One: Ethnographic narrative. Volume Two: Florilegium Toraja—A selection of Toraja songs. Volume Three [DVD]: Multimedia argument/multimedia musical anthology.* Paris: Editions Epistèmes/Editions de la Maison des Sciences de L'Homme.

Read, K. E. 1955. 'Morality and the concept of the person among the Gahuku-Gama'. *Oceania* 25(4): 233–82. doi.org/10.1002/j.1834-4461.1955.tb00651.x.

Rizzolatti, Giacomo and Laila Craighero. 2004. 'The mirror neuron system'. *Annual Review of Neuroscience* 27: 169–92. doi.org/10.1146/annurev.neuro.27.070203.144230.

Robins, Joel and Alan Rumsey. 2008. 'Introduction: Cultural and linguistic anthropology and the opacity of other minds'. *Anthropological Quarterly* 81(2): 407–20. doi.org/10.1353/anq.0.0005.

Rollason, Will. 2012. 'Review of D. Hollan & C. J. Throop (eds). The Anthropology of Empathy: Experiencing the Lives of Others in Pacific Societies'. *Journal of the Royal Anthropological Institute* (NS)18(3): 706–7. doi.org/10.1111/j.1467-9655.2012.01787_15.x.

Rosaldo, Michelle. 1980. *Knowledge and Passion: Ilongot notions of self and social life*. Cambridge: Cambridge University Press. doi.org/10.1017/CBO9780511621833.

Rosaldo, Renato. 1984. 'Grief and a headhunter's rage: On the cultural force of emotions'. In Edward M. Bruner (ed.) *Text, Play, and Story: The construction and reconstruction of self and society*. Stanford, CA: Stanford University Press.

Smith, Adam. 1759. *The Theory of Moral Sentiments*. London: A. Millar.

Stamenov, Maxim and Vittorio Gallese. 2002. *Mirror Neurons and the Evolution of Brain and Language*. Amsterdam: John Benjamins. doi.org/10.1075/aicr.42.

Stearns, Peter and Deborah Stearns. 1994. 'Historical issues in emotions research: Causation and timing'. In David Franks, William Wentworth and John Ryan (eds) *Social Perspectives on Emotion. Volume 2*, pp. 239–66. Greenwich, CT: JAI Press.

Stewart, Pamela J. and Andrew Strathern (eds). 2009. *Religious and Ritual Change: Cosmologies and histories*. Durham, NC: Carolina Academic Press.

Stueber, Karsten. 2006. *Rediscovering Empathy: Agency, folk psychology, and the human sciences*. Cambridge, MA: MIT Press.

Throop, C. Jason. 2011. 'Suffering, empathy, and ethical modalities of being in Yap (Waqab), Federated States of Micronesia'. In Douglas W. Hollan and C. Jason Throop (eds) *The Anthropology of Empathy: Experiencing the lives of others in Pacific societies*, pp. 118–49. New York: Berghahn Books.

Toren, Christina. 1990. *Making Sense of Hierarchy: Cognition as social process in Fiji*. Basingstoke, UK: Palgrave Macmillan.

Toren, Christina. 1993. 'Making history: The significance of childhood cognition for a comparative anthropology of mind'. *Man* (NS)28(3): 461–78. doi.org/10.2307/2804235.

Toren, Christina. 1999. 'Compassion for one another: Constituting kinship as intentionality in Fiji'. *Journal of the Royal Anthropological Institute* 5(2): 265–80. doi.org/10.2307/2660697.

Toren, Christina. 2006. 'The effectiveness of ritual'. In Fenella Cannell (ed.) *The Anthropology of Christianity*, pp. 185–210. Durham, NC: Duke University Press. doi.org/10.1215/9780822388159-007.

Vischer, Robert. 1994 [1873]. 'On the optical sense of form: A contribution to aesthetics'. In Harry Francis Mallgrave and Eleftherios Ikonomon (eds) *Empathy, Form and Space: Problems in German aesthetics, 1873–1893*. Santa Monica, CA: Getty Centre for the History of Art and the Humanities.

Volkman, Toby. 1979. 'The riches of the undertaker'. *Indonesia* 28: 1–16. doi.org/10.2307/3350893.

Volkman, Toby. 1985. *Feasts of Honour: Ritual and change in the Toraja highlands*. Chicago: University of Illinois Press.

Volkman, Toby. 1987. 'Mortuary tourism in Tana Toraja'. In Rita Smith Kipp and Susan Rodgers (eds) *Indonesian Religions in Transition*, pp. 161–7. Tucson: University of Arizona Press.

Wassmann, Jürg, Birgit Träuble and Joachim Funke (eds). 2013. *Theory of Mind in the Pacific: Reasoning across cultures*. Heidelberg: Universitätsverlag Winter.

Waterson, Roxana. 1984. 'Rites of east and west: Ritual, gender and status in Tana Toraja'. In Roxana Waterson *Ritual and belief among the Sa'dan Toraja*. Occasional Paper No. 2, pp. 3–33. Canterbury, UK: University of Kent Centre of South-East Asian Studies.

Waterson, Roxana. 1993. 'Taking the place of sorrow: The dynamics of mortuary rites among the Sa'dan Toraja'. *Southeast Asian Journal of Social Science* 21(2): 73–96. doi.org/10.1163/030382493X00125.

Waterson, Roxana. 1995. 'Entertaining a dangerous guest: Sacrifice and play in the Ma'pakorong ritual of the Sa'dan Toraja'. *Oceania* 66(2): 81–102. doi.org/10.1002/j.1834-4461.1995.tb02538.x.

Waterson, Roxana. 2009. *Paths and Rivers: Sa'dan Toraja society in transformation*. Leiden: KITLV Press. doi.org/10.1163/9789004253858.

Waterson, Roxana. 2015. 'Children's perspectives on ritual and its responsibilities among the Sa'dan Toraja of Sulawesi (Indonesia)'. *Journal of Ritual Studies* 29(1): 49–69.

Wellenkamp, Jane. 1984. 'A psychocultural study of loss and death among the Toraja'. PhD thesis. University of California, San Diego.

Wellenkamp, Jane. 1988. 'Notions of grief and catharsis among the Toraja'. *American Ethnologist* 15: 486–500. doi.org/10.1525/ae.1988. 15.3.02a00050.

Wellenkamp, Jane. 1991. 'Fallen leaves: Death and grieving in Toraja'. In David R. Counts and Dorothy A. Counts (eds) *Coping with the Final Tragedy: Cultural variation in dying and grieving*, pp. 113–34. Amityville, NY: Baywood.

Wellenkamp, Jane. 1992. 'Variation in the social and cultural organization of emotions: The meaning of crying and the importance of compassion in Toraja, Indonesia'. In D. D. Franks and V. Gecas (eds) *Social Perspectives on Emotion. Volume 1*. Greenwich, CT: JAI.

White, Geoffrey. 1993. 'Emotions inside out: The anthropology of affect'. In Michael Lewis and Jeannette M. Haviland (eds) *Handbook of Emotions*, pp. 29–40. New York: Guilford Press.

White, Geoffrey and John Kirkpatrick (eds). 1985. *Person, Self and Experience: Exploring Pacific ethnopsychologies*. Berkeley, CA: University of California Press.

Yamashita, Shinji. 1997. 'Manipulating ethnic tradition: The funeral ceremony, tourism, and television among the Toraja of Sulawesi, Indonesia'. In Shinji Yamashita, Kadir H. Din and J. S. Eades (eds) *Tourism and Cultural Development in Asia and Oceania*, pp. 83–103. Bangi, Malaysia: University of Malaysia Press.

Young, Allan. 2012. 'The social brain and the myth of empathy'. *Science in Context* 25(3): 401–24. doi.org/10.1017/S0269889712000129.

Appendix 4.1: Numerical figures

Question 4: What is the purpose of that ceremony (funeral rites)?

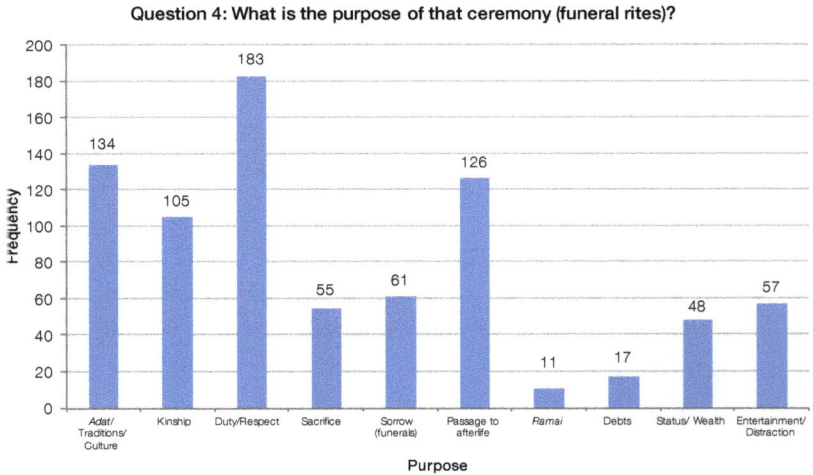

Figure A4.1 Answers to Question 4

Notes: n = 436. Most children gave multiple answers, therefore frequencies exceed the total number of participants; 15 gave no answer.

Source: Author's data.

Question 5: What did you learn from attending the ceremony?

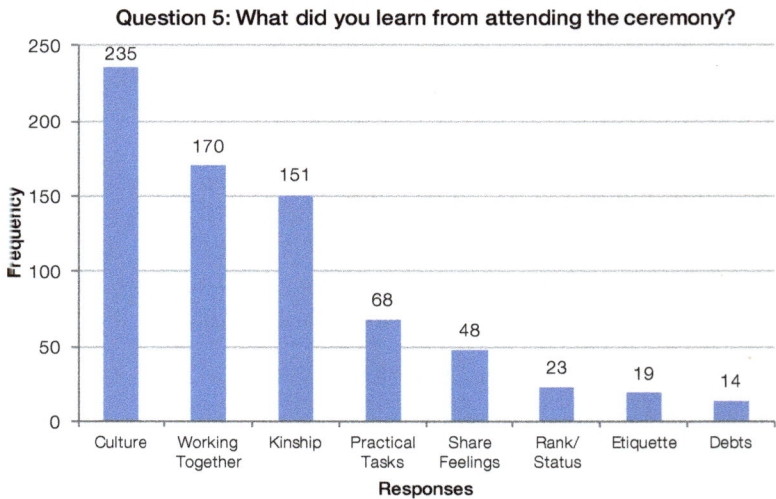

Figure A4.2 Answers to Question 5

Notes: n = 441; most children gave multiple answers, therefore frequencies exceed total number of participants; 10 gave no answer.

Source: Author's data.

Question 6: What will you do when you are grown up if someone in your family is having a ceremony?

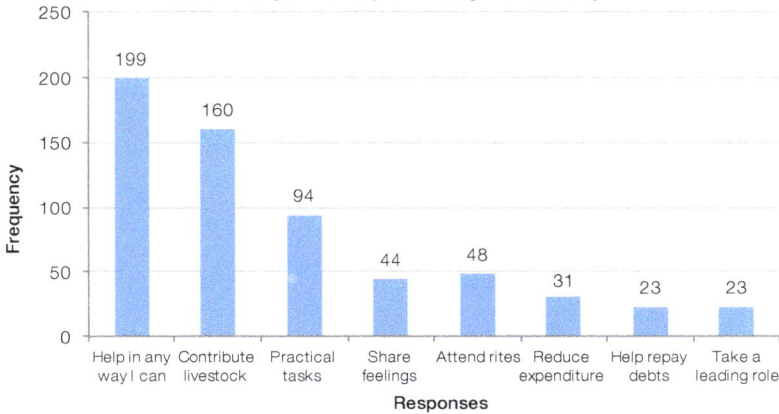

Figure A4.3 Answers to Question 6

Notes: n = 424; most children gave multiple answers, therefore frequencies exceed total number of participants; 27 gave no answer.

Source: Author's data.

Question 7: Is there anything else you would like to tell me about ceremonies?

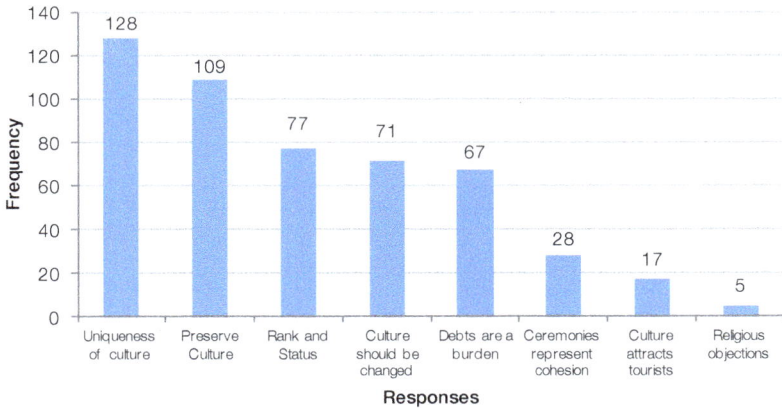

Figure A4.4 Answers to Question 7

Notes: n = 282; most children gave multiple answers, therefore frequencies do not match the number of participants; 169 gave no answer.

Source: Author's data.

5

The body of thinking and of emotions among the Rotenese

James J. Fox

Introduction

This chapter examines the language of thinking and feeling among the Rotenese of eastern Indonesia. It is divided into two complementary parts. Initially, I focus on the specific terms, idioms and ritual expressions that constitute the linguistic basis for the articulation of thinking and for the social expression of emotions.

Among the Rotenese, thinking and the emotions are intimately located within an 'inner person'. This 'inner person' is distinguished from the social semblance that the person presents to the world. Both the inner self and the semblance it presents are associated with specific parts of the body. One of the chief purposes in this section of the chapter is to explore, in some detail, the use of bodily metaphors in the expression of emotions and of thinking.

In this analysis, I combine an examination of ordinary language usage with ritual language usage. Ritual language as a formal register highlights key modes of thought and emotion. Although these thoughts and emotions are those spoken of in ordinary language, ritual language gives emphasis to their particular qualities and, because of its formal dyadic structure, it pairs specific forms of thinking and feeling, often grounding them in metaphoric imagery. This is particularly the case in the ritual admonitions that encourage moral behaviour and insist on proper modes of action.

In the second part of this chapter, I endeavour to locate the use of such metaphors in their social context. Social context is essential to understanding such linguistic usage. This discussion requires the grounding of thought and emotions in notions of the person and in the ideals and values that are given emphasis in Rotenese society. It also requires consideration of the historical development of Rotenese society, where such ideals and values have served as a motivating force for action.

Underlying the expression of the emotions and of thinking among the Rotenese is a specific cultural conception of the person. This conception credits maternal relatives with responsibility for a person's physical being. Through the gift of a woman, wife-givers become life-givers. In the Rotenese botanic idiom, they are regarded as 'planting' (sele) progeny among their wife-takers. These children are explicitly described as 'plants' (sele-dadi). A specific ritual relationship is established between the 'mother's brother of origin' (or 'trunk mother's brother': to'o-huk) and the 'plants', his sister's children, whom he tends throughout their life. All the rituals of the life cycle, which he directs, are concerned with promoting the vitality of the physical person and eventually conclude with the rituals of burial and the dispatch of that person. The mother's brother of origin is duly acknowledged and compensated for his ministration to the physical person to the extent that, were a person to accidentally injure himself by drawing blood, the 'mother's brother of origin' would demand compensation for the injury. This relationship continues for another generation. The 'grandfather of origin' (ba'i-huk) retains specific ritual rights over the children of his sister's children.[1]

---

1   I have discussed these ideas, the idioms that give expression to them and social consequences of these ideas in a long paper entitled 'Sister's child as plant: Metaphors in an idiom of consanguinity' (Fox 1971: 219–52).

The distinction between 'inside' (*dalek*) and 'outside' (*de'ak*)

A Rotenese will often preface a well-considered opinion with the remark that it comes from 'within' (*neme dale-na*) or offer a reflection that has been 'pondered within' (*afi nai dalek*). Such comments are to be taken seriously because they are purposely distinguished from the ordinary, but almost continuous, flow of talk that characterises Rotenese social life.

To converse, dispute, countercomment and qualify another's statement are what give pleasure to social engagement. These diverse sorts of speaking are all classified as *dede'ak*, based on the reduplicated form of the root term, *de'ak*, meaning 'outside'. Such 'out-outside talk' (if one were to translate *dede'ak* literally) is regarded as a less serious form of speaking, expressed as enjoyment in the art of speaking and in response to a present but passing occasion. *Dede'ak* can also be applied in disputes where the arguments may be as diverse and various as the situation allows. To be able to speak cleverly and manipulatively is highly valued and is cultivated as the face of the social person.

In this flood of talk and argument, the distinction is made between what comes from 'within' and what is for show to the 'outside'. Much of everyday life is about this show—a steady verbal performance that need not come from the heart. One of the common narrative devices in Rotenese folktales—and in many of the histories as well, which take the form of 'trickster tales'—hinges on being told what an ancestral character is thinking, feeling or planning 'within' and what that same character says or does to disguise their intended stratagem.

This dichotomy between 'inside' (*dalek*) and 'outside' (*de'ak*) is fundamental and is applied widely in Rotenese classification. Thus, for example, this dichotomy is used to distinguish 'ancestral spirits' (*nitu dale*: 'inside spirits') from all other varieties of generally malevolent spirits (*nitu de'ak*: 'outside spirits') (Fox 1971). Similarly, the house, which, according to Rotenese, has a structure analogous to the human body, is divided into an outside portion (*uma de'ak*: 'outer house'), which can be made accessible to visitors, and an inner sanctum (*uma dalek*: 'inside house'), which contains the hearth and access to the loft—a place open only to the inner family, where the harvest is stored, where healing occurs and where the ancestors can be approached. I once asked an elder who still sacrificed to the ancestors about this part of the house. His reply was that no one knows what anyone does in their inner house; the inside is closed to outside scrutiny.

Similarly, a person's identity is associated with a person's name (*nade*), but a 'name' is itself divided into an inner aspect and an outer aspect. The inner aspect is one's 'hard name' (*nade balakaik*). This hard name is one's ancestral name. It links a person to a succession of ancestors whose names are shared most closely among lineal relatives. These names do not 'descend' but rather 'ascend' from a 'trunk' ancestor (*huk*). The model is that of a tree; the term *balakaik* is an adjective most often used to describe the hard inner core of a tree.

Hard names have two parts, the second of which is the name that 'ascends' from the trunk. The first part of the name is one part of the hard name of a close relative (not necessarily a lineal relative) to whom the newborn child is believed to have some intimate connection. This second component of a person's name is called the *tamok* name and it may occur—indeed, it often occurs—that contemporaries of roughly the same age may share a connection by name to the same *tamok* relative. In this case, there exists a living connection between them.

A person's hard name should never be spoken or uttered outside a ritual context. To speak the hard name is not just to identify the person, but also to invoke a person's ancestral core. Instead, there exist various means for according a person a 'soft name' (*nade manganauk*)—an everyday designation that can change as the circumstances of life change. The possibilities are considerable. Teknonyms are one such possibility; another possibility is a soft name that links a person to the placename of prominence or to some unusual event; yet another possibility are names that hint at the *tamok* name of a person. In one instance, a person I knew well in Termanu was called by the teknonym that was used by his *tamok* ancestor at the time of his death. As a result, he became known as the 'grandfather' of his older brother.

This distinction between 'hard' and 'soft' names parallels the distinction between 'inside' (*dalek*) and 'outside' (*de'ak*). The innermost part of a person is that person's hard name.

The 'inside' (*dalek*) as source of the emotions

In numerous ordinary language contexts, the term *dale*(*k*) refers to a specific inner part of the human person—a physical component of the body that can be associated with 'inner core' or 'heart'. (For translation purposes, in English, the term 'heart' serves better than 'inner core', but it must be realised this gloss is at best an appropriate approximation of the Rotenese term.) As a source of thinking and feeling, the 'heart' (*dale*(*k*)) is the primary locus of numerous expressions that define particular emotional states and basic human qualities. Thus, for example, a good person may be referred to as having 'a good heart' (*dale malole*); a gentle person has a 'soft heart' (*dale mangana'uk*); someone who is open and socially engaged is said to have 'a broad heart' (*dale maloak*); someone who is sad or distressed is said to be 'sick at heart' (*dale hedi*); a caring person has a 'loving heart' (*dale sue/susue*); someone who is satisfied or feels fulfilled has his or her 'heart full' (*dale ketemak*). When people agree with one another, they are 'of one heart' (*dale esak*).[2]

Among the older generation of Rotenese, there is no indication of an idea of romantic love. *Sue*, which is the Rotenese term that most closely approximates the notion of 'love', is a complex, wideranging emotion that embraces notions of 'care' and 'sympathy'—a willingness to share in others' feelings, sentiments and suffering. While *sue* may be used, for example, to describe a mother's love for her child or a brother's love for his sister, *sue* is preeminently a social emotion of empathy that extends well beyond the family. In ritual language, *sue* is combined with the verb *lai*. Relying on a play on words, Rotenese compare the qualities of *sue*//*lai* to the seeming care that swarming fish show for each other. Such fish never appear alone but always in close and intimate contact with one another.

---

2   The Indonesian translation for many (though not all) of these expressions involves a simple substitution of *hati* ('liver') for *dale*(*k*), thus: *dale malole: hati baik*; *dale maloak: hati terbuka*; *dale hedi: sakit hati*.

A common expression based on *dale//tei* is the phrase *dale sue ma tei lai* or, more emphatically, in its reduplicated form, *dale susue ma tei lalai*. This phrase covers a wide gambit of emotions involving 'love and affection' and is often used to express 'sympathy' and indeed 'empathy' as well as 'sorrow' in a time of mourning.[3]

Sadness and anger are also matters of the heart. Instead of necessarily personalising either sadness or anger, these emotions can be idiomatically attributed to the 'heart': *dale nama-hoko* is 'the heart is happy' (but also, in other contexts, 'the heart has sympathy'); another expression for being 'happy, joyful' is the verb *nata-dale*, 'to be particularly happy'. By contrast, someone whose 'heart' is continually inclined to be angry is *dale nasa-meluk* ('bitter-hearted'). Someone who is envious or jealous literally 'places or sequesters the heart' (*napeda dalek*), while someone who covets another's possessions is *dale-salak* ('false-hearted').

Ritual admonitions are cultural assertions on what to do and what not to do. These admonitions occur within long ritual recitations, but, by their nature and format, they are often excerpted from such contexts and used to make moral assertions in ordinary discourse. Many of these admonitions are recognisable by their format: 'Do not ... and do not' (*Boso ... ma boso*). In ritual language, *dale(k)* forms a canonical pair with *tei(k)*, a term that refers to 'the stomach, womb, innards'. These two terms are a set pair and form the basis for many dyadic expressions. One of the most common of these expressions that occurs frequently as a ritual admonition is the phrase *boso madalek dua ma boso matei telu*. Translated literally, it means 'do not have two hearts and do not have three stomachs'. Although this phrase can take on various contextual meanings, its message is to not be of 'two minds'—do not be hesitant, fickle, reluctant, wavering or uncertain. In most contexts, this admonition is used to urge someone to carry out their social obligations without hesitation.

---

3 One of the characteristic features of Rotenese discourse is that it regularly draws on and alludes to well-known ritual sayings. These sayings are taken from traditional ritual narratives associated with different 'chant characters' who embody various moral qualities. In one such narrative, for example, the dual name Sio Meda ma Lepa Lifu occurs in reference to a friend and companion, who is described as a *sio sena ma tio falu* ('a nine-fold friend and eight-fold companion'). Love and affection for this companion evoke the phrase *dale sue Sio Meda ma tei lai Lepa Lifu* ('the love of Sio Meda and the affection of Lepa Lifu'). This association is enough to link the emotion of affection to this particular chant character, whose name serves as a common literary evocation.

Another common dual expression is *tesa tei ma tama dale*, which evokes a sought-after state of 'peace and tranquillity'—a sense of contentment and satisfaction and release from anxiety and worry. In ritual contexts, the sense of wellbeing that these terms imply is achieved only in the close company of lineage mates and companions. Hence it denotes a sense of personal peacefulness in a social milieu.

Yet another such dual expression is that for 'sadness and distress': *dale hedi ma tei susa*. Literally, this phrase translates as being 'sick at heart and troubled in the stomach', but it, too, covers a range of emotions of personal sadness, loss and disappointment.

A further expression is *dale hi ma tei nauk*, which, roughly translated, means 'heart's desire and stomach's wish'. It refers to being 'self-centred' and 'selfish'. Yet another expression is *sale dale ma tuke tei*. The literal translation of this phrase is 'misdirection of the heart and regret/sourness of the stomach'. This phrase refers to emotions of 'regret', 'frustration' and 'disappointment' and has been taken up, in Christian rituals, to refer to notions of 'repentance'. A similar dyadic expression that carries much the same import, but without invoking 'heart and stomach' but instead that of 'rock and tree', is *ai sale ma batu tuke*. Its literal translation is 'tree's misdirection and rock's regret'.

Similarly, the 'heart' is the locus of thought. The idiom *dale dudu'a ma a'afina* is a typical comment that translates as 'according to [my] heart's thoughts and reflections'. The expression is often used as a preface to what purports to be a considered opinion. Another set of verbs used to express serious thought is the reduplicated pair: *dodo ma ndanda*. These verbs may best be translated as 'to consider and to ponder' and are often combined with adverbial expressions that enforce their seriousness: *dodo doak lon ma ndanda sota lon* ('to consider for a long time and to ponder deeply'). This pair is one of the most frequently used expressions in describing serious planning or judgement. Formerly, they were the verbs used to describe the assessment process in divination, but they can be used in all sorts of deliberations that require forethought or careful study.

The head and brain are implicated in a person's capacity for thought. A stupid person is said to have a 'hard[-wood] brain' (*dodole matea*), while someone who is clever and quick in understanding has a *dodole dauk* ('light/easy brain'). Someone who is stubborn and, by implication, stupid has a 'rock head' (*langa batu*).

Each of these expressions has a focus, but together they embrace a spectrum of related emotions: reluctance and hesitancy, inner peace, love, sympathy and sorrow, sadness and distress, selfishness, regret, consideration, deliberation and memory.

Mata as the bodily locus for the outward expression of emotions

The term *mata*, in various contexts, carries multiple meanings: 'eye', 'source', 'focus', 'countenance' or 'expression'.[4] In reference to individuals—whether specifically to the 'eyes' (*mata*) or, more generally, to the countenance (*mata dalek*)—*mata* are where Rotenese see manifest particular qualities of the person. Thus, for example, a pretty face has pleasing eyes (*mata mana'a*); an ugly face shows 'rubbish, lowly eyes' (*mata mangala'uk*). A good person is spoken of as having 'good eyes/face' (*mata lolek*); a person who is reliable has 'straightforward eyes/face' (*mata ndos*).

More interestingly, an individual can be described positively as having 'shame eyes' (*mata mae*), meaning that person is respectable and knows how to behave. More often, this expression is used in the negative as a criticism for someone who knows no shame (*mata mae ta*). The terms, *tema*//*tetu* are frequently used as a contrastive pair: *tema* implies 'fullness' and 'integrity' while *tetu* implies 'order' and 'erectness'. In Rotenese, a virgin girl is a *mata tema*, while the equivalent for a young boy is *mata tetu*. The Dutch, as outsiders, were originally viewed with suspicion and were described as having 'cat eyes' (*mata meok*). This expression is less used at present. In terms of facial appearance, 'doubt' is shown on the forehead (*dedeik*) and 'anger' in the tightening of the neck (*boto-lik*).

Among the most revealing of ritual admonitions are those that offer counsel on shame and fear, doubt and anger. A common admonition during formal visits between houses—for example, in the case of marriage negotiations—is addressed by the household head to his guests before they enter the house: *boso bi ma boso mae* ('do not be afraid and do not be ashamed'). Here the emotions of fear and shame are directly and explicitly linked. Another common admonition is *boso ma-oda dedeik do manasa boto-lik* ('do not show a frown on your forehead or do not show anger in your neck'). Here, 'doubt' is explicitly linked with 'anger'.

---

4   Robert Barnes's 'Mata in Austronesia' (1977) examines the range of uses of *mata* among Austronesian languages.

Anger is a complex emotion. The paired expression for anger in Rotenese is *namanasa ma nggenggele*. *Nama-nasa* ('to become angry') requires a verb stem for 'becoming'; it is not a static condition but a process. The verb *nggele*, or its reduplicated form, *nggenggele*, combines notions of shrieking and forced violence. Anger is explicitly likened to a 'storm' that arises in the person. Although it sweeps over a person, it is not specifically located within the heart (*dalek*). On Rote, the control of physical anger is essential in social contexts, especially when talk becomes aggressive. A repeated admonition is: *Boso mama-nasa maboso nggenggele* ('Do not grow angry and do not grow furious').

Fear is another powerful emotion. Fear (*bi*) and shame (*mae*) are linked, but fear has other associations. The feeling of being terrified is associated with a feeling of cold (*lini*): *momou ma malini* ('to be cold with fear'). Normally, the term *lini* ('cool') describes a positive state of personal tranquillity and ritual neutrality. Rituals—including, in particular, the chanting and oratory that accompany them—are intended to produce a condition of 'heat'. When they achieve this state, these rituals are said to 'boil':

> *Sio laka-doto*: 'The feasts of nine boil.'
> *Ma hus-sala laka-se*: 'The origin rituals bubble.'

Having achieved this state of ritual heat, it is essential to return life to a condition of 'coolness'. This involves a set of calming rituals using coconut water and other plants to render conditions to a tranquil coolness. In ordinary life, intense argument produces a 'heated' state. Sermons, particularly those by an able preacher, are expected to reach a heated crescendo and then, with song and prayer, to taper off to a less intensive state. All such intensity must be controlled and carefully bounded; however, its existence is part of the pattern of life itself.

Living in an oratorical culture

One Rotenese botanic metaphor for sociality is that of a forest of trees whose branches continuously rub against each other (*nula kekek//lasi nggio-nggio*). On an island with relatively little forest cover, this metaphor reflects an image of the ideal society, which, as described in the Rotenese botanic idiom, is:

Tema toe-ao lasin na: 'Intact like a thick wood.'
Teman losa don na: 'Intact for a long time.'
Ma tetu lelei nulan na: 'And in order like a dense forest.'
Tetun nduku nete na: 'Ordered for an age.'

The chaffing and rubbing of branches in this forest refer to the social interaction between individuals that is part and parcel of ongoing social life. A feature of this interaction is verbal interaction—a torrent of talk and argument that brings people together. The verb *kekek*, used to describe the 'rubbing' of branches, is also the verb 'to tease and annoy'.

In any opportunity to talk, there is much on show: the 'outer' semblance of the person and an intense inner sense of personal character. There are implicit rules of speaking: elders dominate assembled gatherings and men speak more than women, although older women can be quite forthcoming. But the younger generation among themselves are as talkative and argumentative as their elders. I have even encountered young children giving 'speeches' to one another in imitation of what they encounter daily.

In this elaborate talk, there is also considerable control. As Dutch travellers noted in the nineteenth century, everywhere on Rote there were local courts whose activities were the source of exuberant argument (see Kate 1894: 221). Each of the 18 domains on the island had a court as its focus. In most domains, disputes were the order of the day and were dealt with at various levels; lineage and clan lords and local elders were called up to hear a variety of disputes. Only a select few cases—the most intractable—made their way to the domain court.

Court cases were a regular function of life during my first period of fieldwork, as were a plethora of lesser local disputes. The disputes at Termanu's court, though often fiercely contested, were hedged by court procedures. When a case was eventually settled, often after several sittings, there occurred the provision of '*paku* [nail] payments' to the court, which were intended to fix judgement in the case. These payments generally consisted of several bottles of gin that were drunk by all who were present, including the litigants.

Funerals are another regular occasion for disputes. Funerals are large social gatherings at which, formally and publicly, all a person's debts and ritual obligations to maternal relatives must be acquitted before burial can occur. (Formerly, when the court existed, members of the court and elders would convene, in ad hoc fashion during the funeral feast, to settle such matters.)

At such gatherings, and indeed at many court cases, the satisfactory settlement is usually a verbal one. Ritual payments must follow strict verbal frames, which are grandiose labels that set out exchange payments in terms of rice fields, herds of water buffalo and quantities of gold—all of which must be fulfilled. The question is not about ritual payment since payment must be fulfilled, but rather about what will be accepted as the agreed on 'substitute' for the ritually designated label. In the end, after a great deal of argument, a chicken or goat may be given as a substitute for a buffalo and a relatively small amount of money provided in place of gold. In retrospect, however, only the grand ritual exchange payments tend to be remembered and the efforts that went into achieving these payments.[5]

In local disputes, there are fewer fixed procedures than at a court hearing and, as a consequence, disputes can often become quite heated. Rotenese have at their disposal a rich, robust scatological repertoire for mockery and abuse and they can resort to this whenever an argument escalates.[6] This mockery language is called *dede'ak a'ali-o'olek* and, as Rotenese explain, it is explicitly intended to 'arouse anger' (*nafofoa nasak*). Significantly, it is also said 'to pierce the liver/heart' (*natola boa-de'ek*). Here a specific body part, the *boa-de'ek*, normally associated with the 'liver' (but sometimes also associated with the 'heart' as a physical organ and not as *dalek*) is identified as a target. The purpose is 'to wound' another.

Most expressions of abuse refer to parts of the body—a person's body or that of a parent. In particular, they refer to the arse or genitalia and link these body parts to qualities of condition, size and smell. Reference to the skull of a parent is also abusive. Reference can also be made to disabilities. Many expressions translate easily into English: *moe-ao* ('piss-self') or *tei-ao* ('shit-self'). My favourite is *pake-tilak* ('vagina-deaf'), although I am not sure whether it is applied to a man or a woman. Abuse can also be directed to a person by making comparison with animals, such as *di'i-dok kapa* ('buffalo-eared') or *mata bi'ik* ('goat-eyes'). It is significant that all forms of

---

5   I have discussed the use of these verbal frames in a paper, '"Chicken bones and buffalo sinews": Verbal frames and the organization of Rotinese mortuary performances' (Fox 1988). The persistence of these formulae gives continuity to social life—or at least to the remembrance of social life—despite enormous change over centuries. Such frames allow the Rotenese to claim they continue to conduct themselves in the manner of their ancestors.

6   I have written at length on this mockery language in a paper entitled '"I'll mock you to fine dust": Rotinese language of mockery, abuse, and cursing' (Fox 1992). The paper lists over 100 different expressions of abuse while indicating the formulae by which one might concoct many hundreds of other terms of abuse.

abuse and mockery are directed to the body (*ao*) rather than to the name or to the 'hard name' (*nade balakaik*). Insults to the name are of a whole different order and produce an immediate response that may escalate as others who share that name become involved.

The social control of violence

Given the near daily occurrence of situations that could escalate, there is surprisingly little resort to acts of physical violence when arguing. A strong underlying belief among Rotenese is that, if one cannot win one's verbal argument and succumbs to a physical response, one has lost not only the argument itself but also self-respect, and is publicly shamed. In the only case I heard about where this occurred, the individual in question, who had been drinking at the time, became the source of hilarity for days afterwards.

Similarly, if a husband were to resort to violence and strike his wife, this would be grounds for immediate divorce. The wife is expected to return to her father's or brother's house and the husband, if he wants to regain his wife, must make 'coaxing' payments to her family, which can be the equivalent of the original bride-wealth.

One case to which I had access at all levels is a good illustration of what may happen. A wealthy noble was considering taking a second wife. His wife learned of his plans and asked for a divorce, which he refused. The wife then set out to stalk her husband's every move, particularly when he attended court. The wife sat at a short distance from the mat on which the elders were assembled and let fly a torrent of abuse at her husband, detailing, among a string of inadequacies, the dismal quality of his genitalia and other body parts. I was sitting at that court session and remember one elder turned to tell me that no man could bear such abuse. At the time, I happened to be meeting regularly with the father of the wife. He was well aware of what was happening and was planning with his son to hold the purification ceremony (*songo aok*) for his daughter as soon as the husband could take no more and finally struck her. The wife's verbal abuse of her husband went on for days—longer than anyone predicted—but, as soon as her husband struck her, she left, returned to her family household, had the proper ceremony for purification of her body performed and then waited for her husband to respond. Eventually, he came courting again and was forced to make substantial 'coaxing' payments to convince her to return.

In broad perspective, much of Rotenese social life is about performance. Like rituals, the 'rubbing and chaffing' of social interaction generate a degree of heat that must be controlled and ultimately rendered cool again—if only to reignite another verbal performance.

Yet there are other dimensions to social life and, in particular, the serious quest for knowledge.

Church and school: The quest for knowledge as a fundamental value

An ideal of knowledge (*lela*) is paramount among the Rotenese. One of the highest compliments one can make is to describe an individual as a 'person of knowledge' (*hataholi malelak*). The designation has broad connotations. In traditional terms, it implies a command of ancestral knowledge, of the ancestral narratives of the origins of things and the genealogies of the domain. Significantly, it also indicates a personal capacity to understand how this knowledge relates to everyday life. It implies a wisdom, discernment and deep sagacity that comes with age, status and experience and pertains most pertinently to the senior-most elders.

In ritual language, knowledge (*lela*) is paired and contrasted with (*ndolo*), which is the knowledge of craft and technique. The quest for these two forms of knowledge (*lela/ndolo*) is one of the most frequently cited quests of the ancestors, in particular, in relation to the knowledge of Christianity, but also in relation to knowledge in general.

Christianity became established on Rote in the early part of the eighteenth century and, with Christianity, came schooling in Malay, particularly in the Malay Bible. The first Rotenese ruler to be baptised with his family, in 1729, almost immediately called up the Dutch East India Company to request that a Malay local school be established in his domain. Eventually, the Dutch East India Company granted this ruler from Thie a schoolmaster. The first school was founded in 1735. Other domains immediately began clamouring for schools. By 1754, there were six Malay schools provided by the company in return for a set payment in agricultural produce, but, by 1765, the local Rotenese educated in Malay took over the island's schooling system at the behest of the local rulers. This schooling system went through fits and starts. The first missionary on Rote in the early nineteenth century closed the local schools because he considered them an affront to Christianity, but they were almost immediately reopened and grew in numbers throughout that century. In 1855, a Dutch Government schools inspector visited Rote. In his report, he described the Rotenese as a 'studious, clever and intelligent people' and recommended that a government-financed school be established in each of the 18 domains of Rote (Buddingh 1859–61: Vol. III, p. 326; see Fox 1977: 92–112, 127–39).

By 1871, an additional 16 'village' schools were opened on Rote and a new phase in Rotenese history had begun. In the early part of the nineteenth century, small groups of Rotenese had been moved to the area around Kupang to ring the Dutch settlement with strategically located populations who could serve as a buffer against marauding Timorese. By the end of the nineteenth century, a new migration of educated Rotenese began to take up coveted positions in the Dutch administration as clerks and schoolteachers and to join fellow Rotenese in the surrounding region. Schools on Rote were the launching pad for this migration.

At present, there are as many Rotenese living in Timor, particularly in the Kupang area, as there are on Rote. In its linkages to Timor, Rote has remained a relative bastion of tradition while continuing to export much of its population in search of modernity.

In the view of present-day Rotenese, the quest for Christianity was an active pursuit. According to contemporary narratives, three rulers from the western part of Rote journeyed to Batavia and there obtained both the knowledge of Christianity and the knowledge of distilling. By a play on words, the two are equated: Christianity brought the knowledge of Allah; the distilling of local lontar juice gave the Rotenese the knowledge of 'gin' (*ala*, from the Malay word *arak*). Christianity is a tree of knowledge, described in the liturgy by dual names: *Tui Sodak ma Bau Molek* ('The Tui-tree of Wellbeing and Bau-tree of Peace'). Lontar gin, on the other hand, is 'the water of words' that lubricates ceremonial gatherings and was once used, with colouring added, at Christian communion services.

The place of thought in Rotenese discourse

The Rotenese have a rich vocabulary for discussing processes of knowing, thinking, pondering and assessing. Many of the terms for thinking are themselves paired and they can best be grasped by contrast to one another. Thus, the most general term for thinking is *afi*, which pairs with *du'a*. *Afi//*

du'a imply active thought and consideration with the intent of arriving at some conclusion. By contrast, the pair of terms *dodo//ndanda* implies longer, more careful consideration. They convey the notion of a deliberate process in thinking. Often these verbs are accompanied by adverbs that imply both a time and a depth to the considerations involved in such thought. The verb *lela* in its active form, *nalela*, is paired with *bubuluk*. *Nalela//bubuluk* indicate general processes of 'knowing'—whether this might be a knowledge of persons, places or things or a practical knowledge of how to do something. Crucial to all these ideas of thinking are ideas of remembering.

Social memory and the nature of personhood

Among the Rotenese there is a common and recurrent ritual refrain: *Sadi mafa-ndendelek ma sadi masa-nenedak* ('Only do remember and do continually keep in mind'). This expression is a strong admonition to preserve memories of the past and especially the memories of the relations commemorated in rituals. Implied in this admonition is an insistence on social memory.

Rituals are the markers that preserve such memories: they become 'memorials' and can, in some cases, result in physical forms of objects of remembrance—what Rotenese call *koni-keak//hate-haik*.

The admonition 'to remember and to keep in mind' is used, most poignantly, in mortuary chants directed to the deceased, who is guided to leave the world of the living. Lamentations, known in Ringgou as *boreu*, are particularly powerful expressions of memory and its loss.

Addressed directly, the chanter conducts the deceased through all the stages that are believed to occur in the transformation from life to death while at the same time vividly invoking the personal life of the deceased. The chanter insists on remembering the little incidents in the personal life of the deceased while admonishing the deceased to try to remember them as well.

Here are excerpts from a lamentation (*boreu*) for an old woman by the master chanter Ande Ruy. This lamentation is in the dialect of Ringgou and extends for almost 200 lines. It consists of a string of images. I have selected a few segments that provide a mix of these images with the recurrent insistence on remembering.

The chanter repeatedly asserts what he himself remembers, but he also urges the deceased to remember—even as the deceased separates from the living (sailing westward on her funeral boat and *perahu*), decomposes ('falling like an old coconut'//'withered like an areca nut') and becomes unable to remember what only the living continue remember.

In these excerpts, segment VII is significant but difficult to comprehend: the Rotenese believe that the recent dead return briefly for several nights after the funeral. They assume the form of a kind of insect and partake of the offerings of rice porridge set out on their behalf. In this manifestation, their capacity to remember is sadly diminished.

Besides 'remembering and keeping in mind', these few lines also portray other basic Rotenese notions of emotion and thought: loving//having affection (*sue*//*lai*), speaking and talking (*dea-dea*//*kola-kola*) and knowing and understanding (*lela*//*rolu*):

I

Ua ia tao le'e boe	What fortune is this?
Ma nale ia tao le'e, besa	What fate is this, Grandmother?
De rina basa nusa ara boe	There through all the domains
Ma basa iku ra boe, besa	And all the lands, Grandmother
Bei ro dudi no-nara	Still with many relatives
Ma ro tora tuke-nara	And with many kin
Fo au afa rene lolo, besa ei	I do continue to remember, Grandmother
Do ameda rara ...	Or steadily bear in mind ...

II

Mana-sue o nei	So loving
Ma mana-lai o nei,	And so affectionate,
Mata malua ia	The eye of day is dawning now
Ma idu maka ledo ia	The nose of the sun is shining now
Te neuko su'i besi neu ko	But the coffin nails strike for you
Ma koe riti neu ko.	And the coffin lock closes for you.
O besa, londa asa neu dulu	Oh Grandmother, drape cloth in the east
Ma ba pou neu laka.	And wrap the cloth at the head.
He'e au we o neu ko	We lament for you
Tika mala balum lain,	Climb aboard your *perahu*
Balu pao-ma lain	Aboard your sailing *perahu*
Ma hene mala tondam lain	Mount aboard your boat
Tonda ufa-ma lain ...	Aboard your sailing boat ...

III

De au afarene lololo	I do continue to remember
Ma asa neda rara, besa.	And I do continue to keep in mind, oh Grandmother.
Fo hida bei leo hatan	At a time long ago
Ma data bei leo don	At a time since past
Ifa mala buna leo	You cradled the flowers of your clan
Ma o'o mala soro mala leo …	And you carried the descendants of your clan …
Nai lo a dale	Within the home
Ma nai uma a dale	And within the house
Ifa mara upu mara	Cradling your grandchildren
Ma o'o mara soro mara …	And carrying your descendants …

IV

Neuko leko la fo mu	Now set sail to go
Ma pale uli fo mu	And turn your rudder to go
De neuko leko la Safu Muri	Set sail for Savu in the west
Ma pale uli Seba I'o.	And turn your rudder to Seba at the tail.
De tule ta di'u dua so	Do not return, having turned your back
Ma fali ta soro lele so …	And do not come back, having turned round …

V

Ela dea-dea, besa o	Let's speak to one another, oh Grandmother
Ma ela ola-ola dei, besa o.	And let's talk to one another, oh Grandmother.
Sadi rene mafa-rene	Only remember, do remember
Te nai oe ma so	Where your water once was
Ma sadi neda masa neda	And only recall, do recall
Te nai dae ma so …	Where your land once was …

VI

Afa rene lololo	I continually remember
Ma ameda rara	And I constantly recall
Mata esa ko matan	Eye to eye
Ma rolu esa ko rolu	Knowing each other
Ma idu esa ko idu	Nose to nose
De lela esa ko lela …	Understanding each other …

VII

Te neuko fati ara tao lada	But in the middle of the night
Ma boro ara tao do	And late in the night
O tule di'u dua mai	You can return, turning back
Ma fali soro lele mai.	And come back, turning round.
Te ma-mata bupu timu	With the eyes of a bumble bee
Fo mahara bupu timu	The voice of a bumble bee
Ma ma-idu fani lasi	And the nose of a honey bee
Fo ma-dasi fani lasi …	The sound of a honey bee …

VIII

Ami mafarene lolo	We continually remember
Ma masaneda rara	And bear in mind
Ua leo besak ua.	Fortune like the present fortune.
Ma nale besak nale.	Fate like the present fate.
Mama lasi leo no	Mother old as a coconut
Fo ono aom leo no	Your body falls like a coconut
Ma mama latu leo pua	And mother withered as an areca nut
Fo refa aom leo pua.	Your body drops like an areca nut.
Mita mai leo be a	We will see what happens
Fo balaha leo be a	What tomorrow will be
Ma ami bulu mai leo be a	And we will learn what will be
Fo binesa leo be a …	What the day after next will be …

For the Rotenese, memories constitute the social person and these precious memories are what dissolve and disappear when the body dies.

Conclusion

This chapter can, at best, be considered an initial exploration of the complexities of Rotenese expressions of thought and emotion. I have concentrated on what I consider to be key defining notions that are at the core of the Rotenese social person. To enhance my presentation, I have deliberately focused on the use of terms for thought and emotion in Rotenese ritual language. The intellectual and emotive power of Rotenese ritual language is at the core of Rotenese culture. In ritual language, terms are always paired and the remarkable pairings of terms for thought and emotions, I would argue, are revealing.

For a comparative study of the expression of thought and the emotions among the Austronesians, the Rotenese case highlights recognisable, comparable particularities: inside versus outside, the eye as source and the focus of emotions, the linkage between fear and shame and the subtle associations of heat and coolness as emotional states. At this basic level, Rotenese shares an Austronesian emphasis on particular terms that link thought and the emotions to specific parts of the body, but the intellectual elaboration of these notions is distinctively Rotenese.

References

Barnes, Robert H. 1977. 'Mata in Austronesia'. *Oceania* XLVIII(4): 300–19. doi.org/10.1002/j.1834-4461.1977.tb01301.x.

Buddingh, S. A. 1859–61. *Neerlands Oost-Indië*. 3 vols. Rotterdam: M Wojt en Zonen.

Fox, James J. 1971. 'Sister's child as plant: Metaphors in an idiom of consanguinity'. In Rodney Needham (ed.) *Rethinking Kinship and Marriage*, pp. 219–52. London: Tavistock.

Fox, James J. 1977. *Harvest of the Palm: Ecological change in eastern Indonesia*. Cambridge, MA: Harvard University Press. doi.org/10.4159/harvard.9780674331884.

Fox, James J. 1988. '"Chicken bones and buffalo sinews": Verbal frames and the organization of Rotinese mortuary performances'. In David S. Moyer and Henri J. M. Claessen (eds) *Time Past, Time Present, Time Future: Essays in honour of P. E. de Josselin de Jong*, pp. 178–94. Verhandelingen van het Koninklijk Instituut voor Taal-, Land- en Volkenkunde 131. Dordrecht: Foris Publications.

Fox, James J. 1992. '"I'll mock you to fine dust": Rotinese language of mockery, abuse, and cursing'. In Tom Dutton, Malcolm Ross and Darrell Tryon (eds) *The Language Game: Papers in memory of Donald C. Laycock*, pp. 581–8. Canberra: Pacific Linguistics.

Fox, James J. 2007. 'Traditional justice and the "court system" of the island of Roti'. *The Asia Pacific Journal of Anthropology* 8(1): 59–74. doi.org/10.1080/14442210601166665.

Kate, H. F. C. ten. 1894. 'Verslag eener reis in de Timorgroup en Polynesië [An account of a trip through the Timor group and Polynesia]'. *Tijdschrift van den Koninklijk Nederlandsch Aardrijkkundig Genootschap* (2nd series) 11: 195–246; 333–90; 541–638; 659–700; 765–823.

6

Describing the body, disclosing the person: Reflections of Tetun personhood and social-emotional agency

Barbara Dix Grimes

Initially setting out to explore Tetun[1] emotion terms, I soon realised that such an approach was too limiting for the data I was encountering. First, there were the inevitable problems that arise when a second language (such as English) is used to index the meaning of words in another language (such as Tetun). And, while it was not hard to compile a list of Tetun words and phrases that could be equated with emotion terms (in English), I found no overarching category in Tetun equivalent to the notion of 'emotions', making it analytically unsound to speak of Tetun 'emotion terms' as if they constitute an emic category. So, rather than force Tetun concepts into Western culture-bound notions of emotion,

1   The Tetun speakers who graciously taught me their language and provided data for this chapter are from the two regencies (*kabupaten*) of Belu and Malaka in the Indonesian province of Nusa Tenggara Timur on the western side of the Indonesian border with Timor-Leste. There are around 500,000 native speakers of Tetun in these two regencies, with the boundary between the two roughly dividing the two major dialects: Foho in the north and Fehan in the south. This variety of Tetun is also spoken in Timor-Leste, where it is often referred to as 'Tetun Terik', in contrast with the variety of Tetun spoken in and around Dili. I am especially grateful to Gabriel A. Bria, Asnat Halek-Dami, Ludofikus Bria and Emanuel Seran, who worked with me periodically over several years. Charles Grimes provided helpful comments on earlier drafts of this chapter.

I shifted from a focus on emotion terms per se to an analysis of how Tetun speakers talk about inner subjective experience, and what this implies in terms of the conceptualisation of personhood and human agency.

The starting point for analysis thus became what I refer to as Tetun *body talk*—phrases describing parts of the body that are used when talking about inner subjective experiences such as feeling, thinking, remembering and relating socially.[2] In the first section of this chapter, I discuss phrases based on seven different body parts that I have found to be at the core of Tetun body talk. I demonstrate how body talk describes the condition or state of a person without disassociating the physical body from the emotional, intellectual or social person. In the second section of the chapter, I note how body talk is linguistically encoded as noun phrases, disclosing the state of the inner person as a non-agent, in contrast to a set of Tetun 'emotion' verbs that assert social-emotional agency. In the third section, I discuss how morality and social norms are emotionally regulated and restrained through the Tetun concept of shame (*moe*).

The noun phrases of body talk

Tetun body talk shows considerable similarities with what is found in other languages in the region, including in both Austronesian and Papuan languages. In contrast to the seven body parts found in Tetun body talk, Papuan languages appear to use particularly large inventories of body parts. Kratochvíl and Delpada (2012) list 22 different body parts found in 'emotion and cognition predicates' of Abui, a Papuan language of Alor Island just north of Timor. Their database includes over 300 expressions based on these body parts. McElhanon (1977) lists 28 body parts that occur in 'idioms' in Selepet, a Papuan language of Morobe Province in Papua New Guinea.[3] He comments that 'body parts express definite

---

2   This use of body metaphors parallels some of what Fox (Chapter 5, this volume) describes for Rote, Sather (Chapter 3, this volume) for Iban and Kuehling (Chapter 7, this volume) for Dobu, along with other works discussed in this chapter.

3   These are *amun* ('buttocks'), *ândâp* ('ear'), *bât* ('hand, arm'), *biwi* ('inside'), *dihin* ('chest'), *eŋgat* ('neck'), *hahit* ('bone'), *hâk* ('skin'), *hâme* ('nose'), *hep* ('blood'), *kahapoŋ* ('breath, vapour'), *kambe* ('shoulder'), *kambiam* ('liver, heart'), *kâi* ('foot, leg'), *kâkâ* ('molar'), *kun* ('head'), *lau* ('mouth'), *rângân nângân* ('understanding'), *nekam* ('chin'), *nelâm* ('mind'), *nimbilam* ('tongue'), *sât* ('tooth'), *sən* ('eye'), *tâp* ('saliva'), *tep* ('belly'), *umut* ('shadow, image, spirit'), *we* ('soul'[?]) and *wât* ('strength').

psychological and sociological functions' and 'a careful study of the expressions based upon body parts reveal[s] an underlying system with some clearly discernible characteristics' (McElhanon 1977: 117).

McElhanon also addresses the difficulty in trying to classify these expressions as having 'idiomatic' (metaphorical or figurative) meaning in contrast to 'non-idiomatic' (literal) meaning.

The same dilemma could be said to exist in Tetun. Some expressions appear to be used metaphorically or figuratively, such as the phrase *laran malirin* ('cool insides'), which is used to refer to someone who is no longer angry. But other expressions refer to a literal observable state of the body as well as an implied internal state, such as the phrase *nawan naksetik* ('tight/constricted breathing'), used to refer to someone who is frustrated. In this analysis, I do not attempt to distinguish metaphorical from literal meaning, opting instead to see Tetun body talk—metaphorical or otherwise—as describing and revealing both the body and the person. The Tetun concept of personhood is an embodied one, where physical as well as emotional, intellectual and relational states are revealed by talking about the body/person. Body talk simultaneously references both physical (literal) and metaphorical (figurative) states, without creating distinction between the body and the person.

Phrases based on the seven body parts that have been found in Tetun body talk are discussed below. I include example sentences to show how 'body talk' is grammatically represented as descriptive phrases that define the body/person in systematic ways. The Tetun body parts I elaborate on are listed briefly below; a fuller discussion with examples is given below for a more complete sense of what these simple glosses represent.

> *nawa-n*: 'breath, life force'
> *ibu-n*: 'mouth'
> *mata-n*: 'eye'
> *ate-n*: 'liver'
> *kakutak*: 'brain'
> *neo-n*: 'mind'
> *lara-n*: 'insides'

Most of the examples below use the following grammatical frame: subject,[4] [is being described as] body part noun + modifier.[5]

1.1 *Nawan* ('breath, life force')

01 *Nia nawan sa'e*
He breath ascend/increase

'He is angry'

02 *Nia nawan aat*
He breath bad/evil

'He has numerous negative social characteristics'

03 *Nia nawan naruk*
He breath long

1) 'He is an athletic runner or diver who holds his breath a long time' OR

2) 'He is a person who took an unexpectedly long time to die'

04 *Nia nawan tuun*
He breath descend/subside

1) 'He is no longer angry' (resulting state)//'His anger is subsiding' (process) OR

2) 'His breath/life force subsides'[6]

Emi baa, te nawan tuun ti'an
You-pl go, reason his breath descend already

'Just go ahead and go, since he's no longer angry [at you]'

05 *Nia nawan badak*
He breath short

'He is quick to get angry'

06 *Nia nawan naksetik*
He breath tight/constricted

'He is extremely angry and frustrated'

07 *Hakraik nawan lai!*
Lower breath imperative

'Stop being angry!'

08 *Nia nawan kotu*
He breath cut/severed

'He stopped breathing' (Euphemism: he died—refers to the moment of a person's death)[7]

09 *La noo nawan*
NEG exist breath

'There is no breath/life force' (refers to inanimate objects)

10 *La noo nawan ti'an*
NEG exist breath already

'There is no longer any breath/life force' (refers to a dead person or animal)

---

4   *Nia*, the Tetun third person singular pronoun, is not marked for gender. For simplicity and brevity, I only gloss it in English with the male pronoun he/him.

5   This sentence is technically composed of a subject and a nonverbal predicate.

6   This phrase is also used to mean a *liurai* ('king') has died, in the special Tetun register used for talking to/about nobles. The normal phrase used when someone dies, *Nia nawan kotu*, is considered too impolite for talking about nobles.

7   Similar to the term *putus nafas* used in the local variety of Malay.

The link between 'breath' and 'life force' in these Tetun phrases reflects the association between breath and life—an association common in many languages, including English. But, as the phrases about increasing and decreasing anger suggest, in Tetun there is also a close association between the physical state of a person's breathing and the state of his/her emotional *and* social experience. *Nawan sa'e* ('breath ascends') is a multidimensional term that simultaneously implies the physiological experience of rapid breathing, the emotional experience of anger and the social experience of troubled relationships.

1.2 *Ibun* ('mouth')

11	*Nia ibu wa-waan* He mouth DUP-open	'He is amazed/astonished/agape'
12	*Nia ibun boot* He mouth (n) big	'He talks too much, without anything constructive to say' (seen as a negative characteristic such as grandstanding or bragging)
13	*Nia ibun maweek* He mouth watery	'He frequently gossips'
14	*Nia nakmulis ibun* He twists mouth	'He is mocking someone'
15	*Nia ibun naruk, nunun naruk* He mouth long lips long	'He habitually talks badly about people'
16	*Nia ibun luan* He mouth wide	'He is talkative' (descriptive, not negative)
17	*Lia nia keke ti'an nosi ibun baa ibun* Matter its spread already from mouth go/to mouth	'The news has spread all over the place'
18	*Loke ibun* Open mouth	'Begin to talk' (again, after not talking) 'Resume speaking'
19	*Taka ibun* Close mouth	'Refuse to talk' (descriptive) OR 'Shut up!' (imperative)
20	*Daka ibun* Guard mouth	'Be careful what one says'
21	*Ibun-nanaan* Mouth-tongue	'A spokesperson'
22	*Nanaan karuak* Tongue doubled	'Hypocritical, say one thing, then another thing'

In the parallelisms associated with ritual speech, *ibun* ('mouth') pairs with *nanaan* ('tongue'), and the 'mouth-tongue' pair functions as an idiom for a spokesperson, reflecting the physiological association of mouth with speaking. The other phrases show how Tetun body talk of *ibun* ('mouth') and *nanaan* ('tongue') reveals the person as a social person.

1.3 *Matan* ('eye')

23 *Sia titu ema nodi mata baluk dei*
    They look person with eye one side only

'They do not treat people appropriately' (they look down on people, view them disparagingly, treat people with contempt)

24 *Nia mata katar*
    He eye itch

'He habitually flirts with girls'

25 *Nia mata malaik*
    He eye quick

'His eyes move quickly' (Implication: to look at or flirt with girls)

26 *Nia mata mareek*
    He eye seeing

'He sees things in the invisible world'

As the above examples show, Tetun body talk of eyes reflects ways of seeing and interacting with the external social worlds, including the invisible world.

1.4 *Aten* ('liver')

27 *Ema ne'e, ate kabahat*
    Person this liver stingy/miserly

'This person is very selfish/unsharing/stingy'

28 *Ema ne'e, ate fa'ek*
    Person this liver split

'This person is self-centred and causes social divisions'

29 *Ema ne'e, ate kamoruk*
    Person this liver bitter

'This person acts extremely egotistically and bitter towards other people'

My Tetun consultants were quick to point out that, unlike Indonesian and the local variety of Malay, in Tetun there are only a limited number of body-talk phrases relating to *aten* ('liver') and these phrases always portray characteristics that are viewed very negatively. The liver is considered to be located deeply within a person, both physically and socially. When traits such as stingy, divisive and bitter are associated with a person's liver, these traits are considered 'deep' and almost never changeable.

1.5 *Kakutak* ('brain')

30 *Nia kakutak di'ak*
He brain good
'He thinks/remembers well/He is a good thinker/He is clever'

31 *Nia kakutak kro'at*
He brain sharp
'He thinks/remembers perceptively'

32 *Nia kakutak loos*
He brain straight
'He thinks/remembers correctly/wisely/ accurately' (the metaphor of straight implies a contrast to the negative association of twisted/devious)

33 *Nia kakutak monas*
He brain hard
'He is dull-witted, can't remember and respond appropriately to what people tell him'

34 *Nia kakutak ufak*
He brain dull
'He is stupid' (he should remember and respond but does not)

35 *Nia kakutak ktomak*
He brain complete
'He is very stupid' (his brains are complete or closed—not open to comprehend or respond to new information)

36 *Mak bolu lia rai lia iha kakutak*
REL calls out word store word in brain
A traditional poet is 'one who stores up knowledge in his brain'

37 *Lia nia la tama baa kakutak*
Matter its NEG enter go/to brain
'That matter does not make sense'

The above examples show that *kakutak* ('brains') are conceptualised as the place where information and memories are located. As with other parts of the body, brains can be described in a variety of ways, indexing how a person remembers mentally and how they respond socially to information they are expected to know. Interestingly, *kakutak* ('brains') contrasts with *neon* ('mind'), described below.

1.6 *Neon* ('mind/heart')

Phrases with the noun *neo-n* are numerous. Some of the phrases refer to thinking, pondering or coming to a mental conclusion about something, and can be translated with an English gloss like 'mind'. However, many *neon* phrases could also be considered typical emotion terms, more fitting with an English gloss of 'heart' as the seat of emotions and values. This is a significant point: *neon* is best translated as both 'mind' and 'heart'—the place for both thinking and feeling.

Tetun speakers agree that the *neon* is an internal part of the body (often pointing to their chest), but they also agree that there is no physical organ called *neon*. In butchering a pig, for example, there would be no *neon* to point out, in contrast to the previous phrases used above to describe Tetun body talk.

The root of the noun *neo-n* is *neo*, which can appear as the verb *ha-neo*, meaning to 'reason' or 'think'. *Neon* is where the action of *haneo* occurs.

38	*Ita haneo iha neon* We-inc think in mind/heart	'We think in our mind/heart'
39	*Naree nu'unia, sia naneo na'ak …* See like that they think saying	'Seeing like that, they reasoned/ concluded that …'

Another verb associated with *neon* is *horan*, which focuses on the human ability to 'sense' or 'perceive'. *Horan* can be associated with what could be considered emotional feelings such as fear, good fortune or unpleasantness, but it also can be associated with sensing bodily 'feelings', such as the adverse experiencing of tiredness, thirst and hunger.

40	*Ita horan hatauk iha neon laran* We-inc perceive fear in mind inside	'We perceive/sense/experience fear in our mind/heart'
41	*Ita horan salaen* We-inc perceive thirst	'We experience thirst'/'They are thirsty'
42	*Sia horan sotir, tan moris furak* They perceive good fortune because live pleasant	'They experience good fortune, because they live well off'

Both *haneo* and *horan* are considered characteristics of living human beings.

43	*Oras ita moris, ita hatene haneo* *no horan* When we-inc live we know think and perceive	'When we are alive, we are able to think and perceive'

In contrast to the actions of *haneo no horan* ('thinking and perceiving'), which are associated with the *neon* ('heart/mind'), the action of *hanoin* ('remembering') is associated with the *kakutak* ('brain'). *Hanoin* can include a sense of yearning for someone or for a socially positive event.

44 *Hanoin ba oras emi sei ki'ik*   'Remember when you were still small/
     Remember to when you-pl   young'
     still small

45 *Ita hanoin iha kakutak*   'We remember in our brain'
     We-inc remember in brain

46 *Hanoin di'a-di'ak!*   'Pay attention!'/'Think carefully!'
     Remember DUP-good

Remarkably, the Tetun grammatical particle *hola* ('take', when used as a main verb) collocates with the verb *hanoin* ('remember'), but does not collocate with *haneo* ('think'). As a modifier, *hola* is a perfective verbal marker, indicating that the action of the verb is completed and accomplished.[8] Semantically, it cannot co-occur with *haneo*—constrained by the reality that thinking is a continuing process. Remembering, on the other hand, is an action that can be completed or successfully accomplished.

47 *Mais la nanoin nola, teki-tekis*   'He forgot what he came to do, and just
     nia fila mai   went home' (i.e. he did not successfully
     But NEG remember take   remember)
     suddenly he return come

But **naneo nola* ('*accomplish thinking') is not allowable in any contexts according to the native speakers of Tetun with whom I consulted.

The following phrases show productive uses of *neon*.

48 *Nia neon di'ak*   'He is happy/pleased/in a pleasant state
     He mind good   of mind'

49 *Nia neon loos*   'He is honest, does what is right'
     He mind straight

50 *Nia neon monas*   'He is hard-hearted/not compassionate'
     He mind hard   (when the social situation requires it)

---

8   Readers interested in understanding in greater depth how verbal modifiers such as *hola* can make the verb perfective with an accomplishment sense are referred to Jacob and Grimes (2011), which describes this in-depth for several languages in the West Timor region.

51 *Niakaan neon kbiit*
His mind strong
'He is not fearful or easily swayed
to do wrong'

52 *Nia neon ktodan*
He mind heavy
'He is worried, heavy-hearted, sad,
discouraged'

53 *Nia neon ki'i*
He mind sting
'He is troubled, has many concerns'

54 *Nia neon ki'ik*
He mind small
'He is insecure, petty, not self-confident'

55 *Nia neon boot*
He mind big
'He is happy, justifiably proud, delighted'

56 *Nia neon susar*
He mind difficulty
'He is distressed/troubled' (often because
of loss due to death or threat of loss)

57 *Nia neo ruak*
He mind two
'He is undecided' (cf. English idiom:
'he is of two minds')

58 *Nia neon monu*
He mind fall
'He becomes disappointed, loses
enthusiasm'

59 *Nia neon lakon*
He mind disappear
'He is temporarily startled, unable
to think, panics, freezes'

60 *Nia neon mamar*
He mind soft/pliable
'He is easily persuaded and does what
others say [when he should not]' (children
are said to have pliable minds/hearts)

61 *Nia neon noku*
He mind calm
'He is calm, at peace, cool-headed,
not worried'

62 *Nia neon kmetis*
He mind firm
'He is consistent, does not change his
mind'

63 *Nia neon fatuk*
He mind rock
'He is consistent' (similar to 'firm mind/
heart' above)

64 *Nia neon lalek*
He mind without
'He does things thoughtlessly, without
caring about others, and without thought
to the social consequences'

65 *Nia neon lakon ti'an*
He mind disappear already
'He is confused, doesn't know what
to think or do'

66 *Nia noo neon ti'an*
He exist mind already
'He now has a mind/heart' (said of
a young child when he begins to express
cognition; newborns are considered to not
yet have a mind/heart)

67	*Ami hakbiit siakan neon* We-exc strengthen their mind	'We encourage, strengthen their hearts'
68	*Nia taka neon ti'an* He close mind already	'He refuses to listen to advice or input from others'
69	*Nia loke neon ti'an* He open mind already	'He now responds to advice or input from others'/'He is now receptive to guidance'
70	*Nia neon dodok* He mind shatter	'His heart is broken [from failed romantic love]'
71	*Emi lala'o, emi neon moris, o!* You-pl walk you mind live EMPH	'When you are walking/travelling, you must keep your minds alert!'
72	*Nia namina aan nola ema neon* He oils self take person mind	'He acts in a way to deceive someone'
73	*Keta rai neon baa kro'at no kmeik* Don't store mind go/to sharp and pointed	'Don't put your trust in weapons'
74	*Lia nia, lia neon ain* Matter its matter mind foot	'That matter/story is a secret' (lit.: at the foot of the mind; cf. English concept of 'deepest darkest secret')

Another phrase considered by Tetun speakers to be similar to *lia neon ain* ('a matter at the foot of the mind/heart') is *lia kabu laran* ('a matter inside the stomach'). Things that are inside the stomach, or at the foot of the mind/heart, are secret and not known to others; they are hidden in the corners of our inner being, so to speak.

1.7 *Laran* ('inside')

Laran ('inside') is a common Tetun locational term referring to the inside of objects (such as *iha uma laran*: 'inside the house') and is an important concept used in discourse about emotional and social relations.[9] Tetun

---

9   As such, there are parallels with Fox's (Chapter 5, this volume) description of *dalek* ('inside') for Rote languages. Linguistically, Tetun *lara-n* and Rote *dale-k* are cognate, both deriving from Proto-Malayo-Polynesian **daləm* ('inside') (C. Grimes, personal communication). Tetun *laran* ('inside') also contrasts with *luan* ('outside') in spatial and social ways, similar to Fox's description of Rote *dalek* ('inside') and *de'ak* ('outside'). For example, in Tetun, a contrast in the social origin of children is expressed as *oa kabun laran* ('child from inside the stomach/womb') and *oa kabun luan* ('child from outside the stomach/womb').

speakers agree that, similar to *neon* ('mind/heart'), *laran* is internal to the body (and they often point to their chest), but there is also no physical organ called *laran*.[10] The following examples show that *laran* can best be described as the internal reflection of the social person.

75	*Nia laran moras* He insides sick	'He is offended/sickened/upset by the actions of another person'
76	*Nia laran malirin ti'an* He insides cool already	'He is no longer angry'
77	*Nia laran maluak* He insides wide	'He is hospitable, generous, helpful'
78	*Nia laran di'ak* He insides good	'He does good things, does not hold grievances or seek revenge' (cf. English: 'a good-hearted person, a person of good character', but in Tetun it is always with reference to a relation with another person)

It is insightful to contrast the above concept of *laran di'ak* ('good insides') with the concept of *neon di'ak* ('good mind/heart') already noted above.

48	*Nia neon di'ak* He mind good	'He is happy/pleased/in a pleasant state of mind'

These two phrases—both using the descriptive word *di'ak* ('good')—reveal a significant distinction between the concepts of *neon* and *laran*: talk of *neon* is self-referential, indexing the state of internal experience, while talk of *laran* is social, indexing the internal state of external social relations. The body talk of *laran* ('inside') thus indicates that sociality is not constructed as external to the person. Instead, the state of social relations registers 'inside' the body, inside the person.

The fact that *neon* and *laran* are both considered integral parts of the body/person provides another indication that Tetun personhood includes inner subjective experiences (such as thinking and feeling) embodied in the *neon*, as well as social relations embodied 'inside' the body/person.

---

10 Donohue and Grimes (2008: 148–51) observe comparatively that quite a few Austronesian languages in eastern Indonesia and Timor-Leste have shifted away from the Austronesian words for 'liver' as the seat of emotion and character prevalent in the west (cf. Malay: *hati* '1. liver, 2. seat of emotions and character'), adapting to follow one of the common Papuan strategies for using 'inside, insides' as the seat of emotion and character.

In poetic and more eloquent forms of speech, *neon* and *laran* are paired to express the notion of doing something enthusiastically, wholeheartedly and unreservedly. In other words, doing something with complete engagement of the inner and social self.

79 *Serwisu hodi neon no laran*   'Work wholeheartedly'
Work with mind and insides

80 *Simu hodi neon no laran*   'Accept something wholeheartedly'
Receive with mind and
insides

81 *Sala mak sia nalo la nodi*   'Unintentional wrong'
neon no laran
Wrong which they do NEG
take mind and insides

1.8 Summary of Tetun body talk

It is now possible to compare, contrast and summarise how Tetun descriptive noun phrases of body talk define the body/person in systematic ways:

- *nawan* ('breath/life force'): locus for physical and social-emotional states that reveal life and death; registers the danger of anger and frustration

- *ibun* ('mouth'): locus for oral communication; reflects social-emotional states associated with communication

- *matan* ('eye'): locus for perception; reveals how the body/person perceives and interacts with the (visible and invisible) social world

- *aten* ('liver'): locus for semipermanent negatively valued social traits considered to represent flawed character

- *kakutak* ('brain'): locus for retaining information; indicates how information is processed and remembered as well as appropriate/inappropriate social responses to memories

- *neon* ('mind/heart'): locus for thinking, feeling, sensing; reveals numerous social-emotional states

- *laran* ('inside'): internal reflection of social relations.

The verbs of social-emotional agency

The descriptive *noun phrases* of body talk discussed above describe the condition or state of the body/person and include states that would be clearly classed in English as reflecting 'emotion'. There are also Tetun *verbs* that can be considered 'emotion' words. These verbs do not refer overtly to the body, but are frequently associated with the social-emotional states that are described through the noun phrases of body talk.

I propose that the differences between the ways these Tetun noun phrases and verbs are encoded in the grammar are significant in the conceptualisation of personhood. Descriptive noun phrases of body talk (body-part noun + modifier) disclose the subject as a non-agent *experiencing* bodily states such as cool insides, hard brains, a bitter liver and so on. In contrast, when 'emotion' words occur as active verbs, they denote that the subject is acting as an agent *doing* what I will refer to as 'social-emotional agency'.[11]

This grammatically encoded distinction between *experiencing* and *doing* alludes to the analytical distinction made by Strathern (1988: 273) between the Melanesian 'person' and 'agent'. The person is construed from the vantage point of the relations that constitute him or her; she or he objectifies and is thus revealed in those relations. The agent is construed as the one who acts because of those relationships and is revealed in his or her actions.

The active Tetun verbs I discuss below are best understood as involving an agent acting with another in mind. Translations that reflect English notions of emotion can be seriously misleading. *Kanarak*, for example, is said of a person displaying anger, but to translate *kanarak* as 'to be angry' is misleading, because *kanarak* is not a descriptive phrase indicating a subject is *experiencing* anger; it is an active verb indicating that the subject is *doing* anger—acting on another as a social-emotional agent.

82   *Nia kanarak*   'He acts in anger towards someone/
      He act-in-anger   He scolds someone'

---

11   Grammatically, most of the clause-level examples in this chapter follow the simple pattern of subject + predicate. However, there are two kinds of predicates. The noun phrase predicates are nonverbal predicates where the subject is an undergoer in a BE relationship with the quality or characteristic being described in the noun phrase. In contrast, the verbal predicates reflect a DO relationship with the subject as actor.

A person who does anger in this way can be described with body talk as EXPERIENCING a changed body state:

Nia nawan sa'e He breath ascend/increase	'He is angry' (cf. ex. 01)
83 *Nia la kanarak ona* He NEG act-in-anger already	'He no longer acts in anger towards someone/He no longer scolds someone'

This person can be described with body talk as EXPERIENCING:

Nia nawan tuun He breath descend	'He is no longer angry' (resulting state//'His anger is subsiding' (process) (cf. ex. 04)
84 *Nia kratak* He fiercely-acts-in-anger	'He habitually acts in fierce anger towards someone'

A person who acts in this way can be described with body talk as:

Nia nawan aat He breath bad/evil	'He has numerous negative social characteristics'/'He has serious issues' (cf. ex. 02)

Other Tetun verbs expressing social-emotional agency include:

85 *hasuhu* complain/grumble	'complain to someone'
86 *hirus* express anger/display anger	'display anger at someone over a period of time'
87 *rai hirus* store anger	'store anger towards someone, build up resentment' (waiting for an opportunity to take action/revenge)[12]
88 *tinu* be jealous	'be jealous of someone, act out one's jealousy' (because someone is better than you or has the attention of your spouse/lover)

---

12 This is similar, in many ways, to how Malay *simpan hati* ('hold a grudge'; lit.: store away liver) is used in eastern Indonesia.

Verbs of positively valued social interaction include:

89 *hadomi* 'to love, have affection for someone' (Can also imply pity and compassion)[13]

dodan 'to care for someone [often of lower status]'

haloon 'to plead, hope, wait humbly for someone [of higher status] to care of me/us'

hakara 'to like, be fond of someone'

beer 'to sincerely desire, yearn for someone'

The cause or result of these actions can be reflected in the body talk of *neon* ('mind/heart') and *laran* ('inside'). When something is done wholeheartedly and unreservedly, the phrase *hodi neon no laran* ('with mind/heart and insides') is used, highlighting the efficacy of the actor to act with maximum emotional and social agency.

90 *Nia nadomi sia nodi neon no laran*   'He loves them wholeheartedly'
He love them with mind and insides

The social-emotional regulation of morality

The final term I discuss is *moe*, a term that appeared on my initial list of Tetun emotion terms because it is translated as Indonesian *malu*, which is often glossed in English with terms ranging from 'shame' to 'embarrassment' to 'shy'. Tetun examples of *moe* present similarities with Goddard's (1996: 432–5) analysis of Malay *malu* as a negative and inhibiting reaction to real or potential social disapproval.

Tetun discourse suggests that social life is about knowing when and where to reflect the correct degree of relational restraint or *moe*. Such knowledge inherently concerns social norms and morality. At one end of the spectrum, respect is required and the restraint of *moe* is socially necessary. If a person does not show appropriate restraint in the context of a particular relationship, he or she is scolded:

91 *O ne'e, moe lalek*   'You are without shame/social restraint'
You this shame without

---

13 As such, Tetun *hadomi* shares a similar range of meaning to what Sather (Chapter 3, this volume) describes for Iban concepts of 'love' and Fox (Chapter 5, this volume) describes for the Rote terms *sue* and *sue//lai*.

At the other extreme, there are times when people (particularly young children acting 'shy') are seen to inappropriately show excessive social withdrawal or *moe*. This is termed *moe aat* ('bad/excessive restraint'). In these cases, the person is told:

92 *Lalika moe!*   'Don't be so shy/socially withdrawn!'
    Unnecessary shame

A sense of boldness can be associated with disregarding *moe* at times when most people would be too timid.

93 *Ha'u la kmoe baa*   'I am not too timid/socially restrained
    I NEG ashamed go   to go' (e.g. get involved in a dispute)

A causative prefix can be added to *moe*, resulting in a verb causing someone else to become *moe*.

94 *Lia nia na-moe ami*   'That matter causes us to become *moe*'
    Matter its CAUS-shame   That matter causes us to socially withdraw
    we-exc   That matter embarrasses us

Further evidence that *moe* is a term indicating social and emotional withdrawal can be seen by the addition of the reflexive word *aan*. *Moe aan* can be translated as 'embarrass oneself', but it also connotes social retreat or withdrawing oneself.

95 *Dadi ema madiduk, ha'u*   'Becoming a begging person, I *moe*
    kmoe aan   myself' (which means both of the
    Become person beg   following:
    I shame self
                               '[If I were to] become a beggar, I would
                               socially withdraw myself'

                               '[If I were to] become a beggar, I would
                               embarrass/shame myself [= be ashamed]')

96 *Musti hakneter ema nia, nebee* '[We] must respect that person, so he does
    nia la moe aan   not *moe* himself' (which means both of
    Must respect person that   the following:
    RESULT he NEG shame self
                               'We must respect that person, so he does
                               not socially withdraw himself'

                               'We must give that person his due respect,
                               so he is not shamed')

Conclusion: Where have all the emotion terms gone?

I now return to my initial plan to collect and analyse Tetun emotion terms. The approach was problematic and limiting, because an exclusive focus on emotion did not reveal the broader system underlying Tetun body talk and concepts of the person. The English-centric view of emotion terms as abstract nouns (such as 'happiness', 'anger', 'joy', 'sadness') constructs emotions as feelings distinct from the body. Interestingly, emotion terms in Indonesian—an Austronesian language from the west of Timor—are also frequently expressed as abstract nouns (see Appendix 6.1 for a list of 124 Indonesian emotion terms from Shaver et al. 2001). Less than 10 per cent of the Indonesian emotion terms in this list are based on body-part idioms. In contrast, more than 80 per cent of Tetun terms relating to emotions involve body-part idioms.

In conclusion, Tetun body talk does not encode emotions as abstract nouns or construct emotions as abstract 'feelings'. Rather, inner subject experiences (emotions as well as thoughts, memories and sociality) are embodied and disclosed through body talk by describing the condition manifested or associated with a part of the body. In contrast to the noun phrases of body talk are active verbs grammatically asserting social-emotional agency: the actor acting on and in relation to another. An agent is not construed as experiencing the emotion of anger, but as enacting anger in relation to another. And, as agents act, their social-emotional states are read from their bodies.

References

Bugenhagen, Robert D. 1990. 'Experiential constructions in Mangap-Mbula'. *Australian Journal of Linguistics* 10(2): 183–215. doi.org/10.1080/07268609008599441.

Donohue, Mark and Charles E. Grimes. 2008. 'Yet more on the position of the languages of eastern Indonesia and East Timor'. *Oceanic Linguistics* 47(1): 114–58. doi.org/10.1353/ol.0.0008.

Goddard, Cliff. 1996. 'The "social emotions" of Malay (Bahasa Melayu)'. *Ethos* 24(3): 426–64. doi.org/10.1525/eth.1996.24.3.02a00020.

Grimes, Barbara Dix. 2010. 'With our hearts and minds: Exploring Tetun emotion terms'. Paper presented to Sixth East Nusantara Conference, Unit Bahasa & Budaya, Kupang, Indonesia, 5–7 August.

Hemer, Susan R. 2013. *Tracing the Melanesian Person: Emotions and relationships in Lihir*. Adelaide: University of Adelaide Press. doi.org/10.20851/lihir.

Jacob, June and Charles E. Grimes. 2011. 'Aspect and directionality in Kupang Malay serial verb constructions: Calquing on the grammars of substrate languages'. In Claire Lefebvre (ed.) *Creoles, Their Substrates, and Language Typology*, pp. 337–66. Typological Studies in Language 95. Amsterdam: John Benjamins. doi.org/10.1075/tsl.95.20jac.

Kratochvil, František and Benediktus Delpada. 2012. 'Emotion and cognition predicates in Abui'. Presentation to Current Trends of Linguistic Research of Indigenous Languages in Indonesia International Workshop, Research Institute for Languages and Cultures of Asia and Africa, Tokyo University of Foreign Studies, Tokyo, 18 February.

LeVine, Robert A. (ed.). 2010. *Psychological Anthropology: A reader on self in culture*. Malden, MA: Wiley-Blackwell.

Levy, Robert I. 1983. 'Introduction: Self and emotion'. *Ethos* 11(3): 128–34. doi.org/10.1525/eth.1983.11.3.02a00020.

Lutz, Catherine A. 1982. 'The domain of emotion words on Ifaluk'. *American Ethnologist* 9(1): 113–28. doi.org/10.1525/ae.1982.9.1.02a00070.

Lutz, Catherine A. 1989. *Unnatural Emotions: Everyday sentiments on a Micronesian atoll and their challenge to Western theory*. Chicago: University of Chicago Press.

Lutz, Catherine A. and Geoffrey M. White. 1986. 'The anthropology of emotions'. *Annual Review of Anthropology* 15: 405–36. doi.org/10.1146/annurev.an.15.100186.002201.

McElhanon, Kenneth A. 1977. 'Idiomaticity in a Papuan (non-Austronesian) language'. *Kivung* 8(2): 103–44.

Myers, Fred R. 1979. 'Emotions and the self: A theory of personhood and political order among Pintupi Aborigines'. *Ethos* 7: 334–70. doi.org/10.1525/eth.1979.7.4.02a00030.

Senft, Gunter. 1998. 'Body and mind in the Trobriand Islands'. *Ethos* 26(1): 73–104. doi.org/10.1525/eth.1998.26.1.73.

Shaver, Phillip R., Upekkha Murdaya and R. Chris Fraley. 2001. 'Structure of the Indonesian emotion lexicon'. *Asian Journal of Social Psychology* 4: 201–24. doi.org/10.1111/1467-839X.00086.

Strathern, Andrew. 1975. 'Why is shame on the skin?' *Ethnology* 14(4): 347–56. doi.org/10.2307/3773236.

Strathern, Marilyn. 1988. *The Gender of the Gift: Problems with women and problems with society in Melanesia.* Berkeley, CA: University of California Press. doi.org/10.1525/california/9780520064232.001.0001.

Unit Bahasa dan Budaya. 2013. *Maromak Manfatin: Maromak Mamenon Foun no Lia Uluk Fohon hosi Maromak Mamenon Tuan [God's Word: New Testament and Genesis].* Kupang: Unit Bahasa dan Budaya.

van Klinken, Catharina. 1999. *A Grammar of the Fehan Dialect of Tetun, an Austronesian Language of West Timor.* Pacific Linguistics C-155. Canberra: The Australian National University.

White, Geoffrey M. 2010. 'Moral discourse and the rhetoric of emotion'. In Robert A. LeVine (ed.) *Psychological Anthropology: A reader on self in culture*, pp. 68–82. Malden, MA: Wiley-Blackwell.

Williams-van Klinken, Catharina. 2007. 'Is he hot-blooded or hot inside? Expression of emotion and character in Tetun Dili'. Paper presented to Fifth East Nusantara Conference, University of Nusa Cendana, Kupang, Indonesia, 1–3 August.

Appendix 6.1: List of 124 Indonesian emotion words

aman	calmness, safety, security
asik	absorption, fascination, excitement
asmara	romantic love
bahagia	happiness, wellbeing
bangga	feeling rightfully proud of

benci	hatred, extreme dislike, animosity
berahi	sexual desire, lust, infatuation
berang	anger, fury, ire
berani	boldness, courageousness
berat hati	sadness (lit.: heavy-heartedness)
berbesar	feeling expanded with pride
berdebar	heart palpitation, heart flutter
berdengki	hatred, envy
bergaira	passion, arousal, enthusiasm
besar hati	pride, elation
bimbang	worry, hesitation, vacillation, indecision
bingung	confusion; feeling panicky, perplexed, disoriented
bosan	boredom; feeling tired of, sick of
cemas	worry; feeling disturbed, anxious
cemburu	jealousy, envy, dissatisfaction
ceria	cheerfulness, brightness, purity
cinta	love, affection
curiga	suspicion, distrust
damai	peacefulness, tranquillity
demen	liking, fondness for
dendam	vengeance, bearing a grudge, animosity, rancour
dengki	envy, spite
dongkol	resentment, acrimony; feeling irked, vexed
duka	grief, sorrow, misery
dukacita	profound sorrow, heartache, grief
edan kesmaran	being madly in love, infatuated, smitten
emosi	negative emotion, feeling seized by emotion
frustrasi	feeling blocked, frustration
gairah	passion, strong desire
galau	confusion, upset
gelisah	nervousness, restlessness, uneasiness, worry, concern
gemas	annoyance, irritation (held back)

gembira	gaiety, happiness, cheerfulness, bounciness, enthusiasm
gentar	fearful trembling
geram	being infuriated, enraged (growling)
getar hati	feeling moved (in the heart)
girang	elation, glee, delighted
gregetan	feeling tense from restraining pent-up emotions
gundah	anxiety, restlessness
gusar	anxiety, restlessness, agitation, upset
haru	feeling affected, moved, touched, emotional
hasrat	ardour, passion, longing, desire
histeris	feeling hysterically upset
iba	compassion, pity; feeling moved, touched
ikhlas	sincere devotion, complete conviction, full preparedness
ingin	desire, longing
iri	envious resentment
jengkel	vexation, annoyance, irritation
jenuh	feeling surfeited, fed up, sick and tired
kagum	amazed admiration, respect
kalap	beside oneself with anger, possessed, bewitched
kalut	confusion, disturbance, inner chaos
kangen	confusion, disturbance, inner chaos
kasih	affection, love, compassion
kasihan	pity, merciful compassion
kawatir	fear, apprehension, worry
kebat-kebit	nervousness, restlessness, agitation
kecemasan	anxiety, worry, concern, apprehension
kecil hati	hurt, grief, faint-heartedness, discouragement
keharuan	feeling moved emotionally, affected, touched
kemesraan	intimacy, absorption, love
kepingin	desire, eagerness for

kepuasan	satisfaction, contentment
kesal	feeling peeved, fed up, piqued, cross
lega	relaxation, relief
malu	shame, disgrace, mortification
mangkel	annoyance, irritation
marah	wrath, anger, ire, fury
mesra	feeling intimately fused, very close
muak	loathing, revulsion, repugnance
murka	anger, fury, feeling incensed
murung	melancholy, depression, gloom
naik darah	rising anger, becoming hot-headed
naik pitam	becoming enraged, having a fit
ngambek	pouting, anger, sulkiness
panas hati	edginess; quickness to anger, envy or jealousy
patah hati	feeling discouraged, heartbroken
pedih hati	mortification, grief, pain (lit.: stinging, smarting heart)
penyesalan	sorrow, regret, remorse
perasaan	feeling, sentiment
pilu	sadness, heartache, compassion
prihatin	concern, apprehension
puas	satisfaction, complacency
putus asa	hopelessness, being dispirited, disconsolation
putus harapan	hopelessness, despondency, despair
remuk hati	feeling crushed, broken-hearted
rendah hati	humility, modesty
riang	hilarity, gleefulness, dizziness
rindu	yearning, homesickness
risau	restlessness, nervousness, worry
sabar	patience, patient persistence, tolerance, calmness
sakit hati	pain (lit.: hurt heart), displeasure, bitterness

sayang	caring, love (also a term of endearment: sweetie, darling)
sebal	resentment, vexation
sedih	sadness, distress, sorrow, misery
senang	happiness, contentment, liking
sendu	sadness, dejection, melancholy
senewen	nervousness, having a nervous fit
sesal	regret, remorse, sorrow, repentance
setia	loyalty, faithfulness, satisfaction, solidarity
simpati	sympathy
suka	liking, fondness for, enjoyment
sukacita	happiness, joy, merriment
sukaria	happiness, pleasure, delight, celebration
tabah	determination, persistence, steadfastness
takut	fear, apprehension, dread
tenteram	feeling settled, quieted, reassured
terangsang	excitement, stimulation, arousal, titillation
terbuai	blissful oblivion, rapture
terkesiap	being startled, captivated; having one's attention grabbed
terpesona	feeling spellbound, enchanted
terpikat	feeling charmed; attraction, fascination
tersentuh	feeling touched, moved
tersingung	feeling offended, bitter
tertarik	attraction, interest
tinggi hati	conceit, arrogance
tulus	honesty, openness, sincerity, straightforwardness
waswas	doubt, anxiety, suspicion, wariness
yakin	certainty, conviction, confidence

Source: Indonesian data from Shaver et al. (2001).

7

Standing tall: Posture, ethics and emotions in Dobu

Susanne Kuehling

The language of emotions can be revealing, especially when words and expressions relate directly to body imagery. In this chapter, the body is examined as a site of moral judgements. Moral conduct, when discursively framed in body imagery, maps out an individual's options of acting and, perhaps more clearly among Austronesians, leads to almost permanent self-awareness. I argue in this chapter that 'emotion words'— spatial expressions of internal processes—are not merely conventional metaphors, but also deeply embedded in local ethics, sense of place and the concept of personhood. For an emotional geography among Austronesians, language is a key (Bellwood et al. 1995: 3; Fox 1995: 215). Linguistic analysis of features such as the common prefixation of emotion words as an Austronesian strategy (body + emotion) may be a yielding path (Huang 2002), but a large body of data is required for the diverse array of Austronesian-speaking societies. According to Pawley, even within the subgroup of Proto-Oceanic there are 'at least five distinct cognate sets … meaning something like "person, human being"' (1985: 93). Austronesians share the experience of being islanders and sailors—a world view based on island experience. The 'noble' posture and the friendliness of Pacific Islanders are legendary, noted by visitors since the early European explorers and missionaries.

As an ethnographic field of study, emotions are challenging, as we too easily assume that, as humans, we all feel the same way and therefore understand our inner states similarly. Seemingly universal emotion words are often constructed as if a sensation, thought or feeling were localised at a specific spot inside the human body. English speakers, for example, construct the heart as the locus for love and the head as the place of thought. While widespread and seemingly intuitive, the clustering of 'inner states' differs between societies, as the mapping of inner states reflects social principles and patterns that are complexly tied to local ontologies. As ideological practices, emotion states are used in moral discourse and deserve more attention (Lutz 1988: 10). Yet so far, as Hereniko critiques, academic texts express our privilege of written sources over performance in Pacific cultures. The messages conveyed through body language:

> are not overt, and often go unnoticed by academics, who are more adept at reading between the lines on a page than reading the message implicit in the kinds of costumes being worn, the way space is negotiated, the arrangement of dancers, the hand, feet, and facial movements, and other elements of performance that embody a culture's aesthetics and values. (Hereniko 2000: 88)

Based on linguistic data, I suggest that the Austronesian concept of personhood includes a private, 'inside' location where thoughts and feelings are experienced and processed, stored and selectively displayed. Exactly where this is located is open to interpretation and varies even between neighbouring Austronesian societies. Tsou speakers claim to locate knowledge in the ear, as Huang reports (2002: 173). Dobu Islanders locate their thinking/feeling (*nua*) deep inside themselves. To these people, as for other Austronesians, there is no clear distinction between emotions and thought processes: *nua* is the secret area where spells and strategies, feelings, fantasies and memories are located. This 'inside' is further compartmentalised in Dobu, where anger and love are, respectively, constructed as located in the stomach (*gamwa*) and liver (*ate*). It is regarded as virtuous to self-censor one's *nua*, and individuals strive to appear as 'good' persons in spite of their deeper feelings/thoughts. Generally, a wise person keeps these inside locations under vigilant control (Kuehling 2005; Weiner 1984). Such self-discipline is expressed both verbally and literally in a straight posture. Being happy—literally having a straight back—emplaces an emotion as a sociolinguistic pointer of virtue. People control their posture, as they know that failure to keep a straight back is perceived as laziness (a bent back). Overexcitement, a negatively classified feeling, is linguistically constructed as having an overly straight spine, and only the middle ground—a nicely straight back—comes across as evidence of a happy, industrious, well-rounded person.

My data stem from long-term fieldwork and are grounded in intersubjective relationships based on mutual friendship and/or constructed kinship with Dobu Islanders of south-eastern Papua New Guinea. What I here gloss as happiness and laziness are based on the dictionaries (Dixon n.d.: 82; Lithgow 1984: 20) and established use of language by English-speaking islanders. These categories will be discussed in detail here, as they allow us to demonstrate how the corresponding posture can be read as a moral statement. Dobu Islanders keep their back straight and smile not only as a result of feeling happy, but also as a way to perform this positively valued mixture of sentiments to be acknowledged as a 'happy person' by others (and, implicitly, not be regarded as 'lazy' or 'overexcited'). A (German) physiotherapist once told me that this was the right posture to feel proud and free, 'like a queen'. While this may well be an effect of this posture, Dobu Islanders have no intention to 'feel like a queen'. Their upright posture and friendly smile have wider implications than personal feelings, and this may well be specific to an Austronesian way of being in the world, as I will demonstrate here. I will also pay attention to the more subtle and subjective forms of communication, such as body language, to push my sociolinguistic entry point to the moral dimension of happiness and laziness and, ultimately, to ponder how this relates to personhood. Of course, not everyone follows ethical principles in the same way, as Dernbach has pointed out (2005: 333–4), but once I was fluent in the vernacular, I believe I picked up the views and, after a year of residence, shared the feelings and 'understood' some of the islanders in personal, empathetic ways. Here is an example of my learning process:

> Mary had a huge sore on her leg, looking as if a generous tablespoon of strawberry jam had been spread on her thigh. It was so big that the largest band aid was way too small. My British colleague, who pitied the young woman, asked me for gauze, explaining that the wound needed to be at least covered to keep the flies and dust out. Since I had not brought any supplies, he wandered off to look elsewhere, leaving me with Sandra, the in-law from Chimbu who had a somewhat outsider's point of view and was refreshingly open when describing sensitive topics. Sandra smiled and showed me a circular scar on her own thigh, explaining that this had been a sore just like Mary's, and that it took two days to heal completely when her period of punishment was deemed over by the senior villagers. 'They spoke over water, poured it over the sore, already it began

to heal', Sandra remembered. Mary, she added, had not been sufficiently cooperative in the preparations of the feast (that the British colleague and I were observing in Miadeba, Normanby Island, in December 1992). 'She just spent her time in her garden with her husband while we were all working so hard ... this is where the sore comes from and this is why we don't feel sorry for her'. Clearly, at that time, I did not share Sandra's way of looking at pain, but while I did feel sorry for Mary, I had not thought of dressing the wound, knowing well that there are many local ways of doing so if desired, and only providing my very limited medical services when directly asked. The conversation brought the lesson home explicitly—people may choose to show 'no pain' in spite of a gaping wound, and Mary was actually repenting, improving her moral standing, as she completed her chores with an eager posture in spite of the flies eating at her flesh. (Fieldnotes, 17 November 1992; names changed)

A person is an island in a sea of people

Recently, scholars have argued for place-based identities of Austronesians (see Fox 1997a, 1997b)—for example, in Vanuatu (Bolton 1999; Hess 2009), engaging in a debate on shared identities or 'dividual' personhood (Macintyre 1995; Mosko 2009; Strathern 1988). My discussion builds on the understanding that persons and places are deeply linked. Spatial metaphors are at the junction of self-experience and self-expression: as persons, Austronesians may experience themselves in a more connected ('dividual') way, as members of groups and representatives for their lineage in time and space, yet there can be no doubt that, at the end of the day, we feel the pain of our individual body and eventually will suffer its death.

Epeli Hau'ofa has argued that the islands of Oceania should be seen as linked, not separated, by the ocean. In a similar way, I propose, persons can be seen as islands, connected by the environment but separated by individual desires and strategies that are located inside each body. This linguistic geography of the person, I believe, leads to a layered model of intimacy—connected through the environment of water, air and ground—and may serve as an illustration while positioning my argument in a larger framework and, perhaps, within Austronesian social memory and protolanguage (see Ross et al. 2003: 88).

Imagine yourself on a canoe, slowly approaching a Pacific island. Your first impression speaks to the prosperity and fertility of a place. You see a beach or mangroves, the canopy of trees, smoke from a settlement. The 'skin' of an island, just like the skin of a person, allows a surface reckoning.

The outsider's gaze provides knowledge about season and surrounding islands, plants and architecture, just as a view of a person's skin at first encounter, their shape, flesh and hair, can reveal information about their age, health and wealth. This first impression is often misleading: an island may look like paradise or a person may appear nice, but a closer look reveals both agreeable and unpleasant aspects.

Arriving on the beach, entering a village, a clearer, morally painted picture emerges. Are the people content, are they hardworking, well behaved and generous? Is this a 'good' place (see Kahn 1996)? Being part of village life provides insights into the moral standing of individuals, glimpses of the hidden inside in spite of all efforts to keep a 'straight face'—as English speakers would say. Dobu speakers locate this effort in the back as the locus for performance as a self-disciplined, hardworking, motivated, moral person, as, like facial expressions, the back can be manipulated. I have seen feverish people sitting on their verandah all day, without back support, with a straight spine. Friends who had stayed up all night never displayed their tiredness when asked to help with a chore; people who had asked me for painkillers because of severe back pain still maintained a straight posture as we walked to pick up some pills. To control one's posture, to keep a straight back, appears to be an indication of personal qualities: a dignified, calm, hardworking, helpful person is the ideal. Jason Throop's work on pain in Yap is comparable with the case on Dobu: controlling pain is evidence of being a 'good' person. Women giving birth without a sound, under their house, are exemplary, as they do not attract envious spirits, witches, confused ghosts or other airborne creatures of the night. The settlement, like the posture of a person, is a public stage where social relations and personal virtues are performed.

Moving any further than the village is regarded as impolite and intrusive, because the inside of houses (Fox 1997a; Rensel and Rodman 1997) and the central region of an island are private spaces in many Austronesian societies. The English metaphors of the 'heart' of an island and as the locus of emotion almost catch the Austronesian construction of an intimate 'inside' place in the body, where thinking and feeling happen. Closed to the outsider, this 'inside' is opaque, not publicly accessible, yet always in danger of being violated. Trespassing could result in death, as island space may be defended by an enraged landowner who swings a machete, and sorcery practices involve intruding in a victim's 'inside'. Going to the inside of an island is only acceptable when permission to trespass is granted, as the bush, gardens and graveyards are private spaces. Places and persons are protected by ethical principles of privacy. Dobu people are required to 'stay at home and mind their own business', to refrain from 'useless wandering' (*miabaula*) and to work for others in a tireless fashion (*gwaunua*). The ethic of 'self-discipline' (*alamai'ita*, lit.: 'to carry a burden tightly and continuously') enjoins that inner feelings are kept to oneself, no matter whether they are valued negatively—such as greed, lust, anger, pride, envy, shame—or positively—such as joy, sympathy or the feeling of being 'just right and filled up with nice food' (see Kuehling 2005: 33–6; see also Edoni 1989). Many spatial metaphors draw an image of a centre with some mobility that requires regulating attention; thinking/feeling (*nua*) may, for example, be 'descending' to refer to humbleness (*nuamwauta*), it may be 'climbing up' when someone is boastful (*nuatue*), 'heavy' from worries (*nuamwau*), 'calm and quiet' when someone is at peace (*nuasiwalowa*), 'wandering aimlessly' when someone is confused (*nua'iyowana*) or it may be 'returning like a new plant from a seed' (Edoni 1989: 37) when a person is in a retrospective mood (*nua'ila*). It is impolite in most situations to mention inner feelings, just as it is regarded as overly inquisitive to ask about the inside of a house or about details of someone's garden. To be openly angry, yelling at an adult or even banging one's fist on a verandah, is offensive. 'My inside is out [*nuagu i out*], my liver is exploding [*ategu i pisali*]!' snarled the old man when he learned that his lavish gift assembly was inappropriate for the occasion of the feast that was performed. Trying to conceal one's inside, even when angry, leads some people to wear sunglasses when they plan a harangue (which is rare and perceived as embarrassing by everybody concerned). One's inside, in Dobu, tries to get out of its opacity and live out antisocial desires. Feelings such as anger, greed, envy, pain or the urge to just let go, relax one's back and stay away from tiresome work need to be kept under tight control as it is not socially acceptable to be intrusive, whining or lazy (*gwautoyasa*, lit.: 'to have a bent back').

Figure 7.1 distinguishes the three layers of intimacy proposed here: the beach of an island likened to the skin as the outward representation of the person, the inside of an island as a private space likened to the thinking/feeling located as *nua* inside a body and the intermediate zone of village life, where virtues and vices are negotiated and form the moral base of daily life in a small community. In Dobu imagery, this intermediate dimension is linked to the back, which is controlled by a person's willpower unless it slips out of attention, contributing to a mixed performance that is negotiated in terms of 'happiness' and 'laziness', a 'straight' and a 'bent' back. This image is encoded in gift exchanges and moral judgement, bridging wants and deeds.

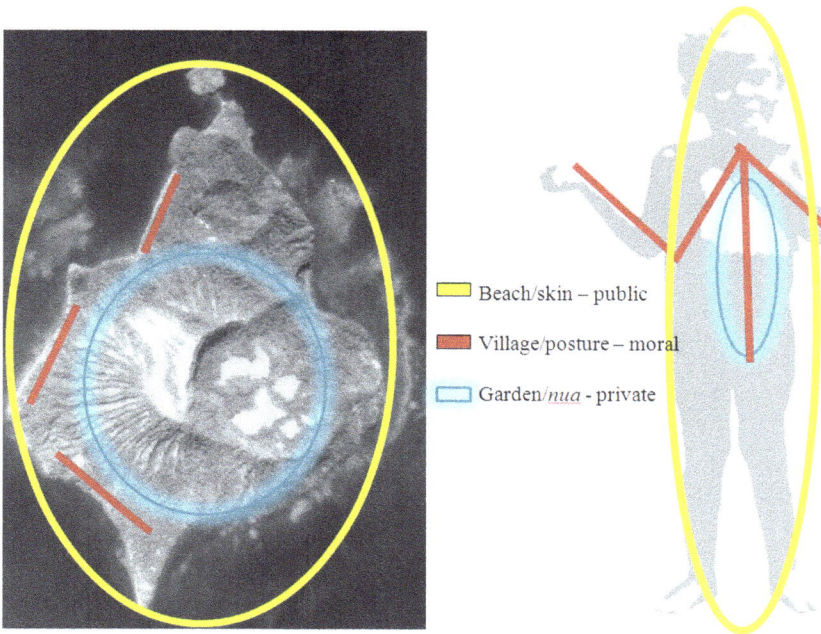

Figure 7.1 Mapping intimacy

Source: Author's figure, overlaid on aerial image from the National Mapping Bureau of Papua New Guinea.

Don't slouch! Be happy!

Restricted spatially and interpersonally, everyday life happens at very few places and around a small number of people, creating strong social pressure to conform and to appear as 'good', hardworking and generous. Annette Weiner's description of Trobriand Islanders' need to protect their 'inside' compares with the Dobu construction, including a general notion that 'truth is being created anew in the telling or the giving' (1984: 163). I have argued elsewhere that the atmosphere of surveillance in a Dobuan village is not too different to that in the Panopticon—British architect Jeremy Bentham's famous model prison (Kuehling 2005: 138–42). The intensity of constant social control is particularly obvious when individuals are expected to share what they wish to keep for themselves, as Dobu ethics favour an egalitarian distribution of wealth (so that 'everybody can have a straight back'). The vernacular term for happiness, *gwauso'ala*, literally means that the 'back' (*gwau*) can 'carry' (*ala*) its weight and keep the body straight. Linguistically, the term is constructed with an alienable possessive prefix—*ma igu gwauso'ala* ('with my happiness')—suggesting the partly external nature of this feeling. It can also be used as a verb—*i gwauso'ala* ('he/she is happy')—as often found in stories.

The back is part of a number of emotion terms serving as a metaphor for upright posture (suggesting a strong, happy or excited feeling) or for a bent and weak posture (suggesting a lazy, bored or listless state). I have elsewhere discussed the use of body parts in emotion words (Kuehling 2005: 38).

Table 7.1 Posture and emotion

Emotion word	Literal meaning	'Translation'
gwauso'ala	back-carry	happy, satisfied, relieved, gay, glad
gwaunua	back-thinking/feeling	hardworking
gwau'a'ala	back-very-straight	excited
gwaugu'itoyase, also *guitoyasa, gwautoyasa*	my back is stiff	lazy, unmotivated, bored, listless

Note: See also Kuehling (2005: 287) As a metaphor, the back (*gwau*) is constructed as the site where the inside becomes visible during episodes of hard work (*gwaunua*, lit.: 'back-inside'). The spine gives away hidden feelings and thoughts when people interpret one another's posture. A person stands either 'straight' (*gwauso'ala, gwau'ala*) or 'bent over' (*gwautoyasa*). The former is an expression of eagerness to work hard (*gwaunua*), of happiness and communality, while the latter stands for the opposite: laziness, exhaustion, sickness and, ultimately, selfishness. The posture of a person, hence, is a moral statement, leading people to control the way they walk and sit and to critically observe how others carry themselves. Women—used to carrying heavy loads on their heads—are known to walk with a straight back without showing signs of exhaustion as they hold a toddler on their hip and climb the muddy paths to the garden for their daily work. No woman complains about the pain, just as they take pride in giving birth silently. Likewise, men who deliver a large bundle of firewood will modestly smile when praised for their *alamai'ita* ('self-discipline'), pretending that it was not painful to bring those logs from a distant garden. A good person is happy, not lazy; this implies holding the spine straight and moving energetically.

The social emotion of happiness, expressed as a matter of posture, deserves more attention and context. To be happy, relaxed and generally at ease is a desired emotional state to Dobu Islanders (as for all humans, I believe). Sadly, it seems so hard to reach such balance, and Dobu Islanders certainly do not live in a state of harmony. Their happiness is the hard-earned result of self-discipline, generosity, respect and labour. I have argued that, in Dobu society, this state can only be achieved 'when the balance between giving and keeping is maintained' (Kuehling 2005: 70). A happy person is strong, stands straight in a dignified manner and works hard—no wonder 'happiness' (*gwauso'ala*) is a welcome character trait. Those happy moments during fieldwork, when I sat with friends and shared a sense of ease and relaxation, are the basis of the following description of the imagery of happiness to the islanders with whom I lived from 1992 to 1994 and whom I keep visiting.

In daily life, happiness arises from various pleasures, such as sensual experiences of the environment. Basking in the morning sun (*eyala*) is a delightful way to shake off the coldness of the night. Other pleasures include sitting in a slight breeze on a hot day (*siwalowa*), seeing the full moon lighting up the hamlet, feeling a gentle rain after the planting of the yams, seeing a magnificent sunrise after a long night of feasting, or tasting a fresh mango and feeling its juice all over one's face and hands. In terms of social life, images of joyful family life come to mind, of parents or peers sitting and sharing food and betel nuts with their children, sending them on little missions to the neighbours or into the kitchen, watching the progress of their babies and telling stories about everyday incidents. Being at ease includes a 'good conscience' (*a- lotona bobo'a-*; in the sense of 'good behaviour': *i- bubuna bobo'a-*) or a 'good name' (*i- ale bobo'a-*). A happy person is healthy, has enough food and objects of wealth and a manageable number of reliable relatives, friends and exchange partners.

Happiness and friendship can be heard from a distance at times—for example, when expressed by a certain way of laughing together that ends with an exclamation of '*hai*' in a higher pitch. This is called *losaila* (lit.: 'to tie it up' or 'to wind it up'). Happiness in women is associated with the sound of cheerful chatter, with *losaila* exclamations; it is characteristic of youths on the beach at sunset or hamlet sisters on a shaded platform watching their toddlers play. Small gifts, such as betel nuts, tobacco and assistance in daily chores, are evidence of a person's ability to 'keep a straight back', to be happy and industrious yet humble and respectful. Such happiness is framed by the absence (or denial) of such internal states as anger, shame, lust, pain, hunger, greed or pride (Kuehling 2005: 90). Apart from *losaila*, happiness is not displayed conspicuously; as such, 'showing off' is despised as a sign of weakness and lack of self-discipline. Happiness is recognised as an emotion, attitude, character trait and social skill; it is a telling sign that a person adheres to the principal ethics. A person who bears no grudges when asked for a small gift, who is willing to form friendships, is praised as *oboboma alena*—a genuinely generous character. A happy person can suffer bodily pain and frustrations, share food and remain affable while hungry—all reasons to praise his or her *alamai'ita* ('self-discipline'). A young, happy person is in a better position to cultivate strong ties with senior people by giving them 'small gifts' with a happy face and an appropriately friendly and obedient demeanour when interacting with them. This kind of conduct shows 'respect'; a straight back never implies a towering attitude, but an energetic eagerness and joyful approach to the tasks at hand.

The back should not be too straight, however, as an overly proud performance is looked down on as 'showing off' (*mokolowai* or *gagasa*). To be openly excited (*gwau'a'ala*) is evidence of a poorly restricted mind that rises too high (*nua'tue*). Wearing bright colours, dancing and singing out of context, shouting and being too talkative are discouraged in children at an early age—simultaneously with their training to bend forward and mutter 'excuse me' or *ya mai* ('I am coming') when passing other people at close distance. Little girls learn to balance a basket on their heads and walk confidently with a straight posture; little boys are encouraged to carry burdens on their shoulder—both genders are praised when they show no pain or fatigue (*Oh, alamai'ita!*: 'Oh, self-discipline!').

Life can be exhausting on small tropical islands, when the humidity is high and the sun burns mercilessly or when it rains and the paths are slippery and people feel cold. Endemic malaria and other diseases cause weakness and death, medicine is often unavailable or ineffective and household chores are plentiful in a world without plumbing and electricity. Sickness of the body, a 'heavy inside' (*nuamwau*) due to conflicts, as well as sorcery-induced debilitation, are normal elements of daily life that should be kept 'inside'. I was certainly fooled by the effortless-seeming work of the women when I was on the island. Later, with my own toddler, I returned to Dobu and complained to my friends that it looked a lot easier when they were parenting. Every time I said this, the proud answer of the mothers from Dobu was the same: 'It is hard work to raise a child, but we don't show it.' When I was tired from running after my 20-month-old son and complained about it, I was performing a very *dimdim* ('Western') way of responding to the challenges of motherhood, but my friends gracefully overlooked my blunder.

The only occasions when I experienced laziness as an accepted and publicly displayed state were during mourning, when receiving a large gift or as a result of the social syndrome called *gwasa* (or *nadiwala*). *Gwasa* (a 'social hangover') is caused by the departure of an overnight visitor or family member. A *gwasa* infestation at a place makes it unsafe to do any physical work and one can often see villagers sitting idly on their platforms, complaining about so-and-so who gave them this *gwasa* 'while we are in the middle of the [gardening] season'. Having *gwasa* can be constructed as 'work', as suffering because of hospitality, but other reasons for idleness mirror selfishness. I remember mentioning that I was feeling sick (*le'oasa*), but received the answer that I was in fact down with '*gwasa*. We all have it' (see below). Feeling admittedly lazy is acceptable only as a comment between friends while on some tiresome project, not as an explanation for days of sleep.

Emotions of exchange: Staging one's back

Work becomes most intense when mortuary ritual needs to be performed, when visitors are hosted or other exchange events (marriage, apologetic gifts, *kula* or gift exchange) take place. Raw yams of high quality (*bebai*), protein (*anina*), pork (*bawe*) and various gifts of lower value are assembled, paraded, set on the ground, thrown down from a platform or publicly prepared and served with decorum. Being a giver during these occasions is licence to be louder and bolder than usual, standing taller and more assertive than at any other time. The act of giving is a register of dominance, while the role of the receiver is characterised by a lower posture, which includes a bent spine and a low voice. A previous gift can legitimise even anger and, during mortuary feasting, when gifts are thrown down from a high platform to a crowd during *'une*, it may be that a large gift comes with a humiliating speech (see Kuehling 2005: Ch. 8).

An embarrassed-looking receiver of a gift may well be scheming about how to assemble a counter gift that will provide an opportunity for an equally bossy response. These roles require self-discipline and temporarily overrule the display of individual virtue; an industrious person with a sunny disposition (and a straight spine) will nevertheless display a body language of lower status when receiving a valuable gift. Since public gift-giving is usually performed by senior men (after counselling by the senior women in most cases I witnessed), it is interesting to observe how a big man bends over, seemingly under the shame and obligation that the act of receiving involves. In everyday life, respectful bending is practised when walking past senior people, as a lower status demands a lower posture and it is seen as impolite to tower over or walk between people who are talking with one another. Respectful bending, unlike lazy bending of the spine, speaks to a humble personality and is valued positively.

While an opportunity to display virtue, exchange rituals and events are also the time to show vice. During the preparation of a feast, as well as the routine of everyday life, there is almost always someone who is to blame for being lazy, slow, disobedient, adulterous and generally not eager to cooperate. The islanders often use the back for their rhetoric strategies—a convenient point of reference that is freely accessible for all to see. There are many ways to describe the strategies of exchange and the ethical principle of hard work ('back-mind', *gwaunua*; more generally, *paisewa*), but one common way is to say that a person is lazy (*gwautoyasa*) or happy (*gwausoala*) (see Kuehling 2017a: 219).

In the confidential negotiations of *kula* exchange, the term *gwauso'ala* is frequently used: 'if you make me happy today, I will make you happy later and we will both be happier than before' (Kuehling 2005: 210 ff.). The Trobriand writer and businessman John Kasaipwalova, following the tradition of sweet-talking an audience by evoking an image of straight spines and bright smiles, called the *kula* a 'development corporation' to 'further human happiness' (1974: 454; Kuehling 2005: 174; 2017b: 203). *Kula* exchange is certainly endowed with the power of creating happiness. My informants stated that hospitality, travel opportunities and the joy of receiving valuables were the 'profit' and, perhaps, the raison d'être of today's *kula* circuits. Going on a *kula* journey is an occasion to feel happiness:

> We all were hungry and thirsty, wanting to bathe and rest. Quietly, we approached the house. I felt unwelcome under the shy gaze of the children who were not used to me (a *dimdim*, after all, they reminded me of my whiteness that was no longer a sensation on Dobu). The wife of our partner came rushing from the garden, alerted by some children. Her husband, she explained, was paying a visit and expected back in the evening. We sat down in the shade of the veranda, chewed betel, smoked and waited—again. In the kitchen hut, girls started to peel yams. We watched the children chasing a chicken and felt happy about the prospect of eating it. (Fieldnotes, 24 May 1993; see Kuehling 2005: 207)

Alexander Meleodi, a *kula* master from Dobu, gave the example of a gift called *eyabala* ('looking across', 'passing on') that begs for a specific *kula* valuable. It consists of a basket (*kwalisi*) of raw yams and other seasonal food that is sent to the *kula* partner through a middleman. The recipient should give a *bagi* or *mwali* to the deliverer, who has to pass it on to the sender of the *eyabala*. At some later opportunity, a matching valuable has to be returned, but the value of the basket of food remains unbalanced;

it was meant to cause happiness—and friendship (Kuehling 2005: 195). Alexander pointed out how nice it was to receive such a thoughtfully composed basket out of the blue and 'for free'. Receiving a *kula* object of high value requires a 'lazy' posture, controlling the joy as perfectly as possible.

Mortuary ritual is another occasion for happiness for the many participants at the margin of these week-long events. Only the principal mourners are heavily involved in the suffering of death and the staging of suffering; they have to bend their backs, cover their heads, hush their voices and refrain from 'happiness' out of love and respect, and are only slowly ritually returned to a happier state when their time of mourning restrictions is terminated. The resident group that organises a mortuary feast will feel happy only after everything is completed, as the work is absorbing and exhausting (see Kuehling 2005: Ch. 8). A wide range of relatives can choose to contribute with produce, valuables and work, finding time to socialise with an even wider range of individuals and a valid reason to visit a wider range of places. Participating fully in mortuary feasting is a way to acquire status, but not everybody is inclined to work hard over several months. As in any society, internal politics are always at play, demotivating some villagers while pushing others to their highest level of performance.

Posture, morals and emotions

As elsewhere, in Dobu, a peaceful time lacking pain and worries makes people happy; the cool evening breeze after a hot day and the cuteness of toddlers are typical examples for this state. Being together with friends and close relatives, joking and laughing together constitute the private joy of happiness. In a more public sense, generosity and hospitality and the physical pleasure of consumption give evidence of the hosts' character and the guests' skills of self-discipline. The back is not an innocent body part in Dobu; it is linked to moral judgements and social benefits and serves as a metaphor for, and marker of, a person's qualities. It may be the underlying reason for gift-giving and provides significant rhetoric in *kula* negotiations. The release of mourning restrictions makes people happy, as they are allowed to quietly enjoy normal life again, just as the unexpected gift from a faraway *kula* partner can bring about a feeling of joy.

Physical and psychic contentment are ideal states of being that are not easy to maintain in the small world of villagers, where conflicts are prone to live long and tensions are not easily resolved. To be happy in spite of everyday troubles gives evidence of a strong character—a back that is stiff and upright even under difficult conditions. A person who can maintain a straight back shows an ability to master negative feelings of greed, anger, laziness and arrogance, and appears to be blessed with a happy character. Such people are better neighbours, affines and exchange partners; they are good to have around.

The Austronesian body as a site of sociality has received increasing attention since the 1980s, but there is room for more inquiry, especially in the field of empathy, emotion and morality. Throop, in his study of pain in Yapese society in Micronesia (2010), has convincingly argued that a Eurocentric perspective of pain has often limited our understanding of the phenomenon. Suffering, in Yap and Dobu, can provide an opportunity to display one's virtue if it is shrugged off with a straight face or a smile. I believe the same is true for other emotions, including feelings of happiness and laziness. Throop proposes an ethnography of subjectivity in which temporality is:

> an imperative that precedes the temporality of reflexive modes of understanding that are invested with the particularities of a given moral order, a particular theodicy, or a particular eschatology whether narratively, metaphorically, or practically conceived. (Throop 2010: 273)

As Throop has demonstrated, situating emotions in their moral context, in time and space, can provide empathetic representation and, ultimately, a better understanding of the underlying motivations of the people with whom we work.

Catherine Lutz, in her discussion of emotion in Ifaluk (Austronesian-speaking islanders of the central Caroline Islands in Micronesia), has demonstrated that an analysis of vernacular constructions of inner states provides a useful perspective, provided the researcher can empathetically 'pick up' the vibes and worries around them, and using vernacular terminology helps to frame thoughts and feelings in locally meaningful ways (1988: 216, 225). Anthropological fieldwork—'deep hanging out'—together with some introspective analysis of the ethnographer's own emotional chartering, will reveal a wide array of understandings for our own terminology. The black box of emotions sits in a black box of our own assumptions, and both need to be handled with care.

The invisible side of ethnography, while difficult to access, is nevertheless important for overall understanding. Austronesia, a sea of islands, is connected not only by the waves, but also by the wind. All living beings share island air—the ubiquitous breeze—transcending the boundaries of bodies and spreading the sounds and scents of life. Ghosts and magicians, witches and spirits travel on this breeze, adding to this emotional and moral space. These invisible beings are believed to have their own *nua*, which they may or may not be able to keep confined. Since yam roots are also endowed with *nua*, it is quite a crowded environment, and how much room the islanders take for themselves, how loud and tall they present themselves depend on their sophistication in self-discipline and silent suffering.

References

Bellwood, Peter, James J. Fox and Darrell Tryon (eds). 1995. *The Austronesians: Historical and comparative perspectives*. Canberra: The Australian National University.

Bolton, Lissant. 1999. 'Women, place and practice in Vanuatu: A view from Ambae'. *Oceania* 70(1): 43–55. doi.org/10.1002/j.1834-4461.1999.tb02988.x.

Brenneis, Donald L. and Fred R. Myers (eds). 1984. *Dangerous Words: Language and politics in the Pacific*. New York: New York University Press.

Colson, Elizabeth. 2012. 'Happiness'. *American Anthropologist* 114(1): 7–8.

Dernbach, Katherine B. 2005. 'Popular religion: A cultural and historical study of Catholicism and spirit possession in Chuuk, Micronesia'. PhD dissertation. University of Iowa, Iowa City.

Dixon, J. W. n.d. *Dobu/English Dictionary*. Salamo, PNG: The United Church Salamo.

Dutton, Tom, Malcolm Ross and Darrell Tryon (eds). 1992. *The Language Game: Papers in memory of Donald C. Laycock*. Canberra: Pacific Linguistics.

Edoni, Gail. 1989. *Head and Shoulders, Knees and Toes*. Ukarumpa, PNG: Summer Institute of Linguistics.

Falgout, Suzanne, Lin Poyer and Laurence M. Carucci. 2008. *Memories of War: Micronesians in the Pacific war*. Honolulu: University of Hawai'i Press.

Fox, James J. (ed.). 1993. *Inside Austronesian Houses: Perspectives on domestic designs for living*. Canberra: The Australian National University.

Fox, James J. 1995. 'Austronesian societies and their transformations'. In Peter Bellwood, James J. Fox and Darrell Tryon (eds) *The Austronesians: Historical and comparative perspectives*, pp. 214–28. Canberra: The Australian National University.

Fox, James J. 1997a. 'Genealogy and topogeny: Towards an ethnography of Rotinese ritual place names'. In James J. Fox (ed.) *The Poetic Power of Place: Comparative perspectives on Austronesian ideas of locality*, pp. 91–102. Canberra: The Australian National University.

Fox, James J. (ed.). 1997b. *The Poetic Power of Place: Comparative perspectives on Austronesian ideas of locality*. Canberra: The Australian National University.

Hau'ofa, Epeli. 1998. 'The ocean in us'. *The Contemporary Pacific* 10(2): 392–410.

Hereniko, Vilsoni. 2000. 'Indigenous knowledge and academic imperialism'. In Robert Borofsky (ed.) *Remembrances of the Past: An invitation to remake history*, pp. 78–91. Honolulu: University of Hawai'i Press.

Hess, Sabine. 2009. *Person and Place: Ideas, ideals and the practice of sociality on Vanua Lava, Vanuatu*. New York: Berghahn Books.

Huang, Shuanfan. 2002. 'Tsou is different: A cognitive perspective on language, emotion, and body'. *Cognitive Linguistics* 13(2): 167–86. doi.org/10.1515/cogl.2002.013.

Jackson, Michael. 1995. *At Home in the World*. Durham, NC: Duke University Press.

Johnston, Barbara Rose. 2012. 'On happiness and transformative change'. *American Anthropologist* 114(1): 15–16.

Kahn, Miriam. 1996. 'Your place and mine: Sharing emotional landscapes in Wamira, Papua New Guinea'. In Steven Feld and Keith H. Basso (eds) *Senses of Place*, pp. 167–96. Santa Fe, NM: School of American Research Press.

Kasaipwalova, John. 1974. '"Modernising" Melanesian society: Why, and for whom?' In Ron May (ed.) *Priorities in Melanesian Development*, pp. 451–4. Canberra: The Australian National University and University of Papua New Guinea.

Kuehling, Susanne. 1996. 'Gwasa: eine soziale Krankheit [Gwasa: A social disease]'. *Invoemagazin* 11: 29–30.

Kuehling, Susanne. 2005. *Dobu: Ethics of exchange on a Massim island, Papua New Guinea*. Honolulu: University of Hawai'i Press.

Kuehling, Susanne. 2014. 'The converted war canoe: Cannibal raiders, missionaries and *pax Britannica* on Dobu Island, Papua New Guinea'. *Anthropologica* 56(2): 269–84.

Kuehling, Susanne. 2017a. 'A fat sow named Skulfi: "Expensive" words in Dobu Island society'. In Elisabetta Gnecchi-Ruscone and Anna Paini (eds) *Tides of Innovation in Oceania: Value, materiality and place*, pp. 193–224. Canberra: ANU Press. doi.org/10.22459/TIO.04.2017.

Kuehling, Susanne. 2017b. '"We die for kula": An object-centred view of motivations and strategies in gift exchange'. *Journal of the Polynesian Society* 126(2): 181–208.

Lithgow, Daphne (ed.). 1984. *Dobu–English Dictionary*. Ukarumpa, PNG: Summer Institute of Linguistics.

Lutz, Catherine A. 1988. *Unnatural Emotions: Everyday sentiments on a Micronesian atoll and their challenge to Western theory*. Chicago: University of Chicago Press.

Macintyre, Martha. 1995. 'Violent bodies and vicious exchanges: Personification and objectification in the Massim'. *Social Analysis* 37: 29–43.

Mosko, Mark. 2009. 'The fractal yam: Botanical imagery and human agency in the Trobriands'. *Journal of the Royal Anthropological Institute* 15(4): 679–700. doi.org/10.1111/j.1467-9655.2009.01579.x.

Nordstrom, Carolyn. 2012. 'Happiness (is not a warm gun)'. *American Anthropologist* 114(1): 13–14.

Pawley, Andrew. 1985. 'Proto-Oceanic terms for "person": A problem in semantic reconstruction'. In Veheeta Z. Acson and Richard L. Leed (eds) *For Gordon H. Fairbanks*, pp. 92–105. Oceanic Linguistics Special Publications No. 20. Honolulu: University of Hawai'i Press.

Pawley, Andrew and Malcolm Ross. 1995. 'The prehistory of Oceanic languages: A current view'. In Peter Bellwood, James J. Fox and Darrell Tryon (eds) *The Austronesians: Historical and comparative perspectives*, pp. 39–74. Canberra: The Australian National University.

Rensel, Jan and Margaret Rodman (eds). 1997. *Home in the Islands: Housing and social change in the Pacific*. Honolulu: University of Hawai'i Press.

Ross, Malcolm, Andrew Pawley and Meredith Osmond (eds). 2003. *The Lexicon of Proto Oceanic. Volume 2: The culture and environment of ancestral Oceanic society. The physical environment*. Canberra: The Australian National University.

Strathern, Marilyn. 1988. *The Gender of the Gift: Problems with women and problems with society in Melanesia*. Berkeley, CA: University of California Press

Throop, C. Jason. 2010. *Suffering and Sentiment: Exploring the vicissitudes of experience and pain in Yap*. Berkeley, CA: University of California Press.

Weiner, Annette B. 1984. 'From words to objects to magic: "Hard words" and the boundaries of social interaction'. In Donald L. Brenneis and F. R. Myers (eds) *Dangerous Words*, pp. 161–91. New York: New York University Press.

Contributors

James J. Fox is an Emeritus Professor at The Australian National University, where he has been Professorial Fellow and Professor since 1975. He was director of the Research School of Pacific and Asian Studies until his retirement in 2006. He was the initiator of the interdisciplinary Comparative Austronesian Project, which was begun in the late 1980s as a major research focus at The Australian National University, and he has edited a number of volumes in the Comparative Austronesian series published by ANU Press. His most recent publications are *Explorations in Semantic Parallelism* (ANU Press, 2014) and *Master Poets, Ritual Masters: The art of oral composition among the Rotenese of Eastern Indonesia* (ANU Press, 2016).

Barbara Dix Grimes received her MA (1990) and PhD (1995) in anthropology from The Australian National University. Her doctoral research focused on social organisation, gender symbolic action and the social construction of health and illness on the island of Buru in eastern Indonesia. She later worked with Tetun Terik–speaking communities in central Timor. Her interests and publications include comparative and historical issues in eastern Indonesia, the social development of pidgins and creole languages in the region and community-based language development in the context of Indonesia. She is currently based in Darwin and is SIL International's Director for Australia and Timor.

Susanne Kuehling is Associate Professor at the University of Regina in Canada. She taught for five years at Heidelberg University, Germany, before moving to Canada in 2008. She received her MA from Göttingen University in Germany. For her doctoral research, she conducted 18 months of fieldwork on Dobu Island in Papua New Guinea. Her PhD thesis, submitted at The Australian National University in 1999, was titled 'The name of the gift: Ethics of exchange on Dobu Island'. She has published a monograph, *Dobu: Ethics of exchange on a Massim island*

(University of Hawai'i Press, 2005), and journal articles on *kula* exchange, value, personhood, morality, gender, emplacement and teaching methods. Her current project on the revitalisation of *kula* exchange was developed during a number of visits to Dobu Island in 2009, 2012 and 2015, and is funded by the Canadian Social Sciences and Humanities Research Council.

Minako Sakai teaches at Southeast Asian Social Inquiry at the School of Humanities and Social Sciences, University of New South Wales, in Canberra. She also holds an Adjunct Associate Professorship at the College of Asia and the Pacific, The Australian National University. She has undertaken longitudinal ethnographic work on Malay-speaking Gumay people of South Sumatra, Indonesia, by exploring the interplay between Islam and ethnic identity. Her recent research focuses on Islamic economy and socioeconomic development policies in contemporary Indonesia.

Clifford Sather received his PhD in social anthropology from Harvard University in 1971. He began fieldwork in Malaysian Borneo in 1964—first, among the Bajau Laut (or Sama Dilaut) in Sabah and, beginning in 1977, among the Iban in Sarawak. His publications include *The Bajau Laut: Adaptation, history, and fate in a maritime fishing society of south-eastern Sabah* (Oxford University Press, 1997) and *Seeds of Play, Words of Power: An ethnographic study of Iban shamanic chants* (Tun Jugah Foundation and Borneo Research Council, 2001). He also co-edited, with James J. Fox, *Origins, Ancestry and Alliance: Explorations in Austronesian ethnography* (The Australian National University, 1996) and, with Timo Kaartinen, *Beyond the Horizon: Essays on myth, history, travel and society* (Finnish Literature Society, 2008). He is currently preparing for publication a monograph on the Sugi Sakit, *Ritual and Romance: The role of ritual storytelling in the Sugi Sakit, a Saribas Iban rite of healing*. Dr Sather retired as Professor Emeritus from the University of Helsinki in 2005 and is currently editor of the *Borneo Research Bulletin*, the annual journal of the Borneo Research Council.

Roxana Waterson gained her PhD in Social Anthropology from New Hall, Cambridge (UK), in 1981. She did field research with the Sa'dan Toraja people of highland South Sulawesi from 1978 to 2009. Her monograph, based on this extensive fieldwork, is *Paths and Rivers: Sa'dan Toraja society in transformation* (NUS Press, 2009). She retired in December 2014 from a position as Associate Professor in the Department of Sociology, National University of Singapore, where she had taught since 1987.

Index